FEMINIST CONVERSATIONS

Women, Trauma, and Empowerment in Post-Transitional Societies

Edited by
Dovile Budryte
Lisa M. Vaughn
Natalya T. Riegg

University Press of America,® Inc.
Lanham · Boulder · New York · Toronto · Plymouth, UK

Copyright © 2009 by
University Press of America,® Inc.
4501 Forbes Boulevard
Suite 200
Lanham, Maryland 20706
UPA Acquisitions Department (301) 459-3366

Estover Road
Plymouth PL6 7PY
United Kingdom

All rights reserved
Printed in the United States of America
British Library Cataloging in Publication Information Available

Library of Congress Control Number: 2008936380
ISBN-13: 978-0-7618-4378-8 (clothbound : alk. paper)
ISBN-10: 0-7618-4378-7 (clothbound : alk. paper)
ISBN-13: 978-0-7618-4379-5 (paperback : alk. paper)
ISBN-10: 0-7618-4379-5 (paperback : alk. paper)
eISBN-13: 978-0-7618-4380-1
eISBN-10: 0-7618-4380-9

∞™ The paper used in this publication meets the minimum
requirements of American National Standard for Information
Sciences—Permanence of Paper for Printed Library Materials,
ANSI Z39.48—1984

For our families and women friends

Contents

Preface		vii
Acknowledgments		ix
Introduction		1
Part I	**Reflecting on Trauma and Empowerment: Theories and Practices**	
Chapter 1	Revision of the Visions: Feminism and Empowerment in Post-Transitional Societies *Natalya T. Riegg*	15
Chapter 2	From "Dirty Laundry" to a Human Rights Concern? International Norms and Gender Violence in Armenia and Lithuania *Dovile Budryte*	33
Chapter 3	Paradoxes of "Gender Equality" in Lithuania: Violence against Women and Equal Opportunities *Vilana Pilinkaite-Sotirovic*	51
Chapter 4	"Come Rape Us!" The Everyday Trauma of Sexual Violence in South Africa *Suzanne Leclerc-Madlala*	63
Chapter 5	Losing Ground: How the Lack of Opportunity for Women to Own Land Impales the Tanzanian Economy *Eric Boos and Karene M. Boos*	73
Chapter 6	Entrepreneurship: Antidote to Women's Economic Oppression *J. Kay Keels*	81

Part II Living Trauma and Empowerment: Stories and Strategies

Chapter 7	Left Alone, the Widows of the War: Trauma Reframed through Community Empowerment in Guatemala *Lisa M. Vaughn and Gabriela de Cabrera*	91
Chapter 8	Dolls with Jobs: A Compelling Response by Traditional KwaZulu-Natal Craftswomen in an Era of HIV/AIDS *Kate Wells*	101
Chapter 9	*Confined Space*: The Simultaneous Installation of Art and the De-Installation of a Relationship *Mary Beth Looney*	111

Part III Authentic Voices: Nothing Lost in Translation!

Chapter 10	Were All Women Born to Suffer? Understanding Resistance to Empowerment: A Lithuanian NGO Activist's Perspective *Dovile Rukaite*	119
Chapter 11	Women and Empowerment in Armenia: Traditions, Transitions and Current Politics *Svetlana Aslanyan*	129
Chapter 12	Zara's Travail: A Life Story *Azniv Eyramjyants*	137
Chapter 13	Gender In/Equality in Egypt and Armenia *Isabella Manassarian*	143
Chapter 14	Addressing Trauma through Political Action: Nineth Montenegro's Story *Gabriela de Cabrera*	151

Conclusion: A Conversation among the Editors	155
Index	169
About the Editors and Contributors	173

Preface

This book is about the ways in which social and political transitions affect women's lives. The essays address traumatic and empowering aspects of structural changes and challenges faced by women in post-transitional societies, including violence against women. We have written this book as a series of conversations among contributors. Toward that purpose, we begin as well as finish the book with conversations among the editors.

Let us start with a simple question: Why did each of us work on this book? What significance did its creation have for each of us personally?

Dovile Budryte: I came to the US from post-Soviet Lithuania sixteen years ago. During my trips "back" to Lithuania, I became painfully aware of my Americanized beliefs about gender roles and feminism. In addition, to tell you the truth, I felt that those newly acquired beliefs were somewhat better, somewhat more progressive than the traditional gender roles practiced by my childhood friends. Sometimes this feeling made me very uncomfortable. This is why I became interested in feminist literature exploring East-West interactions. I felt that despite the declining popularity of the term "feminism," there was a need for more feminist conversations. I also felt that these conversations needed to go beyond the East/West divisions and include feminist scholars and activists from the global South. During my numerous conversations with Lisa, who was my colleague at Brenau University (women's college), we came to a conclusion that similar conversations about gender violence and trauma are already taking place, except that they rarely include community activists and academics in one forum. Lisa introduced me to the idea of "action research," which requires that community activists and academics work together for a common goal. We felt that this should be our guiding philosophy in our interdisciplinary project exploring trauma, gender violence and empowerment in different cultural contexts.

Lisa M. Vaughn: I can't say that I come from post-anywhere, and in fact, by comparison, I have had a privileged life growing up in the United States with many opportunities as a female. This being said, I did grow up understanding the plight of the "underdog" within a socio-cultural context of capitalism, power and money, given that my parents grew up in poor, rural areas and always embodied the notion of never being good enough or having enough in comparison to their peers. Becoming an academic, getting immersed in social psychology was part of this journey—to better understand the social construction of power and dominance whether in relationships or within countries. This book for me represented a special opportunity to work with my dear friend, Dovile. During our time at Brenau University, Dovile and I had regular conversations. To my surprise, one of our recurring themes was that much of what we were interested in was similar, just representing different levels of analysis (I originally thought that her areas of interest were far too "macro" for my smaller, "micro" levels of analysis with relationships and small groups.) It was these discussions, Dovile's international background and my ongoing experience with and in Guatemala and South Africa that led to the conception of the book idea. Dovile was then able to bring her insightful colleague, Natalya T. Riegg, into our project. Natalya's interest in democratic deliberation and communicative action seemed to be synergetic with our interest in action research. For me personally and professionally, this book was a way to really put into "action" my growing interest in participatory action research and give voice to marginalized women and issues affecting them across the globe.

Natalya T. Riegg: To be honest, the writing of works on women's issues in differing societies did not initially appeal to the theoretical and feminist sides of me. Rather, it appealed more to my pragmatic and immigrant sides. Having moved to the US from post-Soviet Armenia some ten years ago, I was painfully aware of the deficiencies and misunderstandings in the mutual perceptions of both my native and my adopted cultures. Both cultures largely constructed each other as "Others," whose ways were perceived as inferior to the way "We" are. There appeared to be a real need for "cultural translation" or a cross-cultural "communicative action," as Jurgen Habermas would put it. But how could one literally create a forum for communicative action or a conceptual space for popular cultural translation? Especially, how could such a forum be created to contribute to the mutual understanding of women from "different worlds"—the First world, the post-communist world, the Third world? This was the set of issues that were at the center of my attention when I met Dovile at the International Studies Association conference in Miami and learned about her and Lisa's project. Your proposal to compose a book of essays written by women in different cultures about the challenges they have faced was similar to my then developing ideas about the possible creation of different forums for undistorted cross-cultural communication. It seemed to me that such a book could serve as a much needed forum for cross-cultural communication among women. I felt inspired when the two of them invited me to become a co-editor.

To start meaningful conversations, we begin with an outline of definitions and theoretical frameworks in *The Introduction*.

Acknowledgments

There are numerous people who helped us in different ways. We would particularly like to thank Dr. Nicholas Riegg, Charles C. Perrin and Evelyn Asher for their help with language editing as well as Carol Reddish and Amy Flaherty for their technical assistance. The project was supported by the University of Saint Mary in Kansas, the Women's Issues Information Center in Vilnius, Lithuania (conference support), and several grants from Brenau University (2006-7).

Introduction

In the contemporary political world, women's issues are treated as a subset of larger democratization projects. More specifically, the state of women's rights in a society is an independent variable that directly affects a country's performance on human rights and democracy. In the words of Phyllis Chesler and Donna Hughes, "Forty years ago American women launched a liberation movement for freedom and equality. They achieved a revolution in the Western world and created a vision for women and girls everywhere. Today, women's economic and social participation is considered a standard requirement for a nation's healthy democratic development" (2004, 396).

However, viewing women's empowerment as a part of democratization makes it clear that women's empowerment is susceptible to variations of the same sorts of problems and subject to the same types of questions as the most recent wave of democratization in general. Accordingly, this book follows the contemporary philosophy of women's empowerment as a part of the larger process of democratization. The essays presented in this volume are related to various aspects of women's empowerment in post-transitional societies. Our essays focus on social phenomena associated with transitions to democracy in various cultural contexts.[1]

The truly diverse, multicultural and multinational approaches of our authors are united by a common denominator: All essays place various women's experiences, hopes, fears and achievements into the context of their pre-democratic histories and the social transformations of their respective countries. This volume includes case studies and essays from post-communist Europe, parts of Africa and Latin America—the areas of the world that have been most affected by the most recent wave of democratization.

In the rest of this introductory chapter we will undertake several tasks. We will briefly outline the controversial character of the most recent wave of democratization. We address that controversy along the lines of a short comparative analysis of democratization and democracy. We look at democratic transitions, with their traumatic as well as empowering aspects, from the point of view of women living in those post-transitional societies. Finally, we explain in this chapter the philosophical basis of the book, which has largely determined the design of the volume.

In preparing this book, we hope to create an interactive, equal and inclusive dialogue on women's issues across the boundaries of countries, cultures and disciplines. We believe that such a dialogue reflects the spirit of democracy and transcends divergence through diversity.

Aporia of Democratization

One of the most paradoxical problems of the most recent wave of democratization is (to a greater or lesser degree) the notable grass-roots rejection of and resistance to certain projects and norms associated with democratization. The most striking example of the popular resistance to democratization can be found in Iraq, where the ambitious American project of "creating a democratic model for the Arab world" has resulted in a catastrophic failure due to a grass-roots insurgency (resistance). Less ostentatious but still a significant example of grass-roots rejection of democratization is the political development of Russia. While the Western world is lamenting the decline of democracy in Russia, according to several comprehensive polls conducted in 2006, "majorities or pluralities of Russians express support for measures that international and domestic critics cite as evidence that [former] President Putin is rolling back democratic reforms." Only 15 percent of Russians strongly agreed with the statement that democracy is the "best form of government."[2]

Additional examples of public distrust of democratization could be given, but the point is simply that, time and again, we see the Western-led efforts of democratic, popular empowerment being rejected in many parts of the world. This strange phenomenon can be called the "aporia of democratization" or "aporia of democratic empowerment." We hope that our volume will help to shed light on this phenomenon. This is why it is important to include detailed case studies and listen to authentic voices.

Democracy versus Democratization

This book tries to address the seemingly counterintuitive "aporia of democratic empowerment" along the lines of democracy versus democratization. Historically, the development of democratic consciousness has been followed by a struggle for the establishment of democratic institutions. In the language of women's rights, the realization of gender power disparity has been historically followed by the struggle for gender equality. The current project of democratization in many non-Western societies, however, is proceeding in the opposite order. It starts from the establishment of democratic institutions (including the legal framework for gender equality) and expects that democratic consciousness will then be generated. This reverse approach to democratization (including women's liberation) tends to underestimate issues of identity (culture, social psychology), and the consequences are often disappointing.

When one views recent democratizations both as an inversion of the historical pattern and as impinging on traditional aspects and interpretations of identity, seemingly remote phenomena like inter-communal violence in Iraq and the continuing culture of gender discrimination in Lithuania or Armenia can be seen as different manifestations of the same problem. Namely, the establishment of democratic institutions is a necessary but not sufficient condition for the development of democratic practices, including real gender equality. The other, equally important requirement for consolidating a democracy is the existence of an appropriate culture (i.e., values, norms, mores, laws, modes of negotiation, dispute resolution procedures, economic processes, religious concepts, etc.). In designing political institutions, a nation's leadership will implicitly be influenced by the prevailing political culture of the society. In the promotion of gender equality, the level of success is probably dependent on the degree of understanding and capacity to deal with a society's prevailing culture of gender relationships.

In any case, if the international community hopes to succeed in democratic consolidation (including women's liberation) in post-transitional societies, it needs to complement institutional development with an understanding of the specific socio-psychological and cultural processes that characterize any given transitional society. This collection of articles is aimed at addressing this need.

Multiple Transitions and Local Women

Mainstream research and policy approaches to democratization (a.k.a. "transitology") have focused on the ways that emerging democratic regimes can be consolidated in order to make democracy the "only game in town." As part of the general democratization process, feminist gender discourse and polity are supposed to become "the only game in town" as well, replacing other "womanly" discourses and polities. However, as Henri Vogt observed in his book *Between Utopia and Disillusionment: A Narrative of the Political Transformation in Eastern Europe,* "most books and articles written about the revolutions (transitions) in Eastern Europe have precious little to say about the interpretations of those who lived through the events; about the mood of the lay people" (2005, 2). A growing body of feminist literature on women and gender in democratizing countries (especially the former USSR) has played an important role in addressing this gap. In addition to recording the stories of women who have experienced transition, this body of literature has yielded some interesting theoretical insights related to gender and structural change.

One of the main insights of this important feminist literature has been, in the words of Janet Elise Johnson and Jean C. Robinson, that in the former Communist countries social, economic and political changes have resulted in "gender multiplication," understood as an increase in "a diverse array of strategies that women and men may use to construct the version of gender that they believe will help them to survive, if not thrive" (2007, 2). Transitional processes empower some individuals and groups, who obtain "the opportunity . . . to negotiate gender in the ways that sometimes can give them more options and choices in their lives" (Johnson and Robinson 2007, 3). Johnson and Robinson's examples of gender negotiations include young women in Russia and Poland using sex and sexual appeal to get better jobs in transitional economies. Another good example of gender identity as a "strategic commodity" is analyzed by Armine Ishkanian in her depiction of the Armenian NGO activists' strategies of interchangeably utilizing feminist and traditional (patriarchal) gender discourses in order "to win grants from donors" (2004, 266).

At the same time, this literature suggests that women are most likely to be marginalized during the time of socio-political transition.[3] Transitional processes may result (and have already resulted) in traumas, such as loss of family members during violent political conflict, increase in domestic violence, sexual trafficking, and difficulties in coping with market pressures. Moreover, societal transition may be perceived as a trauma by itself, by virtue of the inevitable destruction of the familiar life-world and introduction of the new and the unknown. These observations raise important theoretical and practical questions about the impact of transitions, such as: Do most post-transitional societies become more women-friendly as they become more democratic? Which strategies of empowerment can women (especially the ones marginalized during the processes or transition) use to obtain political voice and improve their everyday lives? How do they cope with traumatic experiences and memories?

To gain insight into these questions, we (the authors and the editors) draw on many different disciplines, including gender studies, psychology, and political science. Several chapters focus on the former USSR. (Natalya T. Riegg, Dovile Budryte and many of our authors are intimately familiar with this area.) Inspired by Lisa M. Vaughn, we also include perspectives from post-transitional societies in the global South to place the post-Soviet experience in a comparative framework.

Understanding Trauma and Empowerment

In this book we understand trauma as embedded in the social structure of the community (Martin-Baro 1994). Lykes, Blanche and Hamber suggest that focusing on the individual level of trauma only addresses a small number of those affected while leaving "devastated communities and societies virtually unattended" (2003, 80). If trauma is viewed as socially embedded, that implies that healing and empowerment must encompass various societal spheres and levels, manifesting themselves through economic, social and political phenomena, on community and governmental levels. Different essays in this volume address all of these various dimensions of trauma and empowerment.

In our thinking of empowerment we are inspired by Rappaport's understanding of empowerment as the process whereby people gain control of their own lives in the context of participating with others to change their social and political realities (1987, 122). Empowerment can occur at many levels—individual, community, organizational (Israel et al. 1994). However, most of the empowerment literature tends to over-emphasize empowerment outcomes at the individual, psychological and behavioral levels rather than at the communal level (Labonte 1994). We hope this volume may contribute to a reduction of this shortcoming.

Inspired by the feminist literature, we view empowerment both as a process geared to bringing about positive change and as an outcome. We think that "empowerment must be understood as including both individual conscientization *(power within)* as well as the ability to work collectively, which can lead to politicized *power with* others, which provides *power to* bring change" (Troutner and Smith 2004, 9). The goals of women's empowerment have included challenges to women's subordination, transformation of institutions that have perpetuated gender discrimination and inequality, as well as identification and recognition of institutions that support gender equality (Troutner and Smith 2004, 11).

The focus on trauma and empowerment in this volume logically connects it to concerns of the wider, international women's movement today and feminist literature on democratic transitions. Traumatic experiences and methods of dealing with them are in the center of the (relatively recent) feminist agreement around the issues of violence against women. As Margaret E. Keck and Kathryn Sikkink have argued, by the mid-nineties, violence against women had become "the most important international women's issue, and the most dynamic new international human rights concern" as well as a "common advocacy position" of the women's movement (1998, 11). In this volume, several women's rights activists and feminist scholars reflect on the efficiency of different practices against gender violence, coping with trauma mechanisms and become engaged in dialogue about the applicability to their countries (Dovile Rukaite's, Vilana Pilinkaite-Sotirovic's, Suzanne Leclerc-Madlala's and Kate Wells's contributions and comments).

The relevance of trauma to women's issues, however, goes beyond the cases of physical violence. Various manifestations of traumatic structural violence, the cases of verbal abuse and control, and even the cases of paradoxical disempowerment of women through the process of democratization are also addressed and analyzed in this collection of articles (see contributions and comments by Natalya T. Riegg, Mary Beth Looney, J. Kay Keels, Eric and Karene M. Boos, and Isabella Manassarian).

Design of the Book

This book has been designed to bring together, or act as an interdisciplinary bridge between the action research model, which emphasizes social research for social change, and the deliberative democracy model, which is organized around the idea of discourse ethics.[4] We believe that both models share potential utility as broadly inclusive, analytical and practical aids for the assessment and construction of a feminist discourse.

The book provides a forum for equal, intercultural and inter-subjective discourse among scholars and practitioners coming from diverse and unequal regions of the world and is, particularly, concerned with women's issues in post-transitional countries. The hope is that the book will not just contribute to research on empowerment and its correlation with trauma, but will also help to empower local practitioners and Western theoreticians alike through their equal participation in this scholar-practitioner dialogue.

The intent to act as a bridge across disciplines, across cultures and across the scholar-practitioner divide has determined the criteria for both the contributors and the substance of the book. Our main requirement was that the contributions had to be relevant to traumatic women's issues and the strategies of empowerment of women in post-transitional societies. Other than this, the project was explicitly inclusive and intentionally egalitarian; i.e., it has treated those coming from economically unequal regions of the world and those with different levels of education in a "subject-to-subject" manner. Following the common philosophy of democratic deliberation and participatory action research, instead of merely "analyzing" our "research objects" (women—both practitioners and theoreticians—who are interested in empowerment), we invited them to contribute to our project by writing essays and responding to the ideas of the other participants of the forum. Moreover, to preserve the spirit of "epistemic plurality" and "communicative equality" of this book, the authentic voices of the non-academic authors are preserved to the degree possible. Thus, the contributions (especially—the personal stories) are written in an authentically *different language* rather than being *translated* into the language of Western feminist discourse.

The book is divided into three main parts. Part 1, *Reflecting on Trauma and Empowerment: Theories and Practices*, examines the leading discourses, theories and institutions related to democratization, trauma and empowerment. Part 2, *Living Trauma and Empowerment*, discusses some answers to the questions raised in the previous section by analyzing specific empowerment strategies (art and community activities) in specific cultural contexts. Part 3, *The Authentic Voices* section, is a collection of testimonies of those who have experienced democratization and trauma first hand.

Natalya T. Riegg, in the next chapter, introduces the main questions explored by the other chapters in the book: Why is there so much resistance to Western liberal projects, including women's liberation? Why is there a "collision of visions" between the "West" and the "Rest"? Why do we (the "West") view certain democratization strategies as "empowering," while "others" (the "recipients") see the same strategies as domineering? Riegg's essay outlines a "communicative approach" to the empowerment of women in post-transitional societies. This approach is based on equality, inclusiveness and respect for the local traditions. With Riegg's argument in mind, Dovile Budryte's essay (Chapter 2) focuses on legal dimension of empowerment by exploring the impact of international norms against gender violence in Armenia and Lithuania. Her essay outlines cultural and political obstacles to the incorporation of international norms meant to empower women. Budryte concludes that only the actors who are rooted in post-transitional societies can find ways to make sure that international norms become domestic realities.

Although, under international pressure, transitional democracies may have adopted progressive legislation and policies, this does not mean that those laws and policies are going to be successfully implemented. Vilana Pilinkaite-Sotirovic argues that "formal equality [that is, gender equality guaranteed by rules and legislation] does not automatically translate into substantive equality." Drawing on the case of Lithuania, Pilinkaite-Sotirovic shows how protection of the private sphere from the governmental interference and the ongoing construction of state-supported "gender-neutral" categories leads to the preservation of patriarchal social traditions. Interestingly, Suzanne Leclerc-Madlala makes a similar argument about South Africa. There is no doubt that democracy has resulted in many gains for South African women, particularly in terms of gender legislation and institutional structures. Yet, in terms of the reality of women's lives, South Africa is also a model example of the disjuncture between excellent public policy declarations and lived experience. Many of the country's women live far below the poverty line, cannot find paid employment, are without access to clean water and sanitation, housing, affordable healthcare, food for themselves and their families, and bear the brunt of violence and HIV/AIDS.

Eric Boos and Karene M. Boos's as well as Kay Keels's contributions focus on economic empowerment, which, as Leclerc-Madlala's contribution suggests, is critical in post-transitional societies. The Booses argue that without improving the status of women, democratizing countries cannot expect to establish sustainable democracies. Drawing on their extensive research on land tenure issues in Tanzania, the authors suggest that Tanzania's food security problems could be significantly lessened if women, who bear the brunt of all agricultural labor in Tanzania, were given equal opportunity to hold title to the land they farm. Similarly, Kay Keels makes a case for letting women fully participate in transitional economies. In both cases, the authors suggest that there is "a perception that women are less capable, less entrepreneurial, or perhaps they should not be entrepreneurs at all" (de Bruin et al. 2007). Yet these perceptions must be overcome. Drawing on the case of Lithuania, Kay Keels argues that entrepreneurship can play a significant role in women's development of economic independence.

The chapters in the section *Living Trauma and Empowerment* explore the cultural and psychological dimensions of women's empowerment. Lisa M. Vaughn and Gabriela de Cabrera tell a moving story of Mayan widows of war in Guatemala and the ways in which they confront the "triple oppression"—being a woman, being indigenous and being poor. They participate in community-based groups, including art cooperatives, such as ASOTRAMA, specializing in weaving. Kate Wells's contribution explores a similar initiative in South Africa. She describes how a small group of rural traditional craftswomen from KwaZulu-Natal have attempted to circumvent some of the prescribed societal and cultural requisites with regard to respectable behavior for Zulu women. The article shows how the traditional craftswomen employed their own narrative and traditional medium of expression (beaded cloth doll and tableau making) to exercise their rights as women, and to "speak" openly on sensitive, traumatic and taboo topics. Similarly, Mary Beth Looney's contribution suggests that art can help women to start addressing sensitive and traumatic topics. The heroine of her story is not from a post-transitional society, and perhaps this is why her trauma narrative is distinctly more individualistic when compared with the other two chapters in this section. Looney's contribution raises an important question: How would Amanda's story be different if she lived in a post-transitional society and had to deal with similar personal traumas?

According to Dovile Rukaite, Amanda's story would be very different in a post-transitional society. Amanda's travails would be seen as a personal matter, not deserved to be discussed in a public space. Women's issues, including domestic violence, are still considered to be a "private" matter in post-transitional societies. According to Rukaite's contribution in *The Authentic Voices* section, the inability to discuss domestic violence and similar traumatic issues openly is one of the main obstacles to women's empowerment in Lithuania. Svetlana Aslayan's contribution identifies several other obstacles, such as the tenacity of patriarchal norms and the "Soviet mentality"—feeling like a victim and expecting help from the government. This mentality makes the development of civil society very difficult.

Dealing with the past is the center of a story narrated by Azniv Eyramjyants. This contribution reveals several layers of the traumatic past—the national (experienced by the Armenians), the political (memories of World War II) and the personal (loss of parents). It raises an important question: Is it possible to expect the former victims to embrace democratic norms, such as inclusiveness, tolerance and cooperation?

The story narrated by Eyramjyants shows how women learn how to live with memories and on-going experiences of traumas. Isabella Manassarian's essay describing her life in authoritarian Egypt illustrates a similar trend. When Isabella saw that her Egyptian maid was physically abused and confronted her about it, the maid replied, "If he hits her at times, it is fine as long as he does not cross the accepted boundaries."

Isabella's maid's story raises numerous questions related to empowerment of women: What does it take to change the "accepted boundaries"? And who can do it successfully? The life story of Nineth Montenegro (a human rights activist and politician from Guatemala) provides some answers. Several experiences in Nineth's life—unjust treatment by the government and the abduction of her husband—made her go into the streets and later become a leading politician in Guatemala. Yet, paradoxically, the same traumatic experiences may prevent women activists from being active in transnational feminist movements. As Batya Weinbaum has argued, traumatic experiences may lead women "to regain internal strength by fortifying gender identity that has been thrown into crisis [think about Nineth's attempts to come to terms with single motherhood], using nationalistic contours to reaffirm their sense of self" (2006, 71).

With the possible exception of Rukaite's essay, *The Authentic Voices* section points to the inability of women activists with a previous experience of trauma to overcome the "nationalistic contours" of their narrative. As Nineth's story and Ligia Gomez's commentary show, women who have experienced trauma may find solace in reaffirming their identities as mothers and devout believers, not supporters of equal rights. This insight needs to become integrated into the narratives about the aporia of democratization.

In Closing

The diversity and heterogeneity of the voices presented in this volume reflect the incontrovertible pluralism of the contemporary global, social condition and women's movements. Perhaps, if we approach the multiplicity of reasons and passions, of traumas and empowerments of the various people(s) of the world as equally valid, we will be less puzzled by the aporia of democratization stated in the beginning of this introduction. We hope that the feminist conversations of this volume contribute to that task.

Notes

1. We acknowledge the limits of the term "transitions to democracy," and we are aware of criticisms addressed to the so-called "transitology" literature which suggests that transition to democracy is "over" when "free and fair" elections take place. At the same time, our case studies suggest that there is value to the term of "consolidated" or "quality" democracy. Not only does this term describe a political regime in which democracy is the "only game in town," it also implies popular support and cultural changes, including changes in social relations. The term "post-transitional societies" refers to the states (Lithuania, Poland, Armenia, Guatemala, Tanzania, Côte d'Ivoire and South Africa) which started democratization in the late 20th century. Other cases (Egypt, an electoral authoritarian regime, and the USA, a consolidated democracy) are used for comparison.

2. Worldpublicopinion.org discusses a public opinion poll conducted by WPO/Levada. See worldpublicopinion.org, Russians Support Putin's Re-nationalization of Oil, Control of Media, but See Democratic Future (July 10, 2006), http://www.worldpublicopinion.org/pipa/articles/breuropera/224.php?lb=btgov&pnt=224&nid=&id= (accessed July 1, 2008).

3. Data shows that in the former USSR the situation of women deteriorated significantly after the fall of Communism. According to Roschin and Zubarevich (2005), in 1990s in Russia there were so many registered unemployed women (70 percent) that a term "women's face" of unemployment came into being.

4. PAR (Participatory Action Research) is an approach to social investigation, an educational process and a way to take action to address a problem. In research, PAR is a collaborative, partnership approach that equitably involves all stakeholders (e.g., community members, organizational representatives and researchers) in all aspects of the research process. From the beginning, it was intended (and it still is) to promote social change.

Being one of the most popular ideas of contemporary Western political theory, deliberative democracy is an ideal of political legitimacy. For Jurgen Habermas, one of the leading theorists of deliberative democracy, modern social theory should be couched in terms of the self-other relationship, in which we communicate with the others as subjects, rather than perceiving them as objects. This inter-subjectivity of "undistorted communication" constitutes, according to Habermas, an "ideal speech situation," shaped by a mutual determination to avoid distortion and manipulation and reach understanding and consensus. Habermas substantiated his model through the following logical chain:

> The social world as the totality of legitimately ordered interpersonal relations, is accessible only from the participant's perspective; it is intrinsically historical and hence has, if you will, an ontological constitution different from that of the objective world which can be described from the observer's perspective. The social world is inextricably interwoven with the intentions and beliefs, the practices and languages of its members (1999, 38).

Thus, according to Habermas, if all participants of a certain discourse rationally accept the moral validity of a norm, their rational acceptance makes the claim that the norm should be recognized valid.

Bibliography

Chesler, Phyllis, and Donna M. Hughes. 2004. Feminism in the 21st century. *Washington Post*, February 22.

de Bruin, Anne, Candida G. Brush, and Frederike Welter. 2007. Introduction to the special issue: Towards building cumulative knowledge on women's entrepreneurship. *Entrepreneurship Theory and Practice* (March 12), http://www.allbusiness.com/business-planning-structures/starting-a-business/3900114-1.html (accessed June 29, 2008).

Habermas, Jurgen. 1999. *The inclusion of the Other: Studies in political theory*. Cambridge, MS: MIT Press.

Ishkanian, Armine. 2004. The challenges facing women in Armenia's non-governmental organization sector. In *Post-Soviet women encountering transition, nation building, economic survival and civic activism*, ed. Kathleen Kuehnast and Carol Nechemias, 262-287. Washington, D.C.: Woodrow Wilson Center Press.

Israel, Barbara A., Barry Checkoway, Amy Shulz, Marc Zimmerman. 1994. Health education and community empowerment: Conceptualizing and measuring perceptions of individuals, organizations and community control. *Health Education and Behavior* 21 (2): 149-170.

Johnson, Janet Elise, and Jean C. Robinson. 2007. Living gender. In *Living gender after Communism*, ed. Janet Elise Johnson and Jean C. Robinson, 1-21. Bloomington: Indiana University Press.

Keck, Margaret E., and Kathryn Sikkink. 1998. *Activists beyond borders: Advocacy networks in international politics*. Ithaca, NY: Cornell University Press.

Labonte, Ronald. 1994. Health promotion and empowerment: reflections on professional practice. *Health Education Quarterly* 21 (2): 253-268.

Lykes, Brinton M., Martin Terre Blanche, and Brandon Hamber. 2003. Narrating survival and change in Guatemala and South Africa: The politics of representation and a liberatory community psychology. *American Journal of Community Psychology* 31 (1/2), 79-90.

Martin-Baro, Ignacio. 1994. *Writings for a liberation psychology*, ed. Adrianne Aron and Shawn Corne. Cambridge: Belknap.

Rappoport, Julian. 1987. Terms of empowerment/exemplars of prevention: Toward a theory for community psychology. *American Journal of Community Psychology* 15(2): 121-148.

Roschin, S. Yu., and N. V. Zubarevich. 2005. Gender equality and extension of women rights in Russia in the context of the UN Millennium Development Goals. UNESCO.ru. http://www.unesco.ru/files/docs/shs/publ/gender_mdg_eng.pdf (accessed June 29, 2008).

Troutner, Jennifer L., and Peter H. Smith. 2004. Empowering women: agency, structure, and comparative perspective. In *Promises of empowerment: Women in Asia and Latin America*, ed. Peter H. Smith, Jennifer L. Troutner, and Christine Hunefeldt, 1-30. Lanham, MD: Rowman and Littlefield Publishers.

Vogt, Henri. 2005. *Between utopia and disillusionment: A narrative of the political transformation in Eastern Europe.* New York: Berhahn Books.

Weinbaum, Batya. 2006. How sexual trauma can create obstacles to transnational feminism: The case of Shifra. *NWSA Journal* 18 (3): 71-87.

Part I
Reflecting on Trauma and Empowerment: Theories and Practices

Chapter 1
Revision of the Visions: Feminism and Empowerment in Post-Transitional Societies
Natalya T. Riegg

Power, like love, is easier to experience than to define or measure (Nye 2004, 1).

There are no facts, only interpretations (Nietzsche n.d.).

Last summer I visited my home country, Armenia, after five years of absence. After such a period of separation from everyday cultural encounters, one finds a lot of curious significations that are invisible or mundane to an everyday participant. Two instances, however, seemed to be especially relevant to East-West, North-South cross-cultural translations, including the meaning of women's empowerment.

First, I was surprised by the ubiquitous liquor advertisements in the capital, Yerevan. They read "Nostalgia for the USSR," and contained quaint images of old "Soviet Glory," a picture of the first astronaut Yuri Gagarin and an old-fashioned coat of arms with hammer and sickle. As any advertisement is supposed to be deeply appealing to be effective, and Armenians historically never seemed to be terribly supportive of the Communist regime, I was rather intrigued by the choice of themes.

When I expressed my surprise on the issue to my girlfriends and my sister, they seemed to be shocked by my naiveté. They were nostalgic for a number of features of life under Communism: "Remember everyone was employed at that time and actually received salaries that were enough to buy food. Remember maternity leave? Remember reliable day care?" I had nothing to offer except a vague feeling of the presence of the elements of empowerment within the traumatic powerlessness of Soviet life.

The second eye-opening circumstance was hearing a rather common opinion, most eloquently expressed in a question of an aunt of mine. She asked me: "Is it right that American men are extremely eager to marry Armenian women? I heard that any Armenian woman can catch an American husband in a matter of days." Seeing that I was surprised and puzzled by this question, she explained: "American women are very selfish and individualistic, aren't they? If a woman in America is educated, then she is sure to be aggressively individualistic. So, poor American men have to choose between boring housewives and selfish feminists. No wonder they want to marry foreigners!"

As I listened to her I realized that what Western feminists (de Beauvoir 1989; Kreps 2003; among others) would consider as empowerment and strengths, my aunt viewed as the contrary. During my visit there were other moments of unexpected cultural and cross-cultural significations. These instances led me to think about the meanings of democratic empowerment and the difficulties of their cross-cultural interpretation.

The Problem

At first glance, the ontology of empowerment of women in post-transitional societies appears to be obvious and noble. After all, empowerment is a part of today's sociopolitical meta-project of democratic expansion, which is connected to the ethics of empowering the powerless. However, a second look at the current international situation leaves us less confident. One cannot help but be disturbed by the weakness in the popularity of the current struggle for liberal-democratic transition around the world, including women's liberation as an intrinsic part of democratization. Numerous public opinion polls show a very low regard for the motives and means of American democratization policy. Moreover, Western-style women's liberation and empowerment simply does not seem to be very important to non-Western women. A survey conducted by the Gallup Organization in 2005 suggested that most Muslim women associated gender equality with the West. "A majority of the respondents did not think adopting Western values would help the Muslim world's political and economic progress" (Andrews 2006).

The problem, simply stated is the paradox that those (particularly women) who are the presumptive targets and beneficiaries of liberation and empowerment resist or even oppose such programs. Why is there this apparent collision of visions? Why do some groups see these sociopolitical initiatives as empowering, while others see them as intrusive and domineering?

An Approach

It is the hypothesis of this essay that, first, the successful empowerment of women in any given society is intimately linked to the identity and agency of women in that society. Second, the basis of the "clash of visions" is not necessarily in the adaptive preferences of the oppressed groups, including non-Western women. Rather the grounds for the "clash of visions" between the West and the Rest is seen as resting mainly in the philosophical disparity between the epistemology and the ontology of democratic liberation, including women's liberation. Accordingly, we are not going to seek remedies to the clash through consciousness raising or similar (feminist) techniques.

An approach that will be used will be to offer some non-Western narratives of empowerment from women in transitional and post-transitional societies, in the belief that they will contribute to a mutual cross-cultural understanding of culture-specific meanings and agencies of (women's) empowerment. With increased understanding, the two sides should be better equipped to revise their conflicting visions and move closer to the ideal of "common knowledge." The ideal (and the very idea!) of "common knowledge" may appear suspiciously essentialist and thus epistemologically distasteful for a post-modern mind, but it is an ontological necessity for justification of the moral claims of the global women's movement. Otherwise, the same phenomena may appear as "knowledge of empowerment" to some women, while being the "knowledge of neo-colonial domination" for others.

The Clash of Epistemology and Ontology

On the epistemological level, in the contemporary political philosophy of the post-Dewey era, the theory of the interpretive and contextualized nature of different claims to truth is becoming more and more accepted. Richard Rorty describes the process as "removing any suggestion of inevitability, any hint that the story being told is itself more than another possible interpretation" (2003, xiv). For the feminist epistemology, this general tendency toward "narrativization" of social-democratic theory has been translated into an increasingly sophisticated and nuanced acknowledgement of the differences between different women's experiences and thus acknowledgement of the relativity of different claims to truth. The relativity of truth can be seen in post-modern, post-bellhooks, feminist theories (hooks 2003; Kristeva 1986; Irigaray 2002; Butler et al. 2000; Benhabib 1986, 1996, 2002; among many others).

On the ontological level, however, the present-day situation appears to be quite different. The practice of current international democratization in general, as well as the social movement of empirical feminism in particular, seem to be still indulging in a quaint fondness for "white man's (white woman's) burden" of bringing Truth and enlightenment to the lesser people. In present-day language it should probably be phrased as bringing the Truth of democratic empowerment to the "subalterns" of the autocracies (and patriarchies) of the world. A practical problem with this policy is that the democratically revealed voices and the will of the empowered "subalterns" may present unpleasant surprises to the proponents of the empowerment. Examples include empowering Hamas, bringing to office conservative clerics in Iraq, strengthening the power of the Muslim Brotherhood in Egypt and the rise of populist Socialism and nationalism in Latin America. These unfortunate examples have as much reflected the voice of women as that of men.

Conceptual Approaches to Identity

To understand why such unintended outcomes occur from empowering the masses, it may be useful to consider alternative approaches to the concept of identity. In this regard, let us turn to the thoughts of competing philosophic schools on the subject, particularly the "essentialist" versus "historicist" traditions of (democratic) political philosophy. Flowing from German classical philosophy, the "essentialists" (such as Immanuel Kant, among others) considered humankind in the abstract and posited axioms applicable to beings everywhere. "Historicists" (such as Georg Wilhelm Friedrich Hegel, among others) who came after the "essentialists," contended that nations and peoples differed from one another in accordance with their historical happenstance and, thus, axioms applying to all peoples were generally invalid.

These competing schools put into historical and theoretical perspective the conflicting visions of human freedom and social justice which today are manifest in inter-cultural misunderstandings as well as in the intra-cultural epistemological/ontological disparity described above. Today, the "historicist" tradition is largely reflected in the "anti-authoritarian" theories of Jacques Derrida (1981, 2002), Richard Rorty (2003), Jurgen Habermas (1985a, b) with some reservations and others. Indeed, there has been a general progression from "essentialist" thought to that of the "historicist" to the "anti-authoritarians."

One can see a similar type of progression and diversification in the theories of feminism. Through the second wave of feminism, with such thinkers as Virginia Wolf (1966), Simone de Beauvoir (1989) and Betty Friedan (1997), "essentialism" effectively reigned. In the 1930s, Wolf wrote, "As a woman I have no country. As a woman I want no country. As a woman my country is the whole world" (Wolf 1966). These words were a virtual encapsulation of the credo of the second wave of feminism into the 1970s, with its emphasis on the commonality of experiences and concerns of all women, most famously reflected in Robin Morgan's (1996) pronouncement that "sisterhood is global." However, within the last thirty years significant changes have occurred in the concerns as well as in the approaches employed by Western feminist theory. Some authors consider these changes in feminism as amounting to a paradigm shift (Mohanty 2003, 460).

During the last 30 years feminists more and more often have assimilated new subjective and methodological domains, reflecting the political, cultural and philosophical developments of the period, from the political successes of decolonization and civil rights to the methodological achievements of post-structuralism and deconstruction. The idea that unites these diverse outlooks is the acknowledgement of the multiplicity of women's experiences. One can say that in contemporary feminist theory the initial idea of "woman as other" is being increasingly complemented by the vision of "the other women," i.e., not just white Western women, but women from all cultures and stations of life around the world.

This evolution of feminist theory (i.e., epistemology) mirrors that of general political theory, which is understandable as Euro-American feminism itself is a specific case of the general "democratic expansion" of society and the empowerment of people. Unfortunately, the practice (i.e., ontology) of expanding the empowerment of women *internationally* seems not to have followed the progression seen in the epistemology. Rather, practice seems more to be reflecting the forceful, "essentialist" features of global democratization and appears based on an "essentialist" vision of women that largely ignores differences in their social identities.

Empowerment and Identity

The nexus of empowerment and identity is closely analyzed in the contemporary interdisciplinary studies of Orientalism, as well as in subaltern and postcolonial studies, including their feminist readings. While much discussion of the content and details of this very rich and diverse body of studies is beyond the framework of this essay, suffice it to note that these theories are united by their passion toward the "decolonization of knowledge" (Prakash 1994, 1483) and through the rejection of the perceived Euro-centrism of the normative political, historical, feminist and other discourses. Needless to say, the Orient-Occident, East-West, Subaltern-Elite binary oppositions are laden with power imbalances and perceived Western domination. As Edward Said notes:

> Without examining Orientalism as a discourse one cannot possibly understand the enormously systematic discipline by which European culture was able to manage—and even produce—the Orient politically, sociologically, militarily, ideologically, scientifically, and imaginatively during the post-Enlightenment period (1979, 3).

In a different register, a similar paradigm is displayed by Gyan Prakash who analyzes subalternity in the example of "the paradoxes of the functioning of power" in the representation of the "peasant agency as a spontaneous and prepolitical response to colonial violence" within the dominant discourse (Prakash 1994, 1483). Similar ideas are being translated into the language of feminism in numerous works, from Gayatri Chakravorty Spivak's (1988) famous questioning of the ability of the subaltern to speak, to Meyda Yegenoglu's discussion of "an imperial Western feminist gesture" (1999, 97).

In the light of these ideas one can better perceive the vision of the complex interplay of international power relationships in the field of practical popular empowerment—be it gender or not. In other words, the vision and the version of popular empowerment that are being universally "exported" today have been developed within the liberal-democratic tradition of the Western world. There are, however, other worlds that have developed within different sociopolitical traditions, for example, communitarian, social democratic and Communist ones. They have their own histories, epistemologies, phenomenologies and, thus, their own truths. Given the influence of the differing political environments on personal identity, the feminist slogan "Personal is Political" could probably be complemented by its inverse—"Political is Personal." Numerous findings from social psychology, anthropology and philosophy confirm the significance of the socio-historical and political context of our formative years for the development of our identities (Pennebaker and Banasik 1997; Conway 1997).

The societal and individual context of our life, with all its baggage of historical and personal memories, encounters and significations and even the political structures in which we live (whether we consciously like them or reject them) appear to be more important than we tend to notice. Being internalized, the context of our lives (and especially—of our formative years) essentially becomes part of us, a part of our identity. In many respects our social environment determines our judgments, our interpretations of good and evil, what is just and unjust, sacred and profane, our subjective preferences, the culture of our personal feelings—the entire background ethos of our claims to truth that is often invisible to us until it clashes with different claims to truth.

The baggage of historical (social or personal) memories, whether traumatic or not, may have rather immediate relevance to the meaning and the methodology of the empowerment of women. Real (rather than abstract) women (as well as men) are always concrete, contextual and historical. They can only exist in their flesh and blood, their life-stories and memories, feelings and passions, in their concrete countries and tribes, rather than in an abstract "human nature" or generic "woman's condition." I, as a former Soviet citizen, have an identity that is influenced by my school years and the stories of my Communist grandmother. Native born Americans are also, but differently, influenced by their schooling and received narratives, including different perspectives on Communism.

Identity, Responses and Outcomes

Regarding the meaning of empowerment, the things that I, as a former Soviet, may consider to be empowering and the groups that I may find most competent for advancing the empowerment of women, you as a good American feminist (or as a good social conservative, evangelist, Hindu or Muslim woman) may find unreasonable, banal, or plainly repulsive and vice versa. These sorts of situations, in which disagreement is mutual, however, can be deconstructed, and deconstruction will reveal dominant/sub-dominant relationships of power. So, the meaning and significations of (gender) empowerment appear closely related to non-gender dimensions of identity.

Now let us look at the agency of empowerment. Given all the differences among people of differing life histories, if we were to act on our democratic beliefs when trying to help empower those of another culture, results might be profoundly different than intended. For example, if you as a good proponent of democracy, would try to empower a group of persons who were the opponents of Western democracy, by the use and development of democratic procedures and institutions, the greater likelihood would be that the group would use the opportunity to bring to office former KGB officers or Hamas's "freedom fighters" or the mullahs of Iran. In the case of empowering women, the democratically empowered ones could use their newly found power to transform themselves from traditional Uzbek housewives, for example, into Uzbek female terrorists. In such situations, the beneficiaries of democratic empowerment are able to reveal their true sense of identity. In the words of Richard Rorty, they are able to realize their "respective utopias" (Brandom 2000, 8).

Power and Communicative Action

Further discussion of the empowerment of women in post-transitional societies requires a closer look at the meaning of power. Despite the widespread acknowledgement of the problematic nature of the concept, there is a general agreement on some common features of power. Robert A. Dahl defines power as the ability of one actor to make another do something that s/he "would not otherwise do" (1957, 203). The meaning of power includes the ability to persuade (as in Joseph S. Nye's concept of "soft power").

According to Jurgen Habermas (and in line with the concepts of persuasion and soft power), a proper analysis of power would assume a theory of communication or "communicative action" (Habermas 1985a, b). Different as they are in other respects, the conceptions of power advanced by certain social scientists and by political philosophers such as Hannah Arendt, Jurgen Habermas, Michel Foucault and Anthony Giddens are alike in emphasizing the "communicative" aspect of power" (Ball 2005, 552).

Building upon the findings of these theorists, this essay proposes a communicative approach to the empowerment of women (including the women from post-transitional societies). Theoretically this approach to the empowerment would be closest to (and informed by) Michel Foucault's conceptualization of power. Foucault saw "the general functioning of the wheels of power" as a system of control diffused in numerous societal institutions and phenomena, that hitherto appeared to be irrelevant to power. Structures of medical care, penal institutions, education, sexuality, were seen by Foucault as entangled in the "fine meshes of the web of power" that operate throughout the society and are not limited to the apparent (visible) indications of power, such as economic class or government position (Foucault 2002, 203).

Perhaps today, when the "others" of the world persist in their resentment of and resistance to the liberal-democratic ways of their empowerment, it is time for us to look closer at "the fine meshes of the web of empowerment" that exist globally. In other words, we may need to approach the task of understanding the other mechanisms of empowerment "in themselves" and look at "the general functioning of the wheels of empowerment" within the other worlds' practices, mindsets and institutions. One of the benefits of discovery and better understanding of these mechanisms of empowerment could be a better understanding of why so many women around the world do not buy into Western models of their empowerment, or (in Western eyes) abuse them.

Culture-Specific Mechanisms of Empowerment

In more practical terms, a communicative approach to empowerment should, first, search for *culture-specific and identity-related mechanisms and agencies* that may or may not be immediately obvious to outsiders, but that *empower women in post-transitional societies.* These mechanisms and agencies may be related to intra-cultural language and modes of communication. Second, the proposed communicative approach should emphasize *cross-cultural communication about the variety of mechanisms and agencies for empowerment that exist in the myriad societies of the world.*

Through such communication, women from disparate sectors of the globe can, hopefully, contribute to the empowerment of women through a better understanding of each other and, thus, the development of a truly "common knowledge." Through a truer two-way dialog and Habermasian "subject-to-subject" (as opposed to "subject-to-object") communication, the existing deficiencies of power suffered by women can be addressed in a more case by case, culture-specific fashion, thus achieving more effectiveness than generic, one-size fits all recipes for empowerment of women. In other words, it could be helpful to complement the traditional feminist practice of finding and exposing the structures and strategies of women's oppression in different societies ("search for negatives") with the practice of discovering and communicating the structures and strategies of women's empowerment in those societies ("search for positives").

"Subject-to-Subject" Communication

This essentially discursive or "subject-to-subject" practice for women's empowerment (as opposed to essentially lecturing or the "subject-to-object" practice of many feminist workshops) is based on the ideas of deliberative democracy with its discourse ethic and "narrative constitution of the self." This approach may have many advantages. It could help to transcend the dichotomy between gender and other identities (ethnic, national and/or religious) and the interplay of power relationships embedded in them. If we encourage people to present their narratives, to tell the stories of their lives, rather than to learn the proper way to live, they will not have to choose between allegiances to their groups' ways versus their kinship with other women. They will just present their narratives in their complex unity of different relationships—just as these things exist in all our real lives.

Discursive practices could also better reflect a truly inclusive, equality-based spirit of democracy than does the current, domineering style of the Western-type empowerment. Women even would have a better hope for inspiring each other cross-culturally by expressing their passions and convincing each other by their visionary notions—because they can only exercise the power of conviction through communication.

The importance of truly equal communication and "cultural translation" for overcoming the logic of neocolonial domination within feminism is well articulated by Judith Butler. She indicates "the parochial character" of the norms of "Anglo-feminism" itself and brings attention to "the way in which feminism works in full complicity with US colonial aims in imposing its norms of civility through an effacement and a decimation of local Second and Third World cultures" (Butler 2000, 35).

Empowerment in Former Communist Societies

Let us now try to apply the proposed communicative approach for women's empowerment to the dynamics of cross-cultural interpretations of empowerment that exist between post-transitional and Western societies. There are a number of works dealing with the history of women's issues in the Russian and Eastern European cultural space. Among the best English-language works is Richard Stites's *The Women's Liberation Movement in Russia: Feminism, Nihilism and Bolshevism* (1978). Most interesting, for the purpose of this paper, are the works about women's issues that are written by Eastern European (including Russian) authors themselves. Valuable analysis is offered in the works of Olga Voronina (1993), Hana Havelkova (1993), Dimitrina Petrova (1994) and others. Building upon the findings of these theorists, as well as on my own personal experiences as an Armenian and a former Soviet citizen who lived through the fabulous and turbulent years of the disintegration of the Soviet Union, and who was very active in organizations of the newly forming civil society, I would like to share some impressions and observations of the way in which Western activists (later supported by locals) approached and advocated women's issues in the former Soviet area.

In the 1989-1991 (period of Glasnost, Perestroika and Soviet dissolution), many professional women in the Soviet Union were alternately astonished and overwhelmed by political and economic changes. The Iron Curtain that had separated us from the free world all our lives miraculously disappeared. From behind that curtain and with the intoxicating air of our new freedom, there appeared strangers speaking in a different language—both literally and figuratively. Rather than speaking Russian, they spoke English, and their speech was about civil society, non-governmental organizations, free press and other similar subjects. They rarely knew Russian or any language of the former USSR, so we, the locals, had to struggle hard to understand their language—in both linguistic and symbolic meanings of the word. And some of them seemed to advocate a battle of the sexes, a real conflict between men and women—if only we understood them right, with our limited English.

That was my first encounter with Western feminism. Even now, 15 years later, after the identity shifts, losses and findings, when I no longer can really say "we" about my former compatriots, the impression is still fresh that Western feminism conflated with conflict and the battle of the sexes. In order to understand the depth and the origins of this extreme if not distorted interpretation of the Western feminist message by many ex-Soviet women, we need to look at the historical context that shaped the narratives and perspectives of those women.

Women's Issues during Soviet Times

One the first decrees of the Soviet authorities after the revolution of 1917 was a declaration on sexual equality. Following Marxist criticism of bourgeois, patriarchic society as an institution of women's oppression, the new Soviet authorities tried to implement "Engels's and Bebel's view that women's liberation required bringing women into public industry as full equals to men" (Ferguson 2000, 521). As a result, Soviet legislation in the 1920s was probably the most egalitarian in the world. Young women from all over the country, including from villages and outlying districts, started to work in factories, participated in construction projects, went to school, entered the professions and otherwise became as productive builders of Socialism as men.

It is widely accepted now that this ethos of state-sponsored women's emancipation, as almost everything done by Soviet authorities, should not be taken at face value. The ethos that so thoroughly brought women into all ranks of social and economic life was the result of state-ordered policies that reflected Communist Party philosophy and state interests, rather than the result of a grassroots, gradual development within civil society that might have reflected women's perceptions of their own interests. Consequently, the Soviet women never raised a challenge to their traditional household role or responsibilities and routinely found themselves under the double-burden of being a productive worker as well as a traditional wife/mother. The personal never became political. Moreover, while women were emancipated from male domination by the egalitarian ideology of the Communist state, women, as well as men, were de facto exploited and dominated by the state. As Olga Voronina noted, it was the Soviet women's labor "that held up the extensive economy for many long years at a low cost" (1993, 101).

This situation, of course, created within the Communist societies a gender context and gender agencies that were quite different from Western ones. There was virtually no "little housewife of the 50s." Instead, there was a "super-woman" of the 50s (as well as "super-women" of later decades) desperately trying to combine all the roles, to be it all, to do it all and to do it well. Women did not suffer from "the problem that has no name." It was easy to name their problems: being overworked, underpaid and overwhelmed. For an illustration of the differences between women's concerns in the Communist and liberal worlds of that period, it is interesting (telling) that in the mid-60s, when Betty Friedan's *Feminine Mystique* (1997) was shaping the future of women's issues in the US, a very different writing about Soviet women's lives became popular in the USSR. It was Natal'ia Baranskaia's novel, *A Week Like Any Other* (1989), depicting the typical life of an average Soviet woman, stretched thin between work and family. Women could recognize themselves and their situations in the life of that heroine.

In other words, there was no social context for the rise of a Communist Betty Friedan or Simone de Beauvoir, who would successfully advocate women's emancipation from *male domination*. Both men and women were and felt dominated by the totalitarian state. Moreover, some researchers (Kiczkova and Farkasova 1993; Havelkova 1993) consider that many women in the Communist countries were frequently nostalgic for the security and flexibility (or easiness) of a traditional woman's role, with its agency defined by the leeway of the privacy of family life. As Dasa Duhacek indicated, "The family is almost seen as the site of the public, or at least its compensation, its supplement, which is a reversal of the Western feminist theoretical designation" (2000, 131-32). Hana Havelkova (1993) argued that the family remained the last "bastion" of liberty. Therefore, it took over many functions previously associated with the public sphere.

No wonder that with the beginning of Gorbachev's liberalization and Perestroika women's issues were not a part of the general discourse of liberation. Women felt that liberation was needed from the Communist state, and their situation would improve simply as a consequence of overall democratization. Within the societal reaction against everything Communist, a discourse of return to the "natural role of women" became quite popular in late Soviet-early post-Soviet democratic dialogue. Pettman called these developments "ideologies of housewifization" of the post-Soviet societies (1996, 12).

The Traumas of Transition: Post-Communist Experience

Rather than improving with democracy, the situation of women in the former Communist countries deteriorated significantly after the fall of Communism (Einhorn 1993; Pettman 1996, among others). In response, a large number of women's organizations developed—often with assistance from abroad—to help women cope with the traumas of transition to democracy and capitalism. While these organizations have done and are doing many good deeds, their structures have often been modeled after Western patterns, as have been the sets of issues with which they have been ostensibly concerned. Similarly, their choice and design of programs is more determined by and tailored after the Western foundations' preferences, rather than authentic local needs and demands. In truth, issues, concerns and programs have mainly flowed from the ethos of the Western, not the ex-Soviet, women's discourse. The reason for that orientation has been that the main reason for the existence of most women's organizations, despite their non-profit status, seems to be the solicitation of Western grants, other forms of support and various benefits (e.g., increased access to information, education, travel, jobs and contacts). These women's organizations are usually quite elitist, with their members almost necessarily proficient in English and usually having some academic or bureaucratic background. The choice of members is also understandable given that they need to be able to write competitive grant proposals in a foreign language and within an alien ethos.

At the same time, a large stratum of women in post-communist societies perceives feminism as a manifestation of the Western female mindset that propagates "the battle of the sexes." The message of Western feminism does not seem to be appealing to the average woman of those societies, perhaps precisely because none of them are "little housewives." Diane Duffy writes about this seeming paradox: "Since 1989 I have met many strong feminists from small villages to industrial centers to academic settings who flagrantly eschew the use of the term 'feminism,' denying that the label is applicable to them" (Duffy 2000, 217). The roots of popular anti-feminism in post-communist societies has been analyzed by a number of local and Western researchers, among them Barbara Einhorn and Charlotte Sever (2003), Jirina Siklova (1997), Maria Adamik (1993) and others.

The Discursive Practices of Western Feminists in the Post-Soviet Space

Many of the differences between women's lives in the Communist and capitalist countries have, of course, long been a matter of interest in the West, and there has been a gradual transformation of Western perceptions of those differences. In the beginning of the Soviet period the Communist theory of gender relations seemed to be accepted by the West at its face value. After all, a big part of Western feminist theory itself (Marxist and Socialist feminism) was inspired by and formed after the women's liberation model a'la Engels, Bebel and Alexandra Kollontai. Later, however, more accurate information about the difficulties of the real life of women under Communism became widely available in the West. So, when the Iron Curtain fell, the natural reaction of Western feminists was to offer help to their sisters on the other side. The generic recipes they offered emphasized resistance to male domination.

The ex-Soviets' encounters with Western feminists started as ambivalent and were rather difficult. On the one hand, the message of the necessity to improve the lives of women seemed clear and appealing to the majority of post-Soviet women. That was logical, given the difficult conditions under which most of them lived during and immediately after the Soviet period. However, the generic feminist language of the traditional repression of women and the encouragement of the manifest defiance of male domination seemed rather irrelevant and even suspicious. The discourse of repression and resistance sounded too similar to the discredited Marxist paradigm, and at the same time too foreign.

This reaction also appears quite logical given the historical and political contextualization of the Soviet women's lives discussed above. In other words, the main source of disagreement was not the moral of empowering women but *the modes of agency used in the process*. The inevitable stresses between the viewpoints of Western feminist activists and former Soviet women became evident in various women's leadership and other workshops that were held in the former Soviet and East European states in mid-1990s and later. The logical remedy for the "clash of cultures" could have been a more open discussion within the interested women's communities in order to reveal the different discursive traditions of the participants of those workshops. However, the very atmosphere of those workshops did not encourage such a discussion.

For the Western participants, the politically prescriptive project of women's liberation interfered with the analytic project of better understanding their interlocutors. The Westerners seemed driven mainly by their mission to enlighten and reform their abject counterparts, so the latter could live freer lives. The ex-Soviet participants, in their turn, did not really insist on making themselves heard and understood better. On the one hand, they did not feel very secure, particularly as they were trying to adjust to the new situation of the Western workshops, which were as unfamiliar in their structure as in their content. On the other hand, being trained for years by the Communist authorities to adjust to objectionable conditions rather than to try to change them, many of the ex-Soviet participants treated the language of feminism as just "another language" in which one had to "speak" in order to get Western grants and other benefits. In terms of the Habermasian model of analysis, those sorts of discursive practice constituted a distortion of communication and a breakdown of inter-subjective dialogue with both sides treating each other as objects.

Communicative Approach to Empowerment in the Second World

It is the opinion of this paper that if cross-cultural women's communication were organized on the basis of the communicative approach to empowerment, it would reduce the "clash of visions." It would make visible the specific mechanisms of women's empowerment during Socialism and in post-communist societies. Those mechanisms would probably include non-confrontational (inclusive) if independent (non-submissive) gender identity and an orientation toward cohesion with men (Einhorn and Sever 2003; Duffy 2000) due to (Communist) Socialism's treatment of men and women alike. Another special feature would surely be the empowering ability of the community and kinship networks of the private sphere (Duhacek 2000; Duffy 2000), based on the communitarian traditions of most post-communist societies. One could also mention generous maternity leaves, abortion rights, affordable day care and other features of the former Communist societies that may or may not exist in post-transitional ones and that used to empower women under Communism.

A more subject-to-subject dialogue and communicative approach would yield a more adequate picture of the real lives, aspirations and problems of women in post-transitional societies. Better dialogue, better interaction and better knowledge could not but empower Western and non-Western participants with a more adequate ability to address the problems of women in transition.

Such a process would also surely further empower Western participants with knowledge and understanding of another discourse, one that was neither Western feminist nor patriarchal.

Commentary
Jolanta Reingarde

The author discusses the issues that have been widely debated by Eastern (post-communist) and Western scholars during the last several decades of post-communist transformations. "The collision of visions" of empowerment envisioned by the West and the Rest raises questions about the significance of socio-cultural and political contexts affecting the development of identities and strategies of empowerment. The communicative approach to empowerment (proposed by the author) offers a promising way for cross-cultural communication about various mechanisms and agencies for empowerment on the basis of "subject-to-subject" practices and inclusion of different voices.

During the last several decades of social and political transformations, Eastern European feminist discourse has been confronted with dual tensions and dual exclusions: from the Western feminist thought on one hand and their own societies where their feminist thoughts have been distrusted on the other. To address the first exclusion, both sides must reconsider the reasons behind silences and mutual reservations as well as, in the words of the author, "the modes of agency used in practice." During the 1990s we (feminists in post-communist countries) have internalized the reality of our "absent voice(s)." We understood the necessity to (re)claim our voices internationally to render our reality and experiences understandable and visible, thus breaking the silence that our marginality (globally) imposed on us. It appears that (to a great extent) silences of the West when talking about Eastern Europe result from gaps in communication and information.

Moreover, in the context of democratization, the Western feminist thought was met with widespread resistance in Eastern Europe. Western feminists expected women's organizations in post-communist countries to be the best hope in fighting for retention of women's social rights and benefits. Of course, women's NGOs have enormous influence in shaping the post-communist gendered order in Lithuania and regionally, particularly by drawing attention to important issues and influencing political agendas. Yet there is no large and strong feminist movement in Lithuania and the whole post-communist region. By and large, the most active women's groups have been demobilized. There is very little of what can be called an explicitly feminist activity. Feminism has been publicly stigmatized, ridiculed and marginalized before it was properly understood. The leading liberal women's rights activists in Lithuania and throughout the region do not want to be seen as advocates of feminism. They are often looking for other terms that express their concern with women's issues in order to avoid using the term "feminist." This demonstrates the uncritical acceptance of distorted definitions of feminism rather than a demand for redefinition.

Going back to the strategies of empowerment presented in the chapter, the "subject-to-subject" communication on global and national levels promises to solve the East-West dilemmas presented above and accept the truly inclusive spirit of democracy rooted in equality.

Bibliography

Adamik, Maria. 1993. Feminism and Hungary. In *Gender politics and post-communism: Reflections from Eastern Europe and the former Soviet Union,* ed. Nanette Funk and Magda Mueller, 207-13. New York: Routledge.

Andrews, Helena. 2006. Muslim women don't see themselves as oppressed, survey finds. *New York Times,* June 8.

Ball, Terence. 2005. Power. In *A Companion to Contemporary Political Philosophy,* ed. Robert E. Goodin and Philip Pettit, 548-557. Oxford: Blackwell.

Baranskaia, Natal'ia. 1989. *A week like any other: Novellas and stories.* Seattle, WA: Seal Press.

Benhabib, Seyla. 1986. *Critique, Norm and Utopia: A Study of the Normative Foundations of Critical Theory.* New York: Colombia University Press.

———. 1996. Toward a deliberative model of democratic legitimacy. In *Democracy and difference: Contesting the boundaries of the political,* ed. Seyla Benhabib, 67-94. Princeton: Princeton University Press.

———. 2002. *The Claims of culture.* Princeton: Princeton University Press.

Brandom, Robert B. 2000. *Rorty and his critics.* Oxford: Blackwell.

Butler, Judith, Ernesto Laclau and Slavoj Zizek. 2000. *Contingency, hegemony, universality.* New York: Verso.

Conway, Martin A. 1997. The inventory of experience: Memory and identity. In *Collective memories of political events: Social psychological perspective,* ed. James W. Pennebaker, Dario Paez, and Bernard Rime, 21-46. Mahwah, NJ: Lawrence Erlbaum.

Dahl, Robert A. 1957. The concept of power. *Behavioral Science* 2: 201-215.

de Beauvoir, Simone. 1989. *The second sex,* trans. and ed. H. M. Parshley. New York: Vintage.

Derrida, Jacques. 1981. *Dissemination,* ed. Barbara Johnson. Chicago: University of Chicago Press.

———. 2002. *Acts of religion,* ed. Gil Anidjar. New York: Routledge.

Duffy, Diane M. 2000. Social identity and its influence on women's roles in East-Central Europe. *International Feminist Journal of Politics* 2 (2): 214-243.

Duhacek, Dasa. 2000. Eastern Europe. In *Companion to feminist philosophy,* ed. Alison M. Jaggar and Iris M. Young, 128-136. Oxford: Blackwell.

Einhorn, Barbara. 1993. *Cinderella goes to market: citizenship, gender and women's movements in East Central Europe.* New York: Verso.

Einhorn, Barbara, and Charlotte Sever. 2003. Gender and civil society in Eastern and Central Europe. *International Feminist Journal of Politics* 5 (2): 163-190.

Ferguson, Ann. 2000. Socialism. In *Companion to feminist philosophy,* ed. Alison M. Jaggar and Iris M. Young, 520-529. Oxford: Blackwell.

Foucault, Michel. 2002. Truth and power. In *Contemporary sociological theory*, ed. Craig Calhoun, Joseph Gerteis, James Moody, Steven Pfaff, and Indermonah Virk, 203-210. Oxford: Blackwell.
Friedan, Betty. 1997. *The feminine mystique.* New York: W.W. Norton.
Habermas, Jurgen. 1985a. *The theory of communicative action. Volume I: Reason and rationalization of society.* Boston: Beacon Press.
———. 1985b. *The theory of communicative action. Volume II: Life world and systems. A critique of functionalist reason.* Boston: Beacon Press.
Havelkova, Hanna. 1993. A few prefeminist thoughts. In *Gender politics and post-communism: Reflections from Eastern Europe and the former Soviet Union,* ed. Nanette Funk and Magda Mueller, 62-73. New York: Routledge.
hooks, bell. 2003. Feminism: A movement to end sexist oppression. In *Feminist theory reader. Local and global perspectives,* ed. Carol R. McCann and Kim Seung-Kyung, 50-56. London, New York: Routledge.
Irigaray, Luce. 2002. *The way of love,* trans. Heidi Bostic and Stephen Pluhacek. London, New York: Continuum.
Kiczkova, Zuzana, and Etela Farkasova. 1993. The emancipation of women: A concept that failed. In *Gender politics and post-communism: Reflections from Eastern Europe and the former Soviet Union,* ed. Nanette Funk and Magda Mueller, 84-94. New York: Routledge.
Kreps, Bonnie. 2003. Radical feminism 1. In *Feminist theory reader. Local and global perspectives,* ed. Carole R. McCann and Seung-Kyung Kim, 45-49. New York: Routledge.
Kristeva, Julia. 1986. *The Kristeva reader,* ed. Tori Moi. New York: Colombia University Press.
Mohanty, Chandra Talpade. 2003. Feminist encounters: Locating the politics of experience. In *Feminist theory reader. Local and global perspectives,* ed. Carol R. McCann and Seung-Kyung Kim, 460-471. New York: Routledge.
Morgan, Robin. 1996. *Sisterhood is global: The international women's movement anthology.* New York: Feminist Press at CUNY.
Nietzche, Friedrich. n.d. *Nachlass* (unpublished). Quoted in Stanford Encyclopedia of Philosophy. http://plato.stanford.edu/entries/nietzsche/#NieUnpNot (accessed July 7, 2008).
Nye, Joseph S. 2004. *Soft power. The means to success in world politics.* New York: Public Affairs.
Pennebaker, James W., and Becky L. Banasik. 1997. On the creation and maintenance of the collective memories: History as social psychology." In *Collective memories of political events: Social psychological perspective,* ed. James W. Pennebaker, Dario Paez, and Bernard Rime, 3-20. Mahwah, NJ: Lawrence Erlbaum.
Petrova, Dimitrina. 1994. What can women do to change the totalitarian culture context? *Women's Studies International Forum* 17 (2-3): 267.
Pettman, Jan Jindy. 1996. *Worlding women: A feminist international politics.* New York: Routledge.
Prakash, Gyan. 1994. Subaltern studies as postcolonial criticism. *The American Historical Review* 99 (5): 1475-1490.
Rorty, Richard. 2003. Foreword. In *Nihilism and emancipation,* by Gianni Vattimo, ix-xxiii. New York: Colombia University Press.
Said, Edward W. 1979. *Orientalism.* New York: Vintage.
Siklova, Jirina. 1997. Feminism and the roots of apathy in the Czech Republic. *Social Research* 64 (2): 258-280.

Spivak, Gayatri Chakravorti. 1988. Can the Subaltern Speak? In *Marxism and the interpretation of culture,* ed. Cary Nelson and Lawrence Grossberg, 271-316. Urbana: University of Illinois Press.
Stites, Richard. 1978. *The women's liberation movement in Russia: Feminism, nihilism and bolshevism, 1860-1930.* Princeton: Princeton University Press.
Wolf, Virginia. 1996. *Three guineas.* New York: Harcourt.
Voronina, Olga. 1993. Soviet patriarchy: Past and present. *Hypatia* 8 (4): 97-112.
Yegenoglu, Meyda. 1999. *Colonial fantasies. Toward a feminist reading of Orientalism.* New York: Cambridge University Press.

Chapter 2
From "Dirty Laundry" to a Human Rights Concern? International Norms and Gender Violence in Armenia and Lithuania
Dovile Budryte

During the last decade, the transnational movement against gender violence has gained unprecedented strength. It has mobilized people from different social classes, races, civil society groups and nations. Currently the international community regularly calls on national governments to empower women and give them equal rights to avoid gender violence and discrimination. During the Fourth World Conference on Women in Beijing in 1995, governments were asked to (and agreed) to start fighting violence against women on local, national and international levels. Four years later, the UN (United Nations) General Assembly declared 25 November as the International Day for the Eradication of Violence against Women. In a similar move, in 2007, the CoE (Council of Europe) encouraged all member states to launch campaigns against gender violence.

The influence of this movement and the norms developed by this movement on the status of women needs further research, especially in post-transitional societies. Are governments capable of restructuring their legal systems and sponsoring effective policies to combat different types of gender violence? Are international actors capable of empowering civil societies? Finally, are empowered civil societies capable of transforming the cultures that condone gender violence? In the end, traditional beliefs, historical patterns and local interests may turn out to be more influential variables than international norms because, as Natalya T. Riegg's contribution to this volume suggests, local actors are likely to interpret international norms in their own ways. Consequently, those gauging the success of international norms to fight gender violence need to pay close attention to the sources of domestic resistance to these norms.

With Riegg's argument in mind, this essay explores the impact of international norms associated with the transnational movement against gender violence on the empowerment of women in Armenia and Lithuania. It focuses on domestic violence, which is probably the most problematic type of violence to address.

Lithuania and Armenia are parties to the CEDAW (Convention on the Elimination of All Forms of Discrimination against Women) as well as the Beijing Declaration and the Platform for Action (1995). The Beijing Platform for Action outlined ways to "prevent and eliminate all forms of violence against women and girls" (a statement from the Beijing Declaration) and broadly defined "violence against women" as "any act of gender-based violence that results in, or is likely to result in, physical, sexual or psychological harm or suffering to women, including threats of such acts, coercion or arbitrary deprivation of liberty, whether occurring in public or private life." It outlined several important areas of focus for the governments, which included gender equality, gathering data on the status of women, training officials (including police) in humanitarian and human rights law as well as "mainstreaming a gender perspective in all policies and programs" (Division for the Advancement of Women 1995a).

According to a survey of twenty-six post-communist countries and their compliance with the CEDAW and the Beijing Platform, governments in Lithuania and Armenia demonstrated a "critically low compliance" with these international norms. Thus, the two countries remain a "zone of serious concern in terms of gender justice and safety of women and girls" (Avdeyeva 2007, 891). In both cases, there are strong cultural barriers against speaking out about domestic violence, but under international pressure, both governments tried to accommodate international demands to reduce it. Both societies have experienced a transition from Communism to democracy, which initially pushed many women out of the public sphere, thus making them more vulnerable to abuse at home. On the other hand, Lithuania, as a new member of the EU (European Union), had to adapt to more international rules, including directives to promote women's rights, which, presumably, affected the status and well-being of women in Lithuania.

"Living Gender" in Post-Transitional Lithuanian and Armenian Societies

In a book with a similar title, Janet Elise Johnson and Jean C. Robinson (2007, 3) argue that transitions after Communism have enabled women to "negotiate gender" so that they have more options and choices in their lives. In Armenia and Lithuania, as well as in other post-communist societies, these choices included women starting their own small businesses, emigration, or working at home.[1]

This "multiplication of gender" (Johnson and Robinson's term) has not brought gender equality promoted by transnational feminist groups, the UN, the CoE, the EU and other international actors. Although Lithuania has one of the highest levels of women's employment in the EU (in 2008, women's unemployment rate was 5.1 percent, compared with 4.6 percent for men), there is still discrimination in the labor market.[2] According to the 2006 data, women were paid approximately 18 percent less than men in the private sector and 22 percent less than men in the public sector (Jankauskaite 2007). The UN General Assembly Committee on Elimination of Discrimination against Women (2008) pointed out the need to stimulate "overall women's economic activity, especially in rural areas."

According to Sheldon Yett, UNICEF's representative in Armenia, in 2006 women made 30 percent less money than men in all sectors of Armenia's economy. Furthermore, 60 percent of all unemployed were women. Yett also pointed out low numbers of women in Armenian politics (GINSC.NET 2006). After May 2007 elections, only 12 out of 131 parliamentarians were women (9.2 percent). This number was higher than in 2003 (6, or 4.6 percent) or 1999 (4, or only 3.1 percent), but smaller than in 1995 (12, or 6.3 percent). In Lithuania, the situation is slightly better. After the 2004 parliamentary election, 32 out of 141 parliamentarians were women (22.7 percent). In 2000 there were 15 women parliamentarians (10.6 percent). In 1996, this number was 24 out of 137 (17.5 percent).[3]

A recent (2007) amendment to Armenia's Electoral Code mandated that at least 15 percent of all political party candidates running for seats in the nation's parliament had to be women. The goal of this amendment was to increase the number of women in the Armenian parliament, which is the lowest in the South Caucasus. Although this legal measure did increase the number of women candidates and women parliamentarians in 2007 (their number went up from seven to twelve), it did little to improve their political representation in other branches of power. For example, in 2008, there was only one female minister (out of seventeen) in Armenia (Zastoukhova 2008). In comparison, in Lithuania three (out of thirteen) ministers were women (Cicelis and Pilinkaite-Sotirovic 2007, 4).

According to Lyudmila Harutiunian, a prominent Armenian sociologist who leads a small party called *Arzhanapatvutyun* (Armenian for "dignity"), winning an election or securing a high-level government post is extremely difficult for local women in Armenia because politics "have long been monopolized by wealthy businessmen and other powerful men reliant on brute force, and there is little the women can do about that" (Danielyan 2006). Although "brute force" is absent from Lithuanian politics, cultural beliefs and prevailing socioeconomic structures also deter the Lithuanian women from obtaining more political power.

Despite recent attempts by women's rights' NGOs and international actors such as the EU and the UN to promote gender equality, there is plenty of room for improvement in both societies. As Vilana Pilinkaite-Sotirovic's contribution to this volume suggests, adoption of the EU directives and laws proclaiming gender equality do not guarantee the implementation of the principles of equality in Lithuania. In reality, the country can be described as a "neo-familial society" in which women are given a "choice" to leave the labor market temporarily to take care of young children. Later a woman is expected to go back to work.

However, very few women manage to go back to their former place of employment to work full time and take care of her family at the same time (Davidavicius 2006, 211). Following the neo-familial model, similarly to the Soviet times, women are still expected to balance their activities in private and public spheres.

Family is also very important in Armenian society in which traditional gender hierarchies are seen as crucial for the continued survival of the nation. Official political discourse portrays the family as "a basic unit for viability and self-preservation" of the Armenian nation. Women are expected to be more oriented towards their families and "somewhat less inclined towards an active involvement in politics and social life" (Ishkanian 2004, 267). According to a nation-wide household survey financed by the United Nations Development Program and conducted by the Armenian National Statistical Service in 2004, approximately 70 percent of respondents told the pollsters that their family was "headed by a man." According to this survey, most men continue to avoid house duties because they consider them "a female prerogative." The average time of housework conducted by a man is only four minutes compared with four hours spent on average by an Armenian woman (Atshemian 2006).

Despite the persistent patriarchal norms in society and politics, women in Lithuania and Armenia find ways to participate in social life. Involvement in NGOs is one of them. According to Armine Ishkanian, an Armenian scholar and an NGO activist, there are at least four reasons explaining the feminization of civil society in Armenia. They include exclusion from political parties and government positions in Armenia after the disintegration of the USSR, little if any interest in the non-governmental sector shown by men who were more interested in business or "high" politics, low financial rewards of participation in civil society and interest of international donors in sponsoring projects supporting women's rights (Ishkanian 2004). Similar reasons account for the feminization of civil society in Lithuania.

Given the high level of feminization of the Armenian and Lithuanian NGOs, it is not surprising that they are an important link between the transnational anti-violence network and societies. To measure the effectiveness of the international network (to fight gender violence), Margaret E. Keck and Kathryn Sikkink identified five stages of effectiveness: "1) issue attention, agenda setting, and information generation, 2) discursive change, 3) procedural changes, such as treaty ratification, 4) changes in policies, and 5) influence on behavior of state and nonstate actors"(1998, 192). Olga Avdeyeva's (2007) study of twenty-six post-communist governments and their compliance with international treaties related to violence against women suggested that transmission of international norms is unlikely to be a linear, orderly process. In the post-communist context, governments are likely to sign and ratify international treaties first (the third stage) and only then worry about discursive change (the second stage) and policy implementation. Avdeyeva made a case for using the acculturation approach to study the impact of international pressure on government actions. Acculturation refers to a process whereby actors respond to different social and cultural pressures from international and domestic actors (Avdeyeva 2007, 897). These pressures help to make sure that governments start implementing international norms. The following sections analyze the ways in which social pressures can be applied to increase government responsiveness to fight against gender violence.

Rates of Domestic Violence in Armenia and Lithuania

Although it is difficult to obtain reliable data about domestic violence, it is estimated that half of all women in Armenia may have suffered domestic abuse. In 2004-2005, The Sociometer Center for Independent Sociological Studies surveyed 1,200 women in Yerevan, eight other towns and eight villages. 46 percent of respondents said that "they were exposed to violence in their family." 25 percent of the respondents were physically abused in the presence of their children (Abrahamian 2006).

Most crimes related to domestic violence against women are not reported. According to the survey cited above, 45 percent of the victims kept silent. 0.3 percent had the courage to divorce their husbands, and no more than 0.4 percent contacted the police. The victims are afraid of repeated physical harm from their spouses, scared that the police will return them to their abusive husbands, or simply too embarrassed to "air dirty laundry in public" by making their family issues known to others (US Department of State 2006a). Armenian folk proverbs such as "A woman is like wool; the more you beat it, the softer it becomes," "A woman is made to cry," or "A husband's beating is like a rose's pricking" seem to add to this culture of silence surrounding domestic violence.

However, even in this culture of silence, according to the 2006 data, during seven years of its existence, the Center for Women Rights assisted more than 10,000 women, including over four thousand victims of domestic violence, who called the Center's hotline. The Motherhood Foundation reports having helped 3,000 victims of domestic violence in three years. According to Anna Badalian from the Motherhood Foundation, these numbers are relatively high for Armenia (a country of approximately three million people) because most Armenian women who experience violence tend to seek for help from their relatives and friends. Only the most helpless victims contact NGOs (Abrahamian 2006).

As Dovile Rukaite's contribution to this volume argues, domestic violence plagues Lithuania as well. According to the 1997-1998 research data, 42.4 percent of all married and living with a long term partner women have experienced physical violence, rape or threats from their husbands or partners. 53.5 percent of divorced women were physically or sexually abused and/or experienced threats in the past. According to another survey to assess domestic violence (sponsored by the Women's Information Issues Center and the UNDP), in 2002, 17 percent of respondents acknowledged that they were forced to have sexual relations by their family members. 10 percent of respondents said that they often were subject to physical violence at home, and 25 percent professed that they were "sometimes" subject to such ordeals (Government of Lithuania 2006).

Like in Armenia, most Lithuanian victims have been reluctant to "air dirty laundry in the public," or talk about domestic violence openly. There are sayings such as "he must be in love with you if he beats you" that help to perpetuate gender violence. Domestic violence is prosecuted under general assault laws; thus, there is no reliable data about the real extent of the problem. In 2008, in a country of approximately 3.4 million people, there were 15 "safe emergency shelters" (Council of Europe 2008). They reported the increase in the number of victims of domestic violence applying for help. Reportedly, this increase was not due to the increase in domestic violence but increase in the availability of services provided by these shelters that are supported by local governments and women's rights NGOs. During one year (2006), the Mother and Child Boarding House in Vilnius (a city of approximately 0.5 million people) provided assistance to 287 victims of domestic violence, forced prostitution and human trafficking (US Department of State 2006b).

International Norms against Gender Violence and Government Responses

In both countries, preparation for the 1995 Fourth World Conference on Women in Beijing brought the issue of domestic violence to the attention of governments and non-governmental groups. In the words of the Armenian authors of the 1995 *United Nations Review*, "violence against women, although there are no records kept in Armenia, is a universal phenomenon. . . . Reporting of violence is not customary. The definition of violence is not clear" (Ishkanian 2004, 278). According to Armine Ishkanian, in 1995-96, even the Armenian NGO activists were unwilling to discuss domestic violence, considering it a "private" issue (2004, 278).

In 1996, a transnational network called *The Young Women and Democracy Program*, using the EU funding, started to mobilize the local Armenian NGOs to address violence against women (Ishkanian 2004). During the following year, an Armenian NGO Women's Rights Center, led by Susanna Vardanyan, also started to deal with domestic violence, and immediately encountered resistance. According to Vardanyan, "most people didn't understand what it was all about" and blamed her organization for "destroying Armenian traditional families" (Karapetyan 2006).

Likewise, in Lithuania, the Preparatory Commission for the Beijing Conference started an information campaign to increase the awareness of women's issues in general and gender violence in particular. At that point, it was observed that the Lithuanian society did not understand the scope of domestic violence. It was considered a "private" problem. There were negative attitudes towards victims among policemen, government officials and society in general. During that time, there were no shelters for battered women and no specific legal measures to address the issue (Meltzer et al. 1995, 26-28).

The NGO report about the status of women in Lithuania prepared for the Conference highlighted the issue of rape which, in the words of Lilija Vasiliauskiene, was considered to be a "dirty and shameful" secret of women. The victims were afraid to speak out for fear of being ridiculed. Vasiliauskiene regretted that there was no "community" tradition in Lithuania, encouraging women to get together, talk about their feelings and form self-help groups (Vasiliauskiene 1995). (Such initiatives can be a powerful empowerment strategy; see Kate Wells's, Lisa M. Vaughn and Gabriela de Cabrera's articles in this volume.) Marija Ausrine Pavilioniene, a leading Lithuanian feminist, argued that NGO activities alone will not help to address the issue of violence against women. She called for a comprehensive state policy against this issue (Pavilioniene 1995).

It took more than a decade for the Lithuanian government to develop a comprehensive strategy to address domestic violence. *The National Strategy on Reducing Domestic Violence against Women* was adopted by the Lithuanian government only in December 2006. The text of *The National Strategy* suggests a shift in official discourse about domestic violence. The document acknowledges that domestic violence should not be a private issue. It promises to improve legislation to address violence against women (as of 2008, the Lithuanian law does not criminalize domestic violence separately from other forms of violence[4]), protect the rights of the victims, provide them with temporary shelter, inform society about the status of domestic violence and work on the rehabilitation of the perpetrators. Importantly, the strategy identifies several popular myths, such as "married women cannot be raped by their husbands," and that if women experience violence, they must have "provoked" it themselves. The document acknowledges the link between domestic violence and stereotypes about gender roles, although it does not challenge the legitimacy of the neo-familial model embraced by Lithuania.

How to explain this change in official discourse? As a small state, Lithuania remains sensitive to international opinion and tries to act as a good member of the EU and global international community. The strategy includes a long list of international agreements signed by Lithuania since the early nineties (when the country regained its independence from the USSR), including the CEDAW, the recommendations of the Council of Europe's Human Rights Commissioner after his visit to Lithuania in November 2003 and the Beijing Platform requiring the governments to address violence against women. The Beijing Platform has been binding in the EU since 1996. Therefore, as a new EU member (since 2004), Lithuania is expected to demonstrate respect for women's rights and fight against gender violence.

In addition, in 2006 Lithuania was chosen to host the EU's Gender Equality Institute. This is the first EU institution to be located in Lithuania. In the words of Vilija Blinkeviciute, Lithuania's Minister of Social Security and Labor, this decision made by the EU's Council of Ministers in December 2006 should be seen as "a great [national] achievement" (Vaiseta 2006). To maintain its image as a "good European," the Lithuanian government feels obligated to demonstrate respect for gender equality—one of the most important principles of the European Union. Within this "Europeanization" discourse, gender equality and fight against gender violence cannot be separated. The assumption is that only when both partners are equal, it is possible to expect a reduction in domestic violence.

The Lithuanian Constitution proclaims equal rights for men and women. There is an independent agency, the Equal Opportunities Ombudsman, which investigates complaints regarding gender discrimination. However, it is not sufficient to introduce progressive legislation to combat domestic violence efficiently. The lack of progress in combating domestic violence was noticed by international actors. In November 2003, the Council of Europe's Human Rights Commissioner visited Lithuania and argued that domestic violence was "reportedly widespread, and that the low levels of reporting to the police appeared to be because it was commonly seen as a private matter, not a human rights violation." In May 2004, a similar critique was made by the UN Human Rights Committee which examined the ways in which Lithuania has implemented the International Covenant on Civil and Political Rights. The Committee also urged the country "to take measure to encourage women to report domestic violence" and "to sensitize the police" in handling the cases of domestic violence (Amnesty International USA 2005).

The National Strategy on Reducing Domestic Violence against Women took these concerns into account, proclaiming increased cooperation among different government agencies and women's rights NGOs. Historically, it is possible to trace the cooperation between the Lithuanian government and women's rights NGOs back to the nineties. In 1999, supported by the UNDP (United Nations Development Programme), the Lithuanian government started training police officials on how to address violence against women (Coomaraswamy 2003, 367). This cooperation involving the police and women's rights groups directly assisting the victims of violence has continued since then. Currently the Lithuanian NGOs are running many different programs, such as hotlines, shelters and reintegration programs to help the victims of domestic violence. Some of these projects, e.g., shelters for the victims of domestic violence, are already supported financially by local governments.

These developments suggest that the NGOs combating domestic violence can continue to expect funding from the Lithuanian government, e.g., the Ministry of Social Affairs and Labor. Currently, this Ministry is already supporting some (but not all) women's rights organizations. In addition, the government has already recruited some women's rights activists to advise the government on changes in legislation to reduce domestic violence.

Will this increased cooperation involving the state and women's rights NGOs mean that the country as a whole is likely to become more open to the values embraced by transnational women's movement such as gender equality? In their article about gender and civil society in Central and Eastern Europe, Barbara Einhorn and Charlotte Sever argued in that women's rights organizations' foci on hotlines, shelters and similar projects "indicate a distinct rejection of the monolithic structures and universalized objectives characteristic of broad-based women's 'movement.' These groups often defined their strategies in terms other than gender and rarely as feminist" (2003, 171). Their insight is applicable to the Lithuanian context. Lithuania's women's rights organizations (e.g., *Caritas*, a Catholic group, and WIIC, the Women's Issues Information Center) are already engaged in projects to help the victims of domestic violence and sexual trafficking, but it is impossible to envision their cooperation on, let's say, an abortion rights campaign or a campaign to promote full gender equality. Consequently, more NGO and state projects to address domestic violence will not necessarily challenge the neo-familial model of gender relations.

Compared with Lithuania, domestic violence has received somewhat less attention from the Armenian government and local women's rights groups. According to Armine Ishkanian, "it is an issue deemed important by international donors, and local NGOs therefore began to address it to take advantage of available funding" (2004, 281). Reportedly, there are no state-sponsored shelters for the victims of domestic violence. At the same time, international observers believe that the *de jure* status of women is "generally good" in Armenia because in theory (like in Lithuania) women are supposed to have equal rights in civil, political and economic areas (Coomaraswamy 2003, 339).

To fulfill its international obligations to fight domestic violence, in 1998, the Armenian government adopted its first *National Plan on Improving the Status of Women and Enhancing Their Role in Society*. Another version of this plan was adopted in 2004.

Like Lithuania, Armenia signed the UN Convention against the Discrimination of all Forms of Violence against Women, the Beijing Platform, the UN Millennium declaration and the Council of Europe Committee's for the Equality of the Rights of Women and Men resolutions. The 2004-2010 National Plan makes a reference to these documents. Unlike the Lithuanian *National Strategy on Reducing Domestic Violence against Women*, the 2004-2010 Armenian *National Plan of Action on Enhancement of the Status of Women and Increasing Their Role in Society* refers to "natural" differences between men and women ("peculiarities of women and men, which are driven by nature") as being crucial to "supporting harmony in social life." According to the document, the goal of the plan is to preserve these features (that is, these "natural" gender differences) in "implementing its measures" (Republic of Armenia n.d.).

In Section 5 (which addresses violence against women), the plan notes the absence of reliable data, lack of appropriate legislation and complains about the absence of "an efficient system of moral and sexual education" for the youth. Although the document includes a vague promise to "harmonize" national laws with the requirements of international treaties signed by Armenia, it does not suggest that the Armenian government is interested in cooperation with the local women's rights NGOs. Furthermore, the plan promises to improve training for law enforcement officials and social workers and makes a commitment to protect the rights of the victims, but it does not make a commitment to make domestic violence into a widely discussed public issue (Republic of Armenia). Like in Lithuania, the government appears to be willing to integrate only those international norms that do not challenge or are perceived as challenging traditional social structures (the familial model in the case of Armenia).

Struggle against trafficking of women is another issue related to gender violence that was introduced by international actors. Unlike domestic violence, this issue was eventually earnestly embraced by the governments and civil societies in both countries. According to Hrach Kajhoyan, the Coordinator of the IOM (International Organization for Migration, a UN agency) programs in Armenia, the IOM tried to attract the attention of the Armenian government to this issue in 2001, when the representatives of this organization met with 51 victims of trafficking. However, the initial response of the government was denial that the problem existed. Kajhoyan argues that the US State Department report criticizing the Armenian government made a difference. Only then did the Armenian government agree to cooperate with the IOM. (Yeghiazavyan 2005). In 2006-8 a whole plethora of Armenian NGOs and international actors worked to end trafficking of women, although it is difficult to overcome the corruption of state officials and weakness of state institutions.

The Lithuanian government has adopted its first comprehensive anti-trafficking program in 2002. Several years later, the program was expanded and revised to guarantee cooperation between different government agencies and NGOs. Now this program includes training sessions for policemen and education initiatives in Lithuania's schools. According to Dovile Rukaite from WIIC (Women's Issues Information Center) in Vilnius, policemen are generally interested in cooperation with women's rights' NGOs because they need help with finding shelter for the victims of trafficking, and the NGOs are able to provide such help. This assistance can include counseling and financial support (Rukaite 2007). Since 2003, there is a Criminal Code criminalizing trafficking in human beings, but, like in Armenia, it is still difficult to fully implement the laws in Lithuania (ENATW 2006). Reportedly, the victims of sexual trafficking are still unwilling to testify in the courts for fear of retribution (Zmogaus teisiu stebejimo institutas 2007, 38). At the same time, numerous international awareness campaigns, anti-trafficking images in public places and publications in the leading newspapers about sexual trafficking suggest that the transnational movement against gender violence succeeded not only in drawing attention to sexual trafficking, but also generating a discursive change related to this issue.

Public Discourses about Domestic Violence: Re-Examining Traditions, Looking for Local Solutions

Although Lithuania's *National Strategy on Reducing Domestic Violence against Women* and Armenia's *National Plan on Improving the Status of Women and Enhancing Their Role in Society* dwell on the ways to address domestic violence, thus suggesting a shift in official discourse, it is difficult to argue that the transnational movement against gender violence has resulted in significant changes in public attitudes. In Lithuania, only in June 2007 did Edita Kauzaite, a Lithuanian actress, decide to "air her dirty laundry" in public. She wrote a play about her own experience of domestic violence and shared her family story with the readers of *Lietuvos Rytas*, a leading Lithuanian daily. "My wedding night was horrible," this is the start of Edita's story. "I should have left my husband then, but I suffered for twelve years. . . . I think that it is time to talk about domestic violence openly" (Vileikiene 2007).

Searching for the roots of acceptance of domestic violence in traditional culture, her play daringly reinterprets one of the most famous Lithuanian fairy tales, *Egle Zalciu Karaliene* (in Lithuanian "Egle, the queen of grass snakes"). Edita thinks that Zilvinas, the main male character in *Egle Zalciu Karaliene*, was the first clearly violent husband in Lithuanian literature. (In the story, he tries to restrict Egle's freedom of movement. When his wife expresses interest in visiting her parents, he tells her to perform impossible tasks, such as wearing iron shoes and making silk.) Edita's play reinvents the narrative of this traditional fairy tale: In the end of her play, Egle manages to escape her oppressive husband.

According to the Armenian newspaper publications, public discussions of domestic violence address the role of traditions as well. Thus, for example, when launching a sixteen day campaign against gender violence in 2006 (similar campaigns are held in Lithuania as well), Consuelo Vidal, UN resident coordinator, argued that "Armenian women suffer violence, but they are afraid and keep silent, as they don't believe that anything can be done about it" (Abrahamian 2006). Recently Karine Nalchajyan, an Armenian psychologist, tried to explore the relationship between the breakdown of traditional (patriarchal) Armenian families and the incidents of domestic violence. Apparently, she bemoaned the disintegration of traditional families, arguing that men were likely to be frustrated by the loss of the "traditional image of father" as "an embodiment of strength" (Yeghyazaryan 2005).

Given the strength of the traditionalist discourse in Armenia, it is not surprising that "Armenian women's organizations have gone to great lengths to demonstrate that they are working for the good of the family and hence the nation" (Ishkanian 2004, 281). Susanna Vardanyan, a leading Armenian advocate against domestic violence, has also used references to the "traditional" Armenian family to raise awareness of domestic violence: "They say that Armenian families are so strong that such matters cannot be discussed outside home. I wish our families were so strong. Sometimes they tell me that we [women's rights groups] should not interfere in our traditional family affairs. But do the traditions include beating and offending? Or they say that it's a family—everything happens. So does it mean that family obligations include beating and humiliation? . . . First of all, our traditions do not include beating a woman—Armenian women have always been respected as mothers, and no one ever raised a hand against them" (2006).

Trying to appeal to the respected traditions of the Armenian families is probably one way to find a local approach to domestic violence instead of being viewed as an agent of foreign influence. Those who oppose transnational feminist movement try to argue that the local women's rights activists are merely interested in winning "big grants" and inventing the rates of domestic violence. Their argument is that the problem of domestic violence was artificially imported from foreign countries: "Many organizations just extort grants from abroad; the foreign mediation into Armenian families is quite dangerous. If the woman is constantly told her husband has no right to reprimand [on] her, we will not have families" (Abrahamyan 2006).

One of the greatest dangers of the traditionalist discourse is the temptation to blame the victim for "provoking" the perpetrators: If only the wives were taught to "hold their tongues," they may have been spared the beating (Karapetyan 2006). In April 2007, similar attitudes were examined in a popular Lithuanian TV show *Jeigu* (Lithuanian for "if only"). This program is partially supported by the EU funds. During this show, Nijole Dirsiene, the Director of Mother and Child Boarding House in Vilnius, put forward a passionate argument that the society should change the ways in which the victims of domestic violence are treated. Dirsiene argued that in Lithuania the victims are usually informed about their rights and where to go after they have experienced violence, but police rarely if ever informs the perpetrators that they will be punished. The perpetrator stays at home, and the victim is forced to flee her home and hide (Jankaityte 2007).

In her attempt to empower the victims of domestic violence, Dirsiene decided not to hide the address of the Mother and Child Boarding House. This is a Lithuanian adaptation of the Western model. (According to the latter, the address of shelter should be kept secret.) During our visit to this institution in June 2006, Dirsiene explained that she believes that the victims of domestic violence should not feel like they did something wrong and they should NOT be the ones hiding. The perpetrators, not the victims, should feel ashamed.

Dirsiene's initiative has been supported by the local government, women's rights NGOs, international and local volunteers. It is an example of how local actors have interpreted the international norms and adapted a foreign model to empower women. Hopefully, there will be more such cases in the future.

Conclusions

In summary, this chapter argues that despite cultural obstacles and local interpretations, transnational movement against gender violence helped to introduce change in Lithuania and Armenia—the societies which have traditionally viewed public discussion of domestic violence as inappropriate. International pressure made the governments revise their narratives, especially when their international prestige and status were at stake. The Lithuanian and Armenian governments did respond to international pressure to address domestic violence and especially to fight sexual trafficking.

However, it is unrealistic to expect that international pressure can change the underlying social structures. The Lithuanian neo-familial model and the Armenian familial model survived the international interventions. In fact, these models may have been even strengthened by them. Local women's rights groups, which are sometimes viewed as the "agents" of foreign influence, are unlikely to gain enough strength to challenge these underlying structures any time soon.

Given the relative weakness of local women's rights groups in post-Communist countries (when compared with the power of the government), it is crucial to make the governments sign international agreements and introduce women-friendly policies. At the same time, successful implementation of these policies depends on the strength of state institutions. The more transparent and accountable to its own people as well as to the international community the government is, the more successful it can be in addressing sexual trafficking and domestic violence.

My interpretation of post–transitional experiences in Armenia and Lithuania underlines the need to support local solutions to global problems introduced by international actors. Only the actors who are seen as rooted in post-transitional societies can find ways to make sure that international norms become domestic realities, not short term NGO projects. At the same time, the power of local civil society actors should not be overestimated. Modern governments still have numerous instruments to affect women's empowerment. For example, in Lithuania many projects pursued by women's rights NGOs are dependent on local and national government support. In particular, the Ministry of Social Affairs and Labor is seen as being "in charge" of dealing with domestic violence and women's rights. This suggests that there is a close relationship between civil society groups and the government, and the latter is in charge of resources.

Given the weakness of civil society in post-communist context, it may be helpful to imagine "acculturation" (a process whereby states respond to social pressure) as a two-level game. On one level, the international community encourages the national governments to pay attention to women's rights issues, change discourse, ratify treaties, change and implement policies corresponding to international norms. On the second level, there is interaction between the international community and local women's rights groups. Although these groups may not have enough power to affect the first level game, they are capable of documenting the impact of government policies and introducing new discourses. Their activities are crucial in weaving the international norms into the local social fabric.

I would like to thank Dovile Rukaite (Lithuania's Women's Issues Information Center) and Dr. Vilana Pilinkaite-Sotirovic (Center for Equality Advancement) for their helpful comments.

Commentary
Dovile Rukaite

I agree with the main argument put forward in Dovile Budryte's chapter: It is unrealistic to expect that international pressure can change the underlying social structures. To fight for international causes, such as violence against women, it is important to find local actors who are seen as "rooted" in local communities. At the same time, I would like to suggest that international actors do make a difference. They introduce new issues and inspire some activists to pursue new agendas.

Our organization (WIIC, Women's Issues Information Center) has good connections with women in different parts of the country and outside of it. As I have mentioned in my contribution to this volume, we are engaged in numerous projects to empower women and address violence against women. However, we felt frustrated and even powerless when in June 2008 the Lithuanian parliament overwhelmingly approved the so-called *Concept of the Family Act*, which defines the family as a union between a man and a woman and which provides the conceptual framework for future laws. We wonder what will come next—the prohibition of abortion? (This has been seriously considered by politicians in Lithuania as well.) My story about *The Concept of the Family Act* shows just how powerful traditional beliefs are in post-communist societies and how difficult it is for NGOs to challenge them. Dovile Budryte's article suggests a similar conclusion.

The Concept of the Family Act is a blow to women's rights organizations in Lithuania. In the text of this act traditional families are described as the "backbone" of the state. This family model ignores the approximately 30 percent of children who are born out of wedlock. It also does not recognize civil unions. Interestingly, the legal department of the parliament denounced the proposed Act as discriminatory.

Women's rights organizations in Lithuania argue that this act goes against international norms. We are worried about single mothers. We are worried that this act will trap women in violent relationships. Prior to its approval the Act was publicly denounced by many people and many demonstrations were held in front of the parliament building. The issue was discussed online, suggesting that the younger generation in Lithuania wants to protect individual rights. However, the majority of the public remained passive. The response from parliamentarians, both men and women, to pressure by women's rights organizations was muted. We did receive support from international non-governmental organizations supporting family planning and the rights of women.

This lack of responsiveness to NGO pressure in Lithuania suggests several conclusions. Clearly, the mobilization of NGOs was not the main problem. Women's rights organizations were well organized and well mobilized. Visibility was not an issue: The mass media paid a lot of attention to this problem. There was some international interest. However, there was no real international pressure to change the Act. Personally, I believe that *The Concept of the Family Act* is backward and inappropriate for a country that wants to host the European Gender Equality Institute. At the same time, this incident suggests that the international community cannot do much to challenge the strong traditional beliefs promoted by politicians, although international attention does help to keep this issue in the public sphere.

Notes

1. By and large, these options were not available before Perestroika. Overall, the Soviet society was immune to outside influences. In addition to being responsible for work at home, most women were employed by the state. See Rukaite's, Keels's and Riegg's contributions.

2. This data was provided by the Lithuanian Statistics Department and quoted in a handout prepared by the Center for Equality Advancement in Vilnius, Lithuania. The data for 2008 is from the United Nations Department of Public Information: http://www.un.org/News/Press/docs/2008/wom1690.doc.htm (accessed July 5, 2008).

3. This data was collected by the IPU (international organization of parliaments). It is available from http://www.ipu.org/wmn-e/classif.htm (accessed July 2, 2008). In 2007, there were 33 women in Lithuania's parliament (out of 141).

4. There are several provisions dealing with violence against pregnant women and mothers in the Lithuanian Criminal Code, but, by and large, the concept of domestic violence against women is missing. For a more detailed explanation, see section "Domestic Violence" in *Stop Violence against Women: A project by the Advocates for Human Rights*, http://www.stopvaw.org/Lithuania2.html (accessed July 2, 2008).

Bibliography

Abrahamian, Gayane. 2006. Armenia's silent victims. *Institute for War and Peace Reporting*, December 14, http://www.iwpr.net/?p=crs&s=f&o=326150&apc_state =henpcrs (accessed July 2, 2008).

Abrahamyan, Gayane. 2006. Fighting tradition: Domestic violence is fabric in the family cloth. *ArmeniaNow.com*, April 7, http://www.armenianow.com/?action=printable& AID=1460&CID=1591&lng=eng (accessed July 2, 2008).

Amnesty International USA. 2005. Annual Report for Lithuania. Amnesty International USA. http://www.amnestyusa.org/annualreport.php?id=ar&yr=2005&c=LTU (accessed on July 2, 2008).

Atshemian, Nane. 2006. Survey highlights gender inequality in Armenia. *Armenialiberty.org*, March 28, http://www.armenialiberty.org/armeniareport/report/en/2006/03/ C3455613-178C-4B68-A86F-6D19B2CA346D.asp (accessed July 2, 2008).

Avdeyeva, Olga. 2007. When do states comply with international treaties? Policies on violence against women in post-communist countries. *International Studies Quarterly* 51 (4): 877-900.

Cicelis, Augustas, and Vilana Pilinkaite-Sotirovic. 2007. *Valdzios aritmetika/Arithmetic of power*. Vilnius: Lygiu galimybiu pletros centras.

Coomaraswamy, Radhika. 2003. *Integration of the human rights of women and the gender perspective: Violence against women*. Report of the Special Rapporteur on vio-

lence against women, its causes and consequences. New York: United Nations Economic and Social Council.
Council of Europe. 2008. Parliamentary Assembly Committee on Equal Opportunities for Women and Men. Questionnaire on the implementation of the parliamentary dimension of the Council of Europe campaign to combat violence against women, including domestic violence. Council of Europe. http://www.coe.int/t/pace/campaign/stopviolence/Source/vienna_questionnaire_results_en.pdf (accessed July 5, 2008).
Danielyan, Emil. 2006. U.S. keeps Armenia on human trafficking "watch list." *Armenialiberty.org*, June 6, http://www.armenialiberty.org/armeniareport/report/en/2006/06/D1CAB809-F4F5-4E23-943B-4F4780C8ACF7.asp (accessed July 2, 2008).
Davidavicius, Algis. 2006. Darbo ir seimos suderinimo politikos kryptys bei galimybes ES ir Lietuvoje: vyraujanciu viesosios politikos paradigmu kaitos analize (Lithuanian for "trends and opportunities for policies reconciling work and family in the EU and Lithuania: analysis of changing paradigms in leading public policies"). In *(Ne)apmokamas darbas: seimai palanki darbo aplinka ir lyciu lygybe Europoje* (Lithuanian for "un/paid work: family-friendly policies and gender equality in Europe"), ed. Jolanta Reingarde, 203-236. Vilnius: Vytauto Didziojo Universitetas/Lygiu galimybiu centras.
Division for the Advancement of Women. 1995a. Fourth World Conference on Women: Platform for action. UN. http://www.un.org/womenwatch/daw/beijing/platform/index.html (accessed July 2, 2008).
Division for the Advancement of Women. 1995b. Report of the Fourth World Conference on Women. UN. http://www.un.org/esa/gopher-data/conf/fwcw/off/a--20.en (accessed July 2, 2008).
Einhorn, Barbara, and Charlotte Sever. 2003. Gender and civil society in Central and Eastern Europe. *International Feminist Journal of Politics* 5(2): 163-90.
ENATW (European Network against Trafficking in Women for Sexual Exploitation). 2006. Implementing gender equality principles to combat trafficking and to prevent sexual exploitation of women and children. MONA. http://www.mona-hungary.hu//kepek/upload/2007-06/ENATW%20report%20final.pdf (accessed July 2, 2008).
GINSC.NET (Gender Issues Information Network for the South Caucasus Region). 2006. Zhenskii trud v Armenii oplachivayetsa na 30% men'she chem muzhskoi (Russian for "in Armenia women earn 30 percent less than men"). December 15, http://www.ginsc.net/members/news_details_ru.php?id=2860&sub=region&stat=active (accessed July 2, 2008).
Government of Lithuania. 2006. Nutarimas "Del valstybines smurto pries moteris mazinimo strategijos ir jos igyvendinimo priemoniu 2007-2009 metu patvirtinimo" (Lithuanian for "decision regarding national strategy on reducing domestic violence against women and its implementation in 2007-2009"). Women's Issues Information Center. http://www.lygus.lt/ITC/files_smurtas/Valstybine%20smurtoplanas.doc (accessed July 2, 2008).
Ishkanian, Armine. 2004. The challenges facing women in Armenia's non-governmental organization sector. In *Post-Soviet women encountering transition, nation building, economic survival and civic activism*, ed. Kathleen Kuehnast and Carol Nechemias, 262-287. Washington, D.C.: Woodrow Wilson Center Press.
Jankaityte, Dalia. 2007. TV laida "Jeigu": Didziojo smurto istaku beieskant (Lithuanian for "TV program 'if only': Searching for reasons of massive violence"). *Alfa.lt*, April 25, http://www.alfa.lt/straipsnis/134819 (accessed July 2, 2008).

Jankauskaite, Margarita. 2007. Lyciu lygybe: stereotipai ir diskriminacija (Lithuanian for "gender equality: stereotypes and discrimination"). In *Diskriminuoti draudziama/integruoti* (Lithuanian for "it is forbidden to discriminate/integrate"), ed. Indre Mackeviciute, 11-20. Vilnius: Lygiu galimybiu kontrolieriaus tarnyba.

Johnson, Janet Elise, and Jean C. Robinson. 2007. Living Gender. In *Living gender after Communism*, ed. Janet Elise Johnson and Jean C. Robinson, 1-24. Bloomington: Indiana University Press.

Karapetyan, Astghik. 2006. A family where violence exists has already deteriorated. *Stop Violence against Women*, May 23, http://www.stopvaw.org/Domestic_Violence 4.html#A_Family_Where_Violence_Exists_Is_Already_Deteriorated (accessed July 2, 2008).

Keck, Margaret E., and Kathryn Sikkink. 1998. *Activists beyond borders: Advocacy networks in international politics.* Ithaca, NY: Cornell University Press.

Meltzer, Erica, Dunja Pastizzi-Ferencic, and Patrice Robineau. 1995. *Women in the ECE region: A call for action. Highlights of the ECE high level regional preparatory meeting for the fourth world conference on women.* New York: UN.

Pavilioniene, Ausrine Marija. 1995. Smurtas pries moteris (Lithuanian for "violence against women"). In *Moterys kintancioje visuomeneje—Lietuvos nevyriausybiniu moteru organizaciju ataskaita Jungtiniu tautu organizacijos IV pasaulinei moteru konferencijai Pekine 1995* (Lithuanian for "women in a transitional society: Lithuania's women's NGOs' report to the UN fourth world conference in Beijing"), 52. Vilnius: Pradai.

Republic of Armenia. n.d. 2004-2010 Republic of Armenia National Action Plan on Improving the Status of Women and Enhancing Their Role in Society (unofficial translation). TANDIS-Tolerance and Non-discrimination Information System. http://tandis.odihr.pl/index.php?p=country,arm,nap (accessed on July 2, 2008).

Rukaite, Dovile. 2007. Meeting with the author in Vilnius, Lithuania, June 21.

UN General Assembly Committee on Elimination of Discrimination against Women. 2008. Women's anti-discrimination committee commends Lithuania's gender equality laws but questions the draft bill to severely restrict legal abortion. UN. http://www.un.org/News/Press/docs/2008/wom1690.doc.htm (accessed July 5, 2008).

US Department of State. 2006a. Country Reports on Human Rights Practices: Armenia. US Department of State. http://www.state.gov/g/drl/rls/hrrpt/2006/78799.htm (accessed on July 2, 2008).

US Department of State. 2006b. Country Reports on Human Rights Practices: Lithuania. US Department of State. http://www.state.gov/g/drl/rls/hrrpt/2006/78824.htm (accessed on July 2, 2008).

Vaiseta, Tomas. 2006. Pirmaja ES institucija Lietuvoje taps Lyciu Lygybes institutas (Lithuanian for "Gender Equality Institute will be the first EU institution located in Lithuania"). *Lietuvos Rytas*, December 2.

Vardanyan, Susanna. 2006. Is beating women a national tradition? *Aravot*, March 4.

Vasiliauskiene, Lilija. 1995. Smurtas ir prievarta pries moteris (Lithuanian for "violence and force used against women"). In *Moterys kintancioje visuomeneje—Lietuvos nevyriausybiniu moteru organizaciju ataskaita Jungtiniu tautu organizacijos IV pasaulinei moteru konferencijai Pekine 1995* (Lithuanian for "Women in a transitional society: Lithuania's women's NGOs' report to the UN fourth world conference in Beijing"), 50-51. Vilnius: Pradai.

Vileikiene, Ausra. 2007. Tu siandien dar neverkei, kale, arba tikroji Egles Zalciu karalienes istorija (Lithuanian for "you haven't yet cried today, bitch"). *Lietuvos Rytas*, June 29.

Yeghyazaryan, Aghavni. 2005. Anti-trafficking efforts in Armenia. *HetqOnline*, December 19, http://archive.hetq.am/eng/society/0512-mard.html (accessed July 2, 2008).

Zastoukhova, Nouneh. 2008. Statement during the 52nd session of the Commission on the Status of Women, February 28. UN. http://www2.un.int/Countries/Armenia/12042976712451.doc.

Zmogaus teisiu stebejimo institutas (Lithuanian for "human rights monitoring institute"). 2007. *Zmogaus teisiu igyvendinimas Lietuvoje 2006: Apzvalga* (Lithuanian for "implementation of human rights in Lithuania in 2006: A survey"). Vilnius, Eugrimas.

Chapter 3
Paradoxes of "Gender Equality" in Lithuania: Violence against Women and Equal Opportunities
Vilana Pilinkaite-Sotirovic

This chapter analyzes how dominant culture and institutional forces in Lithuania produce the acceptance of violence against women that gets in the way of gender equality. The rule of law guarantees equal rights for women and men to participate in decision-making processes, seek employment and education, engage in intellectual activities and obtain highly qualified positions. Therefore, the Lithuanian society believes that there are no problems of gender equality in Lithuania. However, everyday experiences of both women and men go beyond the legal and political relationships. They are subject to numerous social, economic and cultural influences. Formal equality does not automatically translate into substantive equality.

The Lithuanian government declares its respect for the right to privacy and its unwillingness to regulate the private sphere of citizens. However, as Nira Yuval-Davis argued, there is no social sphere which is protected from government intervention in modern welfare nation-states (2000, 80). Thus, by conducting this political act (stating its unwillingness to "violate" the private sphere), the Lithuanian state constructs the boundaries of its non/interference. The state dichotomizes these two spheres (private and public) along gender lines, enforces gender differences, gendered labor division and gendered meaning of violence. Violence against men is considered to be a serious crime. Violence against women and discrimination of women continue to be the "silent" problems, treated as "private" and unimportant.

This chapter will draw on legal acts and their interpretations collected for the project *Stop Violence against Women: Monitoring the Actual Situation in Lithuania*.[1] By exploring the so-called "gender-blind" construction of equality and protection of the private sphere from the governmental interference, I will reflect on resistance to women's rights, indifference towards domestic violence and preservation of patriarchal traditions in Lithuania.

This chapter is divided into three parts. The first section describes the social context, depicts social meanings and prevalence of gender inequality in Lithuanian society. The second section focuses on legislation which strengthens patriarchal attitudes towards women. It introduces feminist interpretations of laws by arguing that state-supported "gender-neutral" categories make it difficult to fully support women's rights. Finally, the chapter includes references to several cases of sexual harassment. These cases reveal deeply rooted patriarchal attitudes towards women.

Gender In/Equality in Lithuania: Social Context and Prevalent Beliefs

How does Lithuanian society understand "gender equality"? According to a popular Lithuanian proverb, "A man is the head, and a woman is the neck which directs it." This proverb captures the division of gender roles in Lithuania. In addition, it describes a social hierarchy which is rooted in social and cultural norms. Men are the heads of the household, "natural" leaders in politics and business, and women are expected to take care of mundane household tasks, perform low and middle scale office jobs and other non-essential tasks.

My female friends often use this proverb to argue that women have an "exceptional" place in Lithuanian society. "We, women, they say, are too smart to participate publicly in decision making processes. Therefore, we rule our men indirectly." Counter-arguments pointing out that such "indirect ruling" may consume a lot of time and energy as well as place women below men are usually ignored.

This example shows how gender inequality is "naturalized" within Lithuanian society. This is not an isolated case. In various professional trainings I heard many educated women argue that they do not want to be equal to men because then they will lose their "feminine" attraction, female "privileges" of getting special attention from "their" men in public and being awarded an "exceptional" role of care-giver in private domain. This primitive understanding of equality is usually supported by arguing that equality in Western Europe, and particularly in Scandinavian countries, has already resulted in masculinization of Western women. In addition, memories about the "double burden" of working women during the Soviet period are also brought into conversation (Morvai 2004; Platek 2004; Einhorn 1993; Reingardiene 2001).

Such attitudes are not unique. Many post-communist Eastern and Central European countries have similar memories of how the Communist governments tried (albeit unsuccessfully) to emancipate women. Therefore, it is not surprising that in Lithuania, like other post-communist countries, the public/private divide was "re-traditionalized" after the collapse of the Soviet regime (OSI 2005). Commenting on this phenomenon, Jolanta Reingarde (Reingardiene), a Lithuanian sociologist, argued that when Socialism as a viable political system was rejected, patriarchal gender relations were rearticulated, and patriarchal democracy was reconstructed. Women saw motherhood as a privilege denied to them under Socialism. As a social institution, family became almost a sacred place which gave meaning to the lives of individuals. According to Reingarde, these images are alive and well in modern Lithuania. They are promoted by conservative and even liberal political forces. Those who espouse traditional views of gender roles tend to ignore changes in the family structure, high divorce rates, low fertility rates and increasing domestic violence against women (Reingardiene 2001, 10-11).

Structural Inequalities

As previously stated, many Lithuanian women are convinced that they do not experience gender discrimination. However, they are unable to explain why women, who constitute more than half of Lithuanian society and are better educated than men, are paid less than men, experience higher unemployment and social exclusion. Women can hardly make their voices heard in important political decision making processes. The Lithuanian labor market is segregated along gender lines. Women are more frequently involved in the so-called "feminine" professions in education, healthcare, social work and services, while men are employed in building, transport, information technology and other "masculine" jobs (OSI 2005).

Though unemployment in Lithuania is relatively low, women are most frequently affected by the long-interval unemployment which results in feminization of poverty. Women are less likely to be hired for high level power positions. There are only 48 women leaders listed among the 600 top business leaders in Lithuania (Krutkiene and Silvanaviciute 2005).

Since 1991 (as of 2008), only 7 percent of all ministers were women. In 2007, there were only three women (out of 13) in the Cabinet. They served as the Ministers of Social Security, Agriculture as well as Education and Science. Women hardly occupy the highest positions of law enforcement. There has never been a woman in the position of Prosecutor General, Police Commissioner General or the Chief Justice of the Supreme Court. However, up to 95 percent workforce in notary offices are women. Only 36 percent of women lawyers work as solicitors (Department of Statistics 2006, 18).

According to the 2003-2007 data, there were only three women mayors (out of 60), and only 20 percent of workforce employed by the local government were women (Center for Equality Advancement 2007). Even though some women succeed in obtaining high offices in Parliament, their representation in power structures does not resemble the proportion of women (52 percent) in the Lithuanian population (Department of Statistics 2006, 10-17). To make matters worse, many female politicians have a very limited knowledge of what gender equality is. Therefore, they continue to reproduce the traditional gender role stereotypes by promoting the "traditional" Lithuanian values which suggest that women should be focusing on their homes and family, not their careers.

In contrast, men are the ones who, according to popular beliefs, should focus on their careers. It is not surprising therefore, that paternal leave is very unpopular in Lithuania. Only 1.2 percent of men take paternal leave (Reingardiene et al. 2005, 10). Families explain this trend by arguing that men tend to earn more than women; thus, if they take leave, this decision may have a huge impact on the financial well being of the whole family (Reingardiene 2005). Prevalent social beliefs about hegemonic masculinity also explain the unpopularity of paternal leave. Men are supposed to be the breadwinners, strong enough to compete in the rough world of capitalism and global politics. Women are seen as objects created to give birth. They need to show respect to the gendered "natural" hierarchies. Society respects women who play their prescribed roles in the private realm well.

Women can also be seen a source of pleasure. Then they lose society's respect and become symbols of immorality and indecent behavior. This cultural belief system implies that it is immoral for a "well-respected" woman to divorce her husband even if he is abusive, a drunkard or philanderer because only married women (preferably with children) can be of value to society. However, the same cultural norms do not condemn a man who imposes "discipline" on his wife, drinks, or abandons his family.

The Limited Power of Non-Governmental Actors: The Independent Mass Media and Women's NGOs

Different moral standards for men and women are integrated into the leading social and political discourses. For example, during a seminar focused on women's rights, a battered woman told a story what her life with an abusive husband was like and how law enforcement institutions, municipality officials and other community members ignored her numerous attempts to get help. Finally, she decided to make her story public by contacting a TV program *Prasau Zodzio* (Lithuanian for "I would like to speak out"). During the program, she told the audience that she would kill her husband if he dared to enter her house. After this public statement, she had to face many visitors the next morning—police officers, officers of the Protection of the Child's Rights and many others who warned her about threatening to kill her husband. She was told that she could be arrested or even imprisoned for making threats publicly. This case illustrates how difficult it is to get the state institutions involved to fight domestic violence and try to help the victim, not the perpetrator.

It is extremely rare that victims of domestic violence speak out in the public about their "private" problems. By attempting to use the independent media as a source of empowerment, the victim of domestic violence had to make herself into a perpetrator, at least in the eyes of the public. Clearly, this case did not inspire other victims of domestic violence to make public appearances.

Unfortunately, the victims of domestic violence in Lithuania cannot expect a lot of public support (including public statements) from civil society groups, not even women's rights NGOs. First, there are social norms which condone silence about domestic violence. In Lithuania, as in other post-communist countries, there is a rigid division between the public and private spheres along gender lines. This division means that domestic violence is seen as a "minor" form of aggression. This attitude can be traced back to the times of Socialism when the government strictly controlled individual actions. There was a lot of social pressure to maintain "solidarity" within family as the only alternative to state power. Issues such as domestic violence were treated as "invisible." Therefore, such issues offered little incentive for collective action.

Second, the women's rights NGOs suffer from the lack of funds. My conversations with the heads of women's NGO shelters in Lithuania suggest that their services for battered women are the single source of psychological, social and medical support for the victims. However, this women's non-governmental sector is very weak financially because the government does not view it as important and therefore does not support it financially. (Most Lithuanian NGOs still depend on the state support for survival.) The women's rights NGOs survive from short-term projects supported by the national or local government. It is difficult to obtain money from private donors. One activist told me that funding is limited and often delayed. At the same time, psychological, medical and social services are expected any time when victims seek help.

The Rule of Law: Social Realities and Legal Interpretations

After transition to democracy in 1989, the Lithuanian government concentrated its efforts on joining the UN (United Nations) and the EU (European Union). For this purpose, Lithuania had to implement numerous legal, institutional, social and economic reforms. Gender equality was one of the requirements to join the EU. Like a good student, the Lithuanian government started to introduce gender equality norms into legislation and government institutions. As a result, it is difficult to find a single act or regulation which would be openly discriminatory. The Lithuanian government often boasts that it has successfully met the EU gender equality requirements, introduced appropriate anti-discriminatory laws and promoted equality in the public and private spheres. However, these progressive principles were introduced without a critical analysis of their connection to power relations, gender, class, ethnicity and other social factors.

Many bureaucrats, politicians and the general public believe that the rule of law in Lithuania is objective and neutral. The laws and the legal system are seen as an adequate safeguard for the treatment of women as equal citizens because the legal system is not supposed to favor any gender or other social groups. However, this declared "equality" does not mean that women and men are treated equally in everyday life. Analysis of women's rights in Lithuania suggests that these rights continue to be violated because there is no proper mechanism to implement the laws. For example, in 2004, Article 132 of the Criminal Procedure Code was introduced. It attempted to enforce separation of the perpetrator from the family in the cases of domestic violence. However, in practice, this provision could have been hardly implemented because it was difficult to decide where to place the abuser and how to control him. In addition, it was difficult to find ways to provide psychological support to the abuser and the victim. In practice, when law was applied to separate the perpetrator from his family, he returned and became even more violent towards his wife (Zmogaus teisiu stebejimo institutas 2004). Thus, in many cases, in practice progressive legislation does not mean more than progressive declaration of gender equality.

Gender-Neutral Legal Concepts: Does "Equality" Mean that Women Are Treated Like Men?

In Lithuania, most lawyers and politicians understand the concept of "gender equality" as "gender neutrality." This "neutrality" does not take unique women's experiences into account. Domestic violence falls under the "private accusation procedure," which means that the victim has to write a complaint to the court, collect evidence and provide witnesses. Other cases of violent behavior, even if this behavior occurred in the private space (for example, fight between brothers), are investigated according to the "state accusation procedures." To make matters worse, many police officers think that their job is to investigate "serious" crimes instead of "wasting" their time and energy on *domestic or private conflicts*, such as violence against women.

The officials in law enforcement establishment argue that the existing private accusation practice in the cases of domestic violence is necessary because no one has the right to interfere in the private life of the spouses who frequently quarrel but later reconcile. Many victims of domestic violence withdraw their accusations. Then the pre-trial investigation stops. As a result, perpetrators are not held accountable for their violent behavior. The victims (who are female) have to face social stigma. They are made to feel guilty for the situation in their household. Thus, in practice, "gender-neutral" treatment of violence in the criminal justice system means that those who interpret and implement law focus on male experiences.

Theory is not entirely gender neutral either. In legal academic literature violence as a crime is analyzed and presented only in terms of male experience. Popular case studies analyzing violence in the private and public spheres include only men. Strangely, there are no analyses of domestic violence cases in which women are the victims (Kujalis 2004).

These insights suggest that the boundaries of intervention and nonintervention along gender lines are embedded in law. Legal theorists and practitioners strongly advocate for gender-neutral and objective categories in law, but they treat them from a male perspective. Women's experiences and perspectives are deemed as "subjective," potentially destructive to the "objectivity" of law. Krisztina Morvai, a Hungarian legal theorist, makes a similar case by arguing that male, not female, experience is considered to be the "norm" in legal thought and practice. She suggests that in post-communist Europe feminist analyses and push to take women's experiences into account are deemed as "non-neutral" and potentially challenging the existing social order based on the male dominance (Morvai 2004).

Legal Issues and the Social Context

As previously mentioned, there is a law in Lithuania ordering the perpetrator (who was engaged in domestic violence) to live separately from the victim. On paper, the main objective of this law is to protect the interests of the children and the interests of the victim during divorce. Certain protective measures allow property to be seized for the temporary support of minor children and/or the victim (the other spouse) and to cover the litigation costs of the victim. The law allows the court to determine who should get temporary custody of the minor children and to prohibit one of the spouses from having contact with children and/or from appearing in certain places (presumably places where minor children could be found, such as a school). In summary, the court may decide that the protection of the spouse (victim of domestic violence) and minor children should outweigh the other spouse's rights to property, children and freedom of movement. All of these measures are clearly described as provisional. They depend on the outcome of the divorce lawsuit.

However, the first provisional protective measure includes an additional condition. The court may order one of the spouses to live separately if "circumstances permit." It is unclear what these "circumstances" are—financial conditions or personal preferences expressed by the perpetrator. This phrase could also imply that there is domestic violence in the family; thus, the court could issue an order forcing the violent spouse to move out. Vague wording does not help to protect the right of women and children to live free from domestic violence. Difficulties that may be potentially experienced by an abuser should not be more important than the safety of women and children. According to the Lithuanian law, the court can order a child to live in another household during the divorce proceedings. Consequently, it should be possible to make the abuser find accommodation if he causes harm to his family members.

Two government actors—the Supreme Court and the Advisor to the Committee of Legal Affairs at the Lithuanian Parliament—offered their legal commentary of the law on domestic violence. Both actors argued that the equality principle should apply to both spouses. However, their interpretations revealed that women and men are unlikely to be treated equally in practice. The Advisor argued that when ordering the perpetrator live separately temporarily, the court should consider the perpetrator's financial and other relevant circumstances, because separation from family limits the perpetrator's right to have power over his living quarters (Lietuvos Respublikos Seimas 2005). This comment suggests that an abusive husband may temporarily lose his right to housing. However, I doubt whether the Advisor (or any other legal officer for that matter) has ever considered the fact that many women with small children are frequently forced to run away from their homes with abusive spouses and seek temporary shelter in the crises centers.

In addition, the Advisor argued that the court should take into consideration the possibility of blackmail by the spouse (women) who might use their domestic violence victim status to acquire more property in divorce litigation. This commentary is an example of a typical misogynistic attitude in Lithuania. Women are portrayed as guilty in cases of domestic violence because they are "provoking" men in pursuit of their hidden agenda. In addition, the commentary demonstrates that most legal officials are ignorant of women's issues.

Sexual Harassment: Crime or "Seduction"?

Gender stereotypes and double standards of sexual morals manifest themselves during the investigation of cases related to sexual harassment. Most people believe that women are guilty in these cases because they "provoke" men, including their male supervisors, and later accuse them of sexual harassment.

In 2003, a female student accused her professor at Vilnius University of sexual harassment. She made her accusations public, thus triggering debates on TV, newspapers and informal conversations. These public debates proved once again that women's experiences are not taken seriously in the cases of sexual harassment. During the debates, the student's motives, behavioral patterns, her failures in studying and her physical appearance were scrutinized. In contrast, the male professor was defended. His academic achievements and personal characteristics as a good father and caring husband were highlighted. Eventually, after several months, the professor was fired from Vilnius University. However, society continued to see him as a victim of a selfish provocateur who failed to graduate from the university.

It is unclear how many women are sexually harassed because there is very little reliable data on sexual harassment. Since 2003, only four cases are registered every year. Only a few got some publicity (Dvilaitis 2004, 104-113). In such cases, double standards are applied, even legally. For example, Lithuania's Criminal Code includes an article on sexual harassment. However, according to this Code, only "vulgar" and "rough" behavior is considered to be criminal. The Code states that the abuser will be punished if he raped a woman without her consent. The legal academic literature is heavily focused on physical behavior of the perpetrator and the victim. Other indicators of sexual harassment, such as verbal abuse, psychological pressure or attempts to have sex with the victim are not considered to be "vulgar" behavior and do not fall under the Article 152 of the Criminal Code (Dvilaitis 2004, 110-112). This suggests that sexual harassment can be punished only if there is physical sexual intercourse without consent of the victim. Even worse, the burden of proof falls on the victim who has to initiate the case in court.

In 2006, one case of sexual harassment became public. A woman experienced sexual harassment in her workplace. She recorded the inappropriate actions of her supervisor and complained to the Office of Ombudsperson for Equal Opportunities. After a thorough investigation, the Ombudsperson found the supervisor guilty. However, the supervisor took the case to the civil court. He denied his fault and accused the Ombudsperson of being biased. The court purged him of the charge of sexual harassment due to "the lack of evidence." As a result, hoping to keep their jobs and avoid public embarrassment, many women decide to keep silent about the cases of sexual harassment.

When working on the project *Stop Violence against Women*, I discovered that many female employees do in fact experience sexual harassment by their supervisors. However, they prefer to be silent because they do not believe that there is appropriate support available for them. In addition, they are afraid to damage their reputation. Women feel that their male supervisor will always be able to find support, excuses and power to defend himself, thus making the situation worse for someone who is harassed.

Seeing women as sexual objects in public or private spheres perpetuates double moral standards. If a woman responds to sexual harassment in her workplace, she is considered to be a "provocateur." The absence of strict legal or public opposition to sexual harassment allows the abusers to escape accountability. The whole burden of psychological discomfort falls on the victim's (woman's) shoulders.

Conclusion

In Lithuania, legal mechanisms of gender equality have been created. However, the dominant culture reproduces traditional gender roles and stereotypes that disadvantage and disempower women. This experience is not unique to Lithuania; similar trends prevail in the other post-communist countries which have recently joined the EU.

Following the recommendations of the international community and requirements of the EU, the Lithuanian government has successfully introduced progressive legislation declaring gender equality. However, a formal declaration that women and men are equal does not take into account complex reality. In practice, there is a popular perception that men and women are equal; however, structural inequalities determine that politics and businesses are dominated by men. Women's participation in the top leading institutional positions and top business management is limited.

Culturally, there are numerous everyday practices that diminish the importance of gender equality enshrined in laws, strengthen traditional gender roles and make domestic violence appear trivial. The government is unwilling to regulate the private domain. All these developments prove that gender equality did not become a prevalent democratic value in Lithuania.

Although the legal establishment in Lithuania claims that laws related to violence against women are "objective" and "gender neutral," a closer analysis of relevant documents and legal practices proves that "gender equality" is interpreted from a male perspective, which tends to ignore women's experiences. The state legal apparatus functions without trying to establish a connection to the socio-cultural norms. This is detrimental to women. Furthermore, there is very little critical feminist thought on legislation related to domestic violence and other types of violence against women.

Analysis of several cases that involve domestic violence and sexual harassment proves that civil society is very weak in Lithuania. Usually, individuals (that is, women) are blamed for the problems. Society as a whole is not willing to criticize the state-sanctioned norms. Consolidation of human rights NGOs and their efforts is necessary to start to develop a truly democratic culture in Lithuania.

I would like to thank my friend and colleague Dovile Budryte who encouraged me to write this chapter and reviewed the first draft. Her many useful comments and remarks have vastly improved this chapter. Also, my special thanks are to Natalya T. Riegg and Jolanta Reingarde (Reingardiene) who contributed enormously to the development of the ideas and arguments of this chapter.

Commentary
Suzanne Leclerc-Madlala

For countries that couldn't be further apart geographically or historically, it is indeed striking how similar the present condition of women is in these new democracies. More than being simply an academic curiosity, we might call it a feminist tragedy. But like all such tragedies, it forces us to think about the complexity of the challenges involved in the advancement of women's human rights. As we find, dominant culture in South Africa and institutional forces in Lithuania conspire to produce a social acceptance of gender-based violence, in spite of formal declarations about the equality of men and women. The progressive legislative environment is yet to be reflective of the lived-reality where the status of women is perceived, interpreted and constructed.

During the era of Socialism women in Lithuania were dragged into the labor market through a forced modernization program. During apartheid most of South Africa's women were forced to stay in impoverished rural areas or have their movements in and out of strictly regulated "whites-only" urban areas. Still, in spite of these markedly different political trajectories of "liberation" and democracy, it is striking how, in the post-authoritarian era, women find themselves still wrapped in the old familiar shroud of patriarchal culture and social expectation. With the recent democratization of both countries, there is a noticeable convergence of the conditions, concerns and aspirations of women. The politicians of both countries seem obsessed with matters of global politics. What appears to preoccupy them most is an eagerness to prove themselves to the global powers-that-be as leaders who are serious players in the new world order, true democrats and progressively minded individuals who are well-versed in human rights discourses and contemporary issues of gender equality. This dominant orientation has limited their understanding of the social context as well as their sensitivity to the day-to-day functioning mechanisms of gender relations.

What emerges clearly when comparing the state of gender equality and the normativeness of gender-based violence in these widely divergent settings is evidence that democracy alone cannot free women. Required empowerment strategies must be long-term, sustainable and unequivocal in their goals. Raising awareness of women's issues is the first step towards addressing widespread social ignorance of gender violence and sexual harassment. In both countries the call is made for a consolidation of efforts by NGOs to help grow the desired democratic culture to match the democratic legislation. There is an emerging consciousness that laws alone cannot resolve the problem of gender inequality. It is society that must do this work; as everywhere, that usually means women themselves.

Notes

1. The project *Stop Violence against Women: Monitoring the Actual Situation* was organized by Violence against Women (VAW) Monitoring Program of the Open Society Institute (Budapest, Hungary). It included twenty two Central and Eastern European countries as well as the Caucasus and Central Asia. The Monitoring was completed by the NGOs active in these countries, working in the field of violence against women, aimed to map the situation in their countries and focusing on state responses. The monitoring methodology was based on the recommendations of the Committee of Ministers of the Council of Europe on the protection of women against violence. They covered the governmental responses to VAW, including international state responsibilities, policy documents, national action plans, legislation, institutional bodies, responsible actors and budgets. Research on Lithuania included the analysis of national programs on equal opportunities for women and men and trafficking in human persons, criminal and civil legislation, law enforcement, available services, education and training, media coverage, data collection and statistics and awareness raising campaigns. As a result of the monitoring, twenty two Country factsheets were prepared. These factsheets issued clear recommendations to governments, serving as effective tools for advocacy at national and international levels. The Center for Equality Advancement in Vilnius, Lithuania, was responsible for research on Lithuania. This chapter uses the material collected during this project.

Bibliography

Center for Equality Advancement. 2007. *Savivaldybiu aritmetika* (Lithuanian for "the arithmetic of local government"), http://www.gap.lt/index.php?cid=292 (accessed July 3, 2008).
Department of Statistics. 2006. *Moterys ir vyrai Lietuvoje 2005* (Lithuanian for "women and men in Lithuania 2005"). Vilnius: Department of Statistics.

Dvilaitis, Vidmantas. 2004. Seksualinis priekabiavimas ir teisine atsakomybe uz ji (Lithuanian for "sexual harassment and legal liability"). *Jurisprudencija* 60 (52): 104-113.
Einhorn, Barbara. 1993. *Cinderella goes to market: citizenship, gender and women's movements in East Central Europe*. New York: Verso.
Krutkiene, Izolda, and Simona Silvanaviciute. 2005. Lietuvos moterys įsitvirtina versle (Lithuanian for "Lithuanian women are consolidating their positions in business"). *Lietuvos zinios*, December 13.
Kujalis, Pavelas. 2004. Prievarta—butinojo reikalingumo pavojaus saltinis (Lithuanian for "violence as a source of a necessity threat"). *Jurisprudencija* 60 (52): 74-81.
Lietuvos Respublikos Seimas (Parliament of Lithuania). 2005. Lietuvos Respublikos Civilinio kodekso 3.65 straipsnio pakeitimo istatymo projekto aiskinamasis rastas (Lithuanian for "an explanation for a draft law to change Article 3.65 of the Civil Code of the Lithuanian Republic). Lietuvos Respublikos Seimas. http://www3.lrs.lt/pls/inter2/dokpaieska.showdoc_l?p_id=263853&p_query=Civilinis%20kodeksas%20&p_tr2=0 (accessed July 3, 2008).
Morvai, Kristina. 2004. Women and the rule of law in Hungary. *Feminist Review* 76: 100-109.
OSI (Open Society Institute). 2005. *Lygios moterų ir vyrų galimybės* (Lithuanian for "Equal opportunities for women and men"). Vilnius: Garnelis.
Platek, Monika. 2004. Hostages of destiny: gender issues in today's Poland. *Feminist Review* 76: 5-25.
Reingardiene, Jolanta. 2001. *Socialinis prievartos prieš moterį kontekstas Lietuvoje* (Lithuanian for: "social context of violence against women in Lithuania"), a doctoral dissertation. Kaunas: Vytautas Magnus University.
———. 2005. Fatherhood in question: Attitudes of Lithuanian politicians and state officers towards paternity leave. In *Men and fatherhood: New forms of masculinity in Europe*, ed. by Arturas Tereskinas and Jolanta Reingardiene, 38-58. Vilnius: Eugrimas.
Reingardiene, Jolanta, Arturas Tereskinas, Arnoldas Zdanevicius, Celia Callus, Lea Vedel Drews, Franz Wilhelm Cybulski, Ingolfur V. Gislason, and Gisli Hrafn Atlason. 2005. *Fathers on parental leave/Vyrai ir vaiko prieziuros atostogos*. Vilnius: Lygiu galimybiu pletros centras and Eugrimas.
Zmogaus teisiu stebejimo institutas (Lithuanian for "human rights monitoring institute"). 2004. *Zmogaus teisiu igyvendinimas Lietuvoje 2004: Apzvalga* (Lithuanian for "implementation of human rights in Lithuania in 2004: A survey"). Vilnius, Eugrimas.
Yuval-Davis, Nira. 2000. *Gender and Nation*. London: SAGE Publications.

Chapter 4
"Come Rape Us!" The Everyday Trauma of Sexual Violence in South Africa
Suzanne Leclerc-Madlala

Escalating levels of stress related psychopathologies prompted the South African Society of Psychiatrists in 2006 to call upon government to acknowledge publicly that violent crime in all its forms has taken on proportions of a national disaster. The authors of the report stated that government was failing to uphold peoples' newfound constitutional rights, the result being "the majority of people living in a state of perpetual fear, and if able to afford to, hiding behind walls, high fences and razor wire while the less fortunate are left to the mercy of killers" (Meyer 2006, 5). For the country's women and children the prospect of violence is ever-present, having become a routine consideration when making daily decisions. Which routes to take to school, where to wait for buses and taxis, which clothes to wear, which relatives to trust for child-care, which neighbors to let into homes, which windows to close, doors to bolt, gates to lock—all these thoughts preoccupy South African women who live with the constant threat of violence and violation. This hyper-awareness has become a major new burden for women and girls in the post-apartheid democratic South Africa.

The extent to which gender-based violence in all its forms mars the lives of women and curtails their freedom at a time when they should be enjoying freedom, was highlighted in a recent summary report of crime in the Durban area for the year 2006. Durban is the country's third largest city with a population of approximately 2.5 million situated on the semi-tropical east coast of the Indian Ocean. The report consisted of a long review of specific crime cases, with the most heinous being those involving rape and murder. The following examples are illustrative:

> On December 11, five-year-old Nosini Mnukwa drowned after a knife-yielding man confronted her and her four sisters as they were walking along a river. He tried to get them to undress with the aim of raping them. The panicked child

jumped into the river while her sisters ran away, but found herself in difficulties. She turned to her would-be rapist on the river bank and pleaded with him to help her. The man fled, leaving her to drown.

On October 26, KwaMashu residents took revenge on an alleged serial rapist and his friends, hacking and stoning two suspects to death after dragging them from a police car in which they had been placed after being arrested. Armed with bush knives, axes, hammers, knives and stones, the furious crowd of more than 300 women attacked the man and his friend. The police tried to pull the men back but the crowds were uncontrollable. Soon after the killings the third suspect handed himself over to police (Daily News Reporter 2007).

Official police reports indicate that all types of gender-based violence have greatly increased since the democratic transition of 1994 (Jewkes and Abrahams 2002). Whether or not that increase was due primarily to an increase in reporting (as government officials claimed throughout the 1990s) or to an increase in actual incidence, was a topic that was much debated during the early years of democracy. With the start of the second decade of democratic rule, there is now a wide agreement amongst crime authorities, some government officials and ordinary people that incidences of this kind of violence have indeed increased markedly since the 1994 transition to democracy. Current police statistics reveal that approximately 50,000 rapes are reported nationwide each year, with 20,000 girls and more than 30,000 adult women laying charges at local police stations (Mbongwe 2006). However, rape activists believe that the real figures for rape in the country are at least ten times the official rate, claiming that fewer than 10 percent of all rapes are actually reported to the police. Activists argue that most rape cases are either dealt with privately within the community or family or in cases where an initial reporting took place, the family later decides to withdraw the charge due to bribery or threat.

The increasing rape of children is a worrying trend in the current rape crisis, as is the progressive decline in the age of the perpetrator. A nationwide survey of nearly 300,000 school-going children between the ages of 10 and 19 found that 66 percent of boys and almost 75 percent of girls had experienced forced sex (Andersson et al. 2004). Those abused children were more likely than their non-abused classmates to believe the myth that sex with a virgin could cure AIDS and to report that they would intentionally spread HIV if they learned that they were HIV infected. The researchers concluded that the views of South African youth on sexual violence and HIV/AIDS risks were "compatible with acceptance of sexual coercion and adaptive attitudes of survival in a violent society" (Andersson et al. 2004, 954). Such views may help to explain the persistent rise in children abusing and raping other children.

Power Issues

Theories to help explain why South African boys and men have gained a reputation as amongst the world's leading perpetrators of sexual violence are, for the most part, limited and inadequate. Some researchers have suggested that in many cases rape is used as a form of punishment, and where the victim is a child, it is often punishment of the child's mother (Jewkes et al. 2005). Others have argued that rape is often opportunistic, with men taking chances simply because the opportunity presents itself after having assessed the situation and the unlikelihood of being caught (Wood 2003). Still others draw upon Moore's (1994) ideas of "thwarted male identity," where rape is used to reconfirm fantasies of male powerfulness when structural factors such as poverty and unemployment cause them to feel powerless. The frustrations of the "dethroned male" as described by Rebombo (2006) have also been identified as a possible factor in South Africa's high rates of rape. Feeling emasculated after centuries of colonialism followed by apartheid, the "dethroned males" may be reacting negatively to new discourses and expectations of gender equality by venting their anger and frustrations onto women through rape. While these hypotheses may help to shed light on some aspects of men's motivations for rape, they do not provide adequate explanations for the pervasive and often extremely violent nature of these crimes in South Africa today.

The current inefficiency of the justice system when dealing with cases of sexual violence is yet another reason why many victims of rape do not report the crime and why many men may feel that they can indeed get away with it. Currently not even one out of every nine cases of rape is likely to ever reach the South African courts, and of those that do, fewer than 1 percent ever result in a successful prosecution (Jewkes et al. 2005). It may be the case that a perceived lack of political will on the part of government and lack of commitment shown by formal institutions to act decisively against sexual violence is a major contributor to the problem.

While the experience of gender-based violence has become a defining life experience for millions of South African women and girls, the development of strategies to combat the scourge has not kept pace with the growing problem. In many ways democratic-era efforts to address violence against women have mirrored democratic-era efforts to address HIV/AIDS. Government response to both problems, long recognized by local researchers and activists to be intimately linked, has been mediocre, with some having argued that government's failure to provide strong leadership in addressing these issues is rooted in the very fact that the issues are linked (Leclerc-Madlala 2006). Confronting the twinned epidemics would require a close examination of existing gender inequalities, the attitudes and behaviors that make women and girls so vulnerable to both rape and HIV infection. Such an examination was perhaps too sensitive for the new democratic African leadership that was largely drawn from communities where polygamy was customary practice and the infidelities of married men were accepted. Growing interest locally and internationally in South Africa's rapid rate of increase in HIV infection over the past decade (growing from a 5 percent national prevalence in 1995 to 25 percent in 2005) resulted in a concomitant growing interest in identifying the driving forces behind the virus's spread.

Thus, while government took a denialist stand on both HIV and rape, the extraordinary growth of the country's HIV/AIDS epidemic helped to focus attention on gender-based violence and to propel the crime of sexual violence into the public consciousness. With the close of the first decade of democracy in 2004, South Africans could no longer ignore the violent nature of the society that has emerged in the wake of political change and where an internal war is currently being waged against its women and children.

Beyond Alliance and Legislation

With the release of Nelson Mandela from prison in 1991 and the start of negotiations in preparation for the 1994 elections, South African women formed the WNC (Women's National Coalition) with the expressed purpose of ensuring that their interests would be articulated during the negotiation process. Led by women drawn from the various political parties, the WNC represented a broad front of women politicians and members of various women's groups. The WNC drafted a *Women's Charter* that was intended to inform a democratic constitution and be used as the basis for new legislation to advance gender equality. While the WNC was successful in fulfilling its initial mandate, it collapsed soon after 1994 as many of its leaders moved into state structures. Some political analysts, such as Shireen Hassim (2005), have argued that a major reason for the collapse of the WNC with the dawn of democracy was the unresolved tensions that existed between nationalist and feminist allegiances. Hassim drew upon ideas put forth by Anthias and Yuval-Davis (1989) about women's political activism in many post-colonial or post-authoritarian countries having been enabled by larger struggles against colonial, class or racial oppression. One result was a "politic of alliance" between men and women who fought for liberation as opposed to a "politic of autonomy" that allowed women to organize as women and formed the basis of Western women's liberation movements. In such countries nationalism was the dominant frame for political mobilization, and in South Africa nationalism was overlaid with racial identity as an equally important frame.

One result of South Africa's combined "politic of alliance" has been making women's issues appear as distractions from the primary struggle against the apartheid system and its legacy of white and Western domination. Today, given that gender-based violence is widely perceived to be a women's issue, women who speak out about women's issues can expect to be accused of being unpatriotic, reactionary and, if she is white, racist. The case of journalist Charlene Smith, an internationally acclaimed white South African rape activist, provided what was perhaps the clearest lesson for South African women who dared to speak out. In 2004 Smith published a newspaper article about the local rape crisis and presented nation-wide statistics on the problem. President Mbeki's response to the article was nothing short of explosive. He used the website of the governing African National Congress to launch a searing attack on Smith, accusing her of having "a mind corrupted by the disease of racism" and perpetuating the image of black men as "savage beast unable to control their sexual urges (LaFraniere 2004, 2). Although Smith had been a comrade of President Mbeki during the long struggle against apartheid, this did not seem to matter. At the time only one black woman was courageous enough to publicly defend Smith and confirm that rape was indeed a problem in the country.

There is no doubt that democracy has resulted in many gains for South African women particularly in terms of gender legislation and institutional structures. A Commission on Gender Equality has been established with offices in each of the country's nine provinces, an Office on the Status of Women has been set up as a watchdog body to ensure against gender discriminatory practices, and in November 2007 a Sexual Offences Amendment Bill was approved by the National Council of Provinces. (One goal of this bill was to ensure timely prosecutions and protect the rights of victims.) More than 20 percent of political decision makers are women (a rate only second to Scandinavia), and recognition of the need for gender sensitivity at all levels of government is relatively high (Commission on Gender Equality 2005). Laws are in place to address women's rights in the workplace, domestic violence, child maintenance, customary law and to protect the right of reproductive choice. There is a parliamentary commitment to policy priorities of the national budget in favor of poor women. In all these areas South Africa is referred to as a model country (Govender 2007). Yet, in terms of the reality of women's lives, South Africa is also a model example of the disjuncture between excellent public policy and lived experience. Many of the country's women live far below the poverty line, cannot find paid employment, are without access to clean water and sanitation, housing, affordable healthcare, food for themselves and their families. They also bear the brunt of violence and HIV/AIDS.

A major challenge of the next phase of democracy is to change widespread social attitudes that maintain entrenched patriarchal practices and negate the protection and advancement of women that the new democratic dispensation is intended to promote. With the WNC having failed to develop into the kind of broad-based women's movement needed to advance gender equality and mobilize against the scourges of gender-based violence and HIV/AIDS, many South African women are still eagerly awaiting a space to speak truthfully about their predicament (de Waal 2005).

The Zuma Case

In this second decade of post-apartheid era there is an increasing awareness that the deepening HIV/AIDS crisis will never be adequately addressed without empowering women and confronting the plague of gender-based violence. With this has come a growing interest in finding appropriate triggers that would arouse local women, especially working-class and rural women, to take action to demand the realization of their rights. In March 2006, the rape trial of former Deputy President Jacob Zuma provided such a trigger. A charismatic figure of South Africa's liberation struggle, Mr. Zuma had recently been fired as deputy president after being indicted on bribery charges. Soon thereafter, he had been accused of raping the daughter of a family friend. As part of his testimony, 64-year-old Zuma said that his accuser, a 31-year-old HIV-positive AIDS activist, had signaled a desire to have sex with him by wearing a knee-length skirt to his house and sitting crossed-legged, revealing her thigh. Claiming the privileges that patriarchal Zulu traditions bestow on men, Zuma said he was actually obligated to have sex, seeing that his accuser was aroused. Zuma stated that according to Zulu culture, a man cannot just leave a woman if she is aroused because denying her "pleasure" would be tantamount to rape. Zuma believed that his chances of contracting HIV were small because he had taken a shower soon after sex to minimize his risks.

While much public attention was given to Zuma's insistence that his testimony reflected traditional values, of greater significance to the project of women's emancipation were the statements and comments made by women supporters who gathered outside the court building during the trial. Burning incense on the roadside in an effort to solicit supernatural support for the case, Zuma supporters bore witness to the persistence of outdated patriarchal ways of thinking in a country that boasts one of the world's most progressive constitutions. It was these women supporters who, by revealing the degree to which women had internalized their own oppression, also revealed the extent of the work that is required for correcting current gender imbalances and arresting the co-epidemics of gender-based violence and HIV/AIDS in South Africa. During the trial women supporters of Zuma burned pictures of the accused and danced while shouting "Burn the bitch!"; "Throw her in jail!"; "Zuma, come rape us!" These women insisted that by exposing such a private matter and laying a rape charge, it was the accused who actually was the criminal in this case, guilty of tarnishing the reputation of a respected leader. The aggressive tenor of the comments and actions by these women sent a strong signal to other women that they would face considerable social pressure should they decide to speak out on sexual violence or related matters. Women who transgressed the "boundaries of silence" as defined by the existing patriarchal order could expect to be insulted, degraded and portrayed as attention-seeking traitors. If there was any question about the normativeness of violence in the lives of South African women and the common understanding that rape was something to be quietly tolerated, these doubts were dispelled with a statement made by one of the women supporters who said: "Rape, rape, what rape? We've all been raped. Why is she complaining? Who does she think she is?" (Leclerc-Madlala 2007)

While progressive-minded people found this display of female support for an unapologetic rapist to be deeply disturbing, the Zuma trial served to rivet public attention to the pervasiveness and acceptance of gender-based violence like little else had before. News of the trial was reported throughout the region, provoking what could be described as a show-down between the forces of conservative patriarchy on the one hand and the forces of liberal and radical feminism on the other. The need to lend support to the rape victim resulted in the launch of the *One in Nine Campaign* by seven women's rights and AIDS organizations. The campaign was named as a reminder that only one in every nine local women who are raped actually reports the rape. The campaign message was and remains an encouragement to all women that they must continue to speak out against sexual crimes, despite the backlash by those determined to protect the gender status quo.

The public nature of the trial and the fact that it was a black African woman accusing a black African man of sexual violation provided a unique opportunity for observing not only the role of women in maintaining patriarchy but also the wide occurrence and common social acceptance of gender-based violence, as well as the entrenched nature of misogyny and gender inequality despite a progressive legislative environment.

Conclusion

Calls to build a new women's movement in South Africa had been growing steadily before the Zuma rape trial jettisoned the issue of violence against women into the public domain. On August 9, 2006, National Woman's Day, South Africans celebrated the 50th anniversary of the Woman's Anti-Pass March, when hundreds of women marched to the apartheid government buildings demanding an end to their restrictive movement in what was then "white" urban areas. During the anniversary celebrations, for the very first time since political transition in 1994, it was African women's voices that were the most audible in demanding an end to the gender power imbalances that gave men privileges and curtailed women's autonomy. Writing in a popular weekly newspaper on the eve of National Woman's Day, Pumla Gobodo-Madikizela, a Cape Town academic, stated bluntly: "The enemy is no longer apartheid. The enemy is an old system that unites women across color and class lines—the system of patriarchy" (2006, 25).

If gender issues had been sidelined and women's organizing had been hampered through a "politic of alliance" that was necessary for political mobilization against apartheid, then current trends are towards a definite loosening of that alliance. On National Women's Day of 2006, the Progressive Women's Federation was launched, marking the beginning of an organization that could potentially grow into a women's movement. As an organization for women and led by women, the Progressive Women's Federation represents a symbolic break from struggle-era alliance politics. Women began to see the need for a dedicated women's movement to address gender issues, with violence against women and HIV/AIDS being central gender issues in South Africa today. The success of the Progressive Women's Movement will be largely determined by the extent to which its leaders are able to work with and articulate the aspirations of ordinary South African women, many of whom are suffering at the forefront of the twinned epidemics.

The democratic government's inadequate response to date has meant that the job of addressing these problems and managing the trauma of gender-based violence and HIV/AIDS has been left largely to civil society and its numerous community-based organizations. Women such as those involved in the *Siyazama* Project (see Kate Wells's chapter), who are poor and illiterate could greatly benefit from a national organization that took their plight seriously. Fighting against a long history of patriarchy with its traditions of patrilineal descent, polygamy, wife-inheritance, bridewealth exchange, virginity testing, the sexual cleansing of widows and many other customary practices that reflect social values for male dominance and female servitude will necessarily require long-term vision and collective action. Through hundreds of projects and schemes aimed at empowering, protecting or assisting women, civil society in South Africa has provided the most robust response to women's on-going oppression. The multiple burdens of women are being lifted largely through the actions of many ordinary South African citizens who have come to realize that by doing nothing they are accomplices in the denial that drives violence against women and HIV/AIDS in this part of the world.

Commentary
Vilana Pilinkaite-Sotirovic

If Suzanne Leclerc-Madlala made a presentation on everyday trauma of sexual violence in South Africa to the Lithuanian audience (politicians, law enforcement officials, women's rights NGOs), I would expect the audience to point immediately to different cultural traditions in geographically remote regions and, drawing on those differences, argue that these are "theirs," not "our" problems. Many in the audience may emphasize with the experiences of victims of gender-based violence, but probably nobody would recognize that similar incidents of gender-based violence occur around them. In addition, it would be difficult to recognize that women react to these incidents in similar ways.

Everyday rituals and traditions in South Africa and Lithuania are probably radically different, but there are many similarities in trajectories of transition to consolidated democratic regimes. In both countries, most gender-based violent crimes are ignored or inadequately addressed. Both countries exhibit similar trends in legislative development: The governments have adopted progressive laws on gender equality, but they lack political will to address unpopular "women's problems." At the same time, both countries have coalitions of politically active women interested in common action to promote women's rights, but the level of women's solidarity is insufficient. There is not enough commitment to change the deeply embedded patriarchal attitudes on femininity and masculinity, gender roles in public and private domains and gender stereotypes. Feminism is still considered to be something imposed by Western culture which does not fit "our" unique environment, and therefore is viewed as alien to "our" unique culture.

Perhaps during the next phase of democracy we should think about different ways to change feminist gender equality discourse by taking it out of the domain of relatively closed communities focused on women's issues. It may be difficult to eliminate structural inequalities without changing the symbolic order of patriarchal relations, the culture of heteronormativity and dominant masculinity. Currently both women and men in post-transitional societies are strongly opposed to such changes. Therefore, innovative strategies designed to reach as many individuals as possible, inspire them to transform the dominant masculine perspective and introduce pluralistic models of different gendered identities are a very ambitious but achievable goal.

Bibliography

Andersson, Neil A., Ari Hi-Foster, Judith Mattis, Nobantu Marokoane, Vincent Mashiane, Sharmila Mhatre, Steve Mitchell, Tamara Mohoene, Lorenzo Monasta, Ncumisa Ngxowa, Manuel Pascual Salcedo, and Heidi Sonnecus. 2004. National Cross-sectional study of views on sexual violence and risk of HIV infection and AIDS among South African school pupils. *British Medical Journal* 329: 952-954.

Anthias, Floya, and Yuval-Davis, Nira. 1989. *Women-nation-state*. Houndmills: Macmillan.

Commission on Gender Equality. 2005. *Annual Report 2004-2005*. Johannesburg: Commission on Gender Equality.

Daily News Reporter. 2007. Local crime round-up for 2006. *Daily News*, January 3.

de Wall, M. 2005 Globalising the women's movement in South Africa. *Agenda* 64: 117-125.

Gobodo-Madikizela, Pumla. 2006. Time for women to make history yet again. *Mail and Guardian*, August 4-10.

Govender, P. 2007. UN must take up the cudgels for women. *The Sunday Times*, March 11.

Hassim, Shireen. 2005. Nationalism displaced: Citizenship discourses in the transition. In *(Un)thinking citizenship: Feminist debates in contemporary South Africa*, ed. Amanda Gouws, 55-70. Aldershot: Ashgate.

Jewkes, Rachel, and Naeema Abrahams. 2002. The epidemiology of rape and sexual coercion in South Africa: An overview. *Social Science and Medicine* 55 (7): 1231-1244.

Jewkes, R., L. Penn-Kekanaand, and H. Rose-Junius. 2005. "If they rape me, I can't blame them": Reflections on gender in the social context of child rape in South Africa and Namibia. *Social Science and Medicine* 61 (8): 1809-1820.

LaFraniere, Sharon. 2004. After apartheid: Heated words about rape and AIDS. *New York Times*, November 24.

Leclerc-Madlala, Suzanne. 2006. Popular Responses to AIDS and Policy in South Africa. *Journal of Southern African Studies* 31(4): 845-856.

———. 2008. Global struggles, local contexts: Prospects for a Southern African AIDS Feminism. In *The politics of AIDS: Globalization, the state and civil society*, ed. Maj-Lis Foller and Hakan Thorn, 141-155. Houndmills: Palgrave Macmillan.

Mbongwe, L. 2006. Gender violence helpline shows abuse a growing concern. *Star*, November 24.

Meyer, Jani. 2006. Violence gives South Africa the blues. *Sunday Tribune*, July 23.

Moore, Henrietta L. 1994. *Passion for difference*. Bloomington: Indiana University Press.

Rebombo, Dumisani. 2006. "Dethroned Men" . . . An underlying factor fuelling the pandemic? *AIDS Legal Quarterly* June: 15-18.

Wood, Kate. 2003. *Ethnography of sexual health and violence among township youth in South Africa.* Unpublished Ph.D. thesis. London: University of London.

Chapter 5
Losing Ground: How the Lack of Opportunity for Women to Own Land Impales the Tanzanian Economy

Eric Boos and Karene M. Boos

This chapter is a summation of the authors' research on land tenure issues in Tanzania with a specific emphasis on the plight of women as indicative of the future direction of the country.[1] That research concluded that Tanzania's food security problems could be significantly lessened if women, who bear the brunt of all agricultural labor in Tanzania, were given equal opportunity to hold title to the land they farm. Without clear title to the land they farm, women are caught in a cycle of deprivation and poverty, relying on decades old, labor intensive, agricultural techniques. Such opportunity requires basic legal information and nominal financial support (to complete the actual titling process). This support can be orchestrated by non-government organizations which provide free legal aid and micro-financing. This support must be coupled with a commitment from lending institutions to assist small-holder (women) farmers in the credit process and a commitment from the Tanzanian government to include specific statutory provisions recognizing women's rights to hold property as against the assertion of customary rights by their male counterparts on the local level.

A Traumatic Life: Tatu's Story

Tatu is a typical Tanzanian woman whose story is reflective of the basic reality confronting many young women in Tanzania. As a member of the Waluguru tribe in the Morogoro district in Central Tanzania, she was forced to endure a cliterectomy at age 11 and was given in marriage at age 13. Her abusive and demanding husband, 20 years her senior, had two other wives and 13 children.

Though Tatu was given a separate hut and small garden to tend, nothing was ever her own. She never knew when or in what condition her husband would show up, and if things were not to his liking, she was sure to be beaten. She and the children lived primarily off of what she could grow in the garden. When the children were sick, Tatu would forgo food in order to sell it for the money to buy medication. If the seasonal rains were insufficient, it meant hunger and a period of begging for Tatu and her children. Having no formal education and no job skills, employment outside the home was not an option. Retreating to her family was out of the question since it would bring embarrassment and economic hardship to them.

On one particular occasion, Tatu's husband had gone on a drinking and gambling binge and had wracked up a significant debt. To cover the debt, he allowed three men to gang rape Tatu. Not satisfied with the payment, one of the men took the hut and garden to cover the difference. Tatu was forced to seek refuge with one of her husband's other wives, Rehema. Together the two were able to share child care duties and produce a bountiful crop which they sold portions of for cash. When their husband discovered that they had been "holding out" on them, he beat them, took the money and demanded the same amount of money at regular intervals.

Non-compliance was not an option for the women because "legally" he could divorce them and expel them from the property. Without any title to the property, the women remained at their abuser's mercy. Though they could have pursued title legally, they lacked the financial resources and know-how to do so. Furthermore, state courts are remiss to recognize the claims of women through marriage because it goes against the system of "customary rights" in which legal claims are processed within the tribe through a tribal council and tribal chairman. As Aili Tripp (2004) pointed out in her study of customary law and land rights in Africa: "Because women's ties to land are mediated by their relationship to men in patrilineal societies, women's attempts to assert their rights in ways that challenge customary land tenure systems is often perceived as an attempt to disrupt gender relations, and society more generally."

When their abusive husband died, his creditors showed up to confiscate the hut and garden and what little personal property the women had accumulated. With few options, the women and children moved to a shanty village on the outskirts of Dar es Salaam where they work a "common plot" of ground which produces a few onions, tomatoes and potatoes when the rain is good and when they can defend it against thieves. This is their life. They approach one day at a time and take what comes, surprisingly, with a smile.

When asked about her hopes, dreams and aspirations, Tatu has only one: that her children receive an education so that they don't have to live like her.

That's Life in Tanzania

Tatu's tragic story is all too common in Tanzania and the other countries of sub-Saharan Africa. Even more tragic is that the elements for positive social change are in place, but no one seems to know exactly how to break the cycle of discrimination and oppression.[2]

That cycle dates back to pre-colonial times when patriarchal tribal arrangements were the norm. Women, then, were considered "property." In many instances, the birth of a female in the rugged African wilderness or in a remote village was seen as a curse; or at the very least, a misfortune. In many cases today, women are still looked upon as a liability—as evidenced by the dowry system for marriage which is part of a large number of Tanzanian tribes.

Under colonial rule, the plight of women worsened as politically appointed chieftains and tribal councilors abrogated customary rights in order to secure more wealth and power for their own families.[3] Indirect Rule facilitated the usurping of legitimate customary rights to property with the dubious property claims of unscrupulous leaders, especially against widows, women and pastoralists.

The commoditization of local economies through the introduction of cash crops for export was great for the colonialists, but a disaster for women. As Aili Tripp's (2004) research indicates, "Under colonialism . . . the demise of authority of clans and local elders made women's land rights even more precarious." The result was a direct threat to food security because women then (as is the case now) provided the majority of labor in the production of food (both for domestic consumption and export), and the pressure to dedicate energy to cash crops steadily increased. The practical result was a diversion of energy and resources from the family (women and children) and a reiteration of male dominance through ownership of property.

Tanzania's first post-colonial president, Julius Nyerere, embarked on an ambitious campaign to make Tanzania strong through *Ujaama* ("self-reliance"). He initiated a program of "forced villagization" which aimed at locating people in villages that were centered around state-run schools, hospitals, dispensaries, food co-operatives, transportation and distribution centers.

Nyerere's radical Socialism envisioned the liberation of women from menial lives of agricultural servitude through equal access to education and through equal opportunity for proprietary rights over land. In 1971 Nyerere's government passed *The Marriage Act* which sought to protect women's property and inheritance rights (against the discriminatory customary law perpetuated under the British colonial system of Indirect Rule). Nyerere's government established the Department for Women and Children in 1985 (under the Ministry of Community Development, Women and Children), for the expressed purpose of addressing ways and means of reducing women's workloads, improving their health and increasing productivity, promoting education and training and identifying strategies for women's economic empowerment, advocating the use of gender-sensitive statistics in all government forums and ensuring that women's experiences and concerns were more fully incorporated into the planning process for resource allocation.

Perhaps the most telling aspect of Nyerere's intentions to improve conditions for women in Tanzania was his decision to include a *Women in Decision-Making Focal Point* within the Ministry of Agriculture in 1985 with the specific mandate to train rural women in agricultural credit and how to enhance their entrepreneurial capacities. It likewise sought to provide women with much-needed agricultural science training through extension programs and encouraged women to pursue leadership roles in the agricultural sciences.

In spite of all these programs and the progressive ideal of liberating women as a means of securing the culture (economically and socially), not much progress has been made. The Socialist mechanisms gradually broke down, and the social backlash put women in a worse situation. As people broke free (literally) from the "forced villages," they sought to recover ancestral lands from which they had been forcibly removed. This resulted in competing claims of ownership which overshadowed Nyerere's grand social agenda, and the plight of women worsened: a classic case of the euphemism "one step forward, two steps back."

The post-Socialist government, particularly under President Benjamin Mkapa, implemented some of the most radical land laws in Africa. *The Land Act of 1999* and *The Village Land Act of 1999* shifted administrative responsibility for land tenure matters to the elected officials of each village. These local administrative bodies are in charge of the adjudication, registration, titling and dispute resolution of all land claims in their district. That means there are 9,225 discrete tenure administrations that are in charge of all property except that held directly by the government. The aim of such a radical approach is to avoid "land grabbing" by foreign investors. The problem, however, is history. There are competing claims over the same parcels of land from pre-colonial, colonial, post-colonial Socialism and post-Socialist times. By and large, the claims of women get lost in the shuffle. As Okello (2003) argued in her article *Why East African Women Have No Land Rights*, the fact that Tanzania's land law allows for women's equal right to acquire and hold land (*Section 3(2)* of *The Land Act*) and allows for spousal co-ownership (*Section 161* of *The Land Act*) is negated by the fact that gender-based discrimination in land matters is still allowed in the application of customary rights.

It's All about the Land

"Land tenure and land resource management have been the focus of many debates in Tanzania in recent years as the country moves into market economy. The situation has been particularly so with the formulation of the *1995 National Land Policy*, *The 1999 Land Act* and *The 1999 Village Land Act*, and the *2000 Human Settlements Development Policy*," stated Haruna Masebu (2001), who then served as a land resources management consultant. There are three primary reasons for the intensity of the present debates surrounding land tenure policies in Tanzania.

First of all, land is the central component of life in Tanzania. Tanzania is an agrarian culture with few other natural resources on which to base an economy. Agriculture accounts for 80 percent of the total labor force in Tanzania and more than 40 percent of the nation's GDP (Gross Domestic Product) (CIA 2008). Therefore, most of the wealth generated and kept in Tanzania, as measured by GDP, is directly related to the use of land. Women play a paramount role in

Tanzanian agriculture. Majority of rural women are engaged in subsistence farming. Women's relation to the land has a direct impact on Tanzania's economy and should be taken very seriously.

A second reason for all the recent attention given to Tanzania's land tenure and use policies is because of its 40 million people, significant majority of Tanzania's population lives in rural areas. The majority of these people hold land under customary or deemed rights of occupancy. Likewise, the majority of urban dwellers also own land under such customary rights. These rights are tenuous, at best, because the only specified delineation of these rights, until recently, was in *The Land Ordinance of 1923*. This is problematic because, as Masebu (2001) saw it, "Customary land tenure [as it has been called since 1923] has been left to be interpreted severally, depending upon the customs of the various [120 plus] tribes. This created inconsistency in, and unpredictability of, the land tenure system; especially in the rural areas."

The impact has been negative for the people and the land as well. Without security of tenure, families are reluctant to develop the land with any long-range vision. Consequently, there has been little attention paid to the important ecological issues endemic to an agrarian society. Furthermore, in the urban areas, people without tenure have taken to building "spontaneous settlements," which lack proper urban planning and subsequently contribute to waste management and overcrowding problems.

Finally, the land tenure issues are of great significance in Tanzania because the push is on to conform to the directives of the International Debt Reduction Program for Developing Nations sponsored by the World Bank and the IMF (International Monetary Fund). Tanzania has a 4.4 billion dollar international debt (2007 data; CIA 2008), and the reduction of that debt was premised upon its commitment to reform its land tenure policies. The IMF and World Bank were reticent to relieve the debt burden without individual countries showing political stability and a commitment to democratic and capitalist ideologies (Harsch 2001). That translated into a commitment to reform land policies:

> It is also clear that the driving forces behind the new land laws [in Tanzania] are the current policies of privatization of our resources, liberalization of trade, free market promotion and protection of foreign investments. These are the policies dictated by the International Financial Institutions (IFIs) and implemented by the Government which argues that there is no other alternative. As a result, the land bills are premised on the claim that land has a market value; without regard of the fact that for many Tanzanians the value of land lies in its use. Further, the land bill disregards the fact that small peasants, women, and pastoralists are the main investors in the economy of this country (National Land Forum 1997).

Tanzania's recent land laws, while conforming to the dictates of the international institutions and furthering the cause of globalization, still contributed to the marginalization of women—which does not bode well for the overall economy given the relative importance of women in agriculture. As Kameri-Mbote points out, "Women play a central role in food production. Their activities determine the amount of food available for consumption in the home" (Shimba 2000, 91).

In spite of women's crucial role in the overall food security of the nation, land is typically inherited, bought and sold according to patrilineal tradition (as manifest in the application of customary rights at the local level under the 1999 *Land Act* and *Village Land Act*). Similarly, "the main inputs for agricultural production are provided by the males, and the proceeds from the sale of crops are controlled by the males" (Wagao 1991, 87).

Conclusion

Given the relative importance women play in national food security and the overall gross domestic product of Tanzania, it is fair to assert that the key to empowering women in Tanzania is in the land. If women can gain clear title to land, they will have a source of collateral to borrow money for tools, machinery, seed stock and participation in extension programs to learn about the best agricultural science. While privatization has made ownership theoretically possible for women, the administration of land tenure laws at a local level has done little more than bolster the oppressive bias found in the acknowledgment of customary rights. Women do not have the legal acumen or the financial support to press their property claims—especially given the existing tension between the state courts and local land administrations. Without title, women farmers cannot gain much-needed credit from lending institutions to buy machinery, fertilizer, or seed cover for cash crops. They must consistently engage in cost-sharing between their household, medical and educational needs; thereby perpetuating the cycle of poverty for women since males in the family get first shot at food, medicine and education.

In spite of the progressive political reforms of Julius Nyerere, Tanzania's first president, and the ardent efforts of NGOs to improve conditions for women, the situation has not improved much in the last 40 years. More specifically, in the shift from Nyerere's Socialism to today's democracy, there has been a greater emphasis on capitalism. This perpetuates the commoditization of the land begun in colonial times which in turn perpetuates the social and cultural bias against women as men control the input regarding agricultural practice (emphasizing cash crops over and above food source crops which compromises food security) and the proceeds from agriculture.

The most complete remedy to this situation is contingent upon the government's recognition that the nation's food security is directly linked to the plight of women. There needs to be additional legislation protecting the legal claims of women against the unjust recognition of customary rights asserted in a patrilineal context at the local level. There needs to be additional support from lending institutions to facilitate the loan process for women farmers. There needs to be additional legal and financial support in the form of free legal aid to press claims in state court and nominal funding to acquire legal title. There needs to be a concerted effort on the part of government institutions to create opportunities for women to participate in agricultural science.

Commentary
Gnimbin A. Ouattara

I commend the Booses for addressing the issue of land tenure in Tanzania and particularly the plight of women as it relates to this problem. In the 1990s, following the structural adjustment program, the Tanzanian government implemented the privatization policies of the institutions of Bretton Woods without regard to the social rights of the women peasants:

> The weaker the African economies, the more determinedly were they pressured into structural adjustments that the [World] Bank and the IMF insisted upon. Dependence upon aid donors is made plain when it is pointed out that several, mostly low-income countries . . . depended almost entirely on official development assistance for net capital flows (Arnold 2005, 746).

The 1990s were also the years of structural adjustment for Côte d'Ivoire. The country was forced to abolish most of its social programs. The first victims were the members of the Ivorian working class in general and women in particular. Constance Yai, the leader of AIDF (The Ivorian Association for Women's Rights), the most important Ivorian women's rights organization, emphasized this point during a meeting with President Clinton and his wife in 1998. Yai (2005) argued that modern Ivorian governments were more retrograde than traditional ones:

> Our organization . . . realized that the population is not hostile to women's rights implementation. . . . but I would like to inform you that there is a complicity between the African governments and populations, which are hostile to changes for women. We call it the anti-women conspiracy in Côte d'Ivoire. . . . We have refugees; we have conflicts. But, above all, there is an absence of women in decision-making bodies.

In sum, women were and still are traumatized both in modern Tanzania and Côte d'Ivoire. Their rights are similarly suppressed. The policies discussed above did not help to empower them. However, Ivorian women's plight is directly related to the crisis of modern Ivorian governments and the civil war which has plagued the country since 2002. According to a 2007 report by Amnesty International, numerous women were raped in Côte d'Ivoire with impunity, used as booty of war and political weapons by different armed groups (BBC 2007). We should all be outraged.

Notes

1. In 2003-2004, Eric Boos was appointed by the U.S. State Department to teach and conduct research on land tenure issues at Sokoine University of Agriculture in Morogoro, Tanzania, as a Fulbright Scholar. His research was published in *Property Rights, Pastoral People and Problems with Privatization in Tanzania*. Ndanda, Tanzania: Salvatorian, 2004.

2. Various economists and political scientists view privatization and protection of customary land tenure arrangements as instruments for helping women achieve power. Research (e.g., Tripp 2004) has shown, however, that the recognition of such rights has generally taken place in a context of religious law and customary practice which subordinates women.

3. The British colonial system of "Indirect Rule" sought to administer policy by appointing local leaders. The system was wrought with corruption as the British tended to appoint those individuals who had endeared themselves to various colonial officials in spite of their actual status within the tribe. This led to decades-long corruption and abuse of power.

Bibliography

Arnold, Guy. 2005. *Africa: A modern history*. London: Atlantic Books.
BBC. 2007. Ivorian women "forgotten victims." *BBC News*, March 17, http://news.bbc.co.uk/2/hi/africa/6453123.stm (accessed on July 1, 2008).
CIA. 2008. The World Factbook: Tanzania. CIA. https://www.cia.gov/library/publications/the-world-factbook/geos/tz.html (accessed July 5, 2008).
Harsch, Ernest. 2001. Africa preparing its own recovery plans. *Africa Recovery, United Nations* 15 (1/2), http://www.un.org/ecosocdev/geninfo/afrec/vol15no1/151gov1.htm (accessed July 5, 2008).
Masebu, Haruna. 2001. Land as power and source of wealth. *Guardian*, January 3.
National Land Forum. 1997. *Land rights in Tanzania=Azimio La Uhai (a declaration of NGOs and interested persons on land)*. Oxford: Oxfam.
Okello, Rosemary. 2003. Men's Property: Why East African women have no land rights. *The East African*, http://www.caledonia.org.uk/land/okello.htm (accessed July 5, 2008).
Shimba, H. J. M. 2000. Women, weeding and agriculture in Iringa region, Tanzania, http://www.atnesa.org/weeding/weeding-shimba-women-tz.pdf (accessed July 5, 2008).
Tripp, Aili. 2004. Women's movements, customary law and land rights in Africa. *African Studies Quarterly* 7 (4), http://www.africa.ufl.edu/asq/v7/v7i4a1.htm (accessed July 5, 2008).
Wagao, J. H. 1991. *Household food security and nutrition in Tanzania: A consultancy report submitted to UNICEF regional office*. Nairobi, Kenya: UNICEF.
Yai, Constance. 1998. Remarks at a roundtable discussion on human rights in Africa with United States President Bill Clinton. Gifts of Speech. http://gos.sbc.edu/w/yai.html (accessed on July 1, 2008).

Chapter 6
Entrepreneurship: Antidote to Women's Economic Oppression
J. Kay Keels

Women face a distinct disadvantage in the job market in a transition economy. Entrepreneurship can play a significant role in women's development of economic independence. This paper specifically considers the case of Lithuania.

With the collapse of the Soviet system in the early 1990s, the economies of the former Soviet republics underwent significant transformation. The economic impact on the citizens of these newly independent countries was often severe. Frequently, women, typically the most disadvantaged in the job market, particularly faced difficult challenges during this transition. Often out of necessity, women in these transition economies turned to entrepreneurial endeavors as a means to overcome the dismal job prospects. This paper considers transition economies and how women's entrepreneurship played a significant role in helping women to overcome the economic odds.

Pre-Independence

Before gaining independence in the early 1990s, the Baltic countries had been part of the Soviet industrial machine. Citizens of these countries worked to serve the Soviet centrally planned economy. For women, working was not an option as it was in the pre-Soviet era. Everyone was obliged to work (Kanopiene 1998). However, the work was not the kind that produces self-fulfillment and feelings of achievement. Production efficiency was based on economies of scale and standardized products (Bliss et al. 2003). Everything was tightly controlled; there was no room for innovation (Baumol 2004), no quarter for creativity officially anyway. Unofficially, there was a thriving black market in most Soviet states, but these activities were mostly informal, not full-time work (Hessler 1998). These entrepreneurs, known as *spekulianty* managed to buy materials from other European countries and sell them on the black market.[1] While the shadow market was mostly small market and artisan enterprises, the official state-run work was largely heavy industrial drudgery. The Communist plans for industrial growth and expansion depended upon nearly full employment of both men and women. State-run childcare facilities were provided so that even mothers with small children could work. While the system was touted as a promoter of women's equality, there was something oppressive about being forced into unrewarding work (Kanopiene 1998).

Transition

After independence, the economic landscape changed dramatically. The Baltic countries might have been politically free, but they lacked the infrastructure to achieve economic independence (Misiunas and Taagepera 1983). Following the collapse of the Soviet system, economies of the former Soviet republics underwent significant changes. Many of the large state-owned monopolies were converted to private ownership. These huge new entities found themselves having to cope with a market economy and an entirely different set of demands than those of a Socialist economy. Some countries adapted rather quickly and went on to establish a new economic order while others experienced more difficult transformations (Aidis et al. 2005). Regardless of the path taken, all of these former Socialist countries (in 1990s) were said to be transition economies (Peng 2000). Transition, in this case, implies changing from a planned Socialist economy to a free market economy. In transition, these countries teetered somewhere between Communism and capitalism (Grennes 1994). Even as countries, such as Lithuania, struggled to build a new economic order, vestiges of the old Soviet system remained. Compared to other transition economies, like Ukraine, however, Lithuania experienced a rather rapid transformation, already having gained the EU (European Union) membership in 2004 (Aidis et al. 2005). Poland followed an equally successful trajectory. "Poland is viewed by many as the economic success story of Eastern Europe" (Bliss et al. 2003, 226). Women certainly played a role in this economic transformation. In fact, in the early transition years, Lithuania led many of the transition countries in percentage of business owners who were female (Aidis et al. 2005).

One particularly negative impact of the transition was that the full industrial employment under the Soviet system was quickly replaced with massive unemployment which reached as high as 20 percent in some transition countries (Ruminska-Zimny 2002). Women were impacted by joblessness more severely than men. "The differences ranged from 2-5 percentage points in Armenia, the former Yugoslav Republic of Macedonia or Estonia, to close to 10-13 points in Albania, Lithuania and the Russian Federation. A significant gender gap in employment cuts was also seen in Kazakhstan, Slovenia and Ukraine" (Ruminska-Zimny 2002, 8). This feminization of poverty had a greater impact on women than men, especially single mothers, large families and older women living alone (Ruminska-Zimny 2002).

The cultural norms and values of Lithuanian society made it more difficult for women to find work. A similar scenario was true in Poland. "Many private employers avoided hiring women due to more costly benefits associated with lengthy maternity leave, sick-child leave and other 'pro-family' policies" (Bliss et al. 2003, 229). There was the prevailing notion that the woman's place was in the home attending to child bearing and nurturing. With the loss of state support, women were increasingly required to assume non-paying household and child care duties (Ruminska-Zimny 2002). Furthermore, the job market was blatantly sexist. Job advertisements were explicitly directed to men. Even though Lithuania has made significant progress toward privatization, a larger percentage of women were still employed in state-owned businesses (Aidis et al. 2005). This meant that job losses associated with more privatization and restructuring were likely to affect women disproportionately. Clearly, women now faced a different kind of oppression.

Women and Entrepreneurship

One result of the economic changes in post-Soviet countries was the rise of legalized entrepreneurship in the form of the ownership of private businesses (Aidis et al. 2005). Given this option, it is not surprising that some women turned to self-employment in the form of an entrepreneurial venture. As Welter et al. (2003) argue, in transitional economies, business ownership may have been the only way for women to fight discrimination and avoid poverty. Women are becoming an important facet of the entrepreneurial landscape. "Women are one of the fastest rising populations of entrepreneurs and . . . they make a significant contribution to innovation, job and wealth creation in economies across the globe" (de Bruin et al. 2007). Women's reasons for starting an entrepreneurial venture vary, but necessity often plays a role. In a survey conducted in 2000, many women cited economic reasons and unemployment as the motivation for starting a business. Those who began an enterprise for the challenge or the desire to have their own business cited the same reasons (Aidis et al. 2005).

Lisowska (2002) notes three types of barriers to the development of entrepreneurship: economic, educational and cultural. Economic barriers include bureaucratic difficulties such as taxation, lack of access to funding and slow demand due to a struggling economy. Educational barriers could be problems such as lack of consultation and advisory sources as well as lack of opportunities for training. Lack of social acceptance of private enterprise and occupational gender bias are representative of cultural barriers. Cultural barriers affect women disproportionately.

"If we believe what we read in the press or the media, there is a perception that women are less capable, less entrepreneurial, or perhaps they should not be entrepreneurs at all" (de Bruin et al. 2007). To some, it may seem quite oxymoronic to speak of women's entrepreneurship, since the very term entrepreneur and the way it has been defined historically carry masculine overtones (Bird and Brush 2002). Consequently, expectations for the kinds of organizations that are created are also decidedly masculine.

Bird and Brush (2002) note that masculine impacts on organizations include a low commitment to people, formal centralized structure, personal and financial control, and a culture that values success for self and the firm. By contrast, these authors say that "feminine" organizations feature a high commitment to people, participatory structures, sharing and culture of valuing self and others. Furthermore, women engage in several different types of entrepreneurial businesses, including small and micro-businesses, street trade, co-entrepreneurial businesses with their husband, home-based self-employment or a subsistence combining family and income responsibilities (Welter et al. 2003). Godwin et al. (2006) argue that "a woman entrepreneur within a male-dominated industry of culture may carry the invisible-yet-cumbersome baggage of sex-based stereotypes when she attempts to secure resources, develop business networks, and gain legitimacy for her business venture."

Being a female entrepreneur in Lithuania as well as other transitional and post-transitional countries is said to be more difficult for several reasons (Aidis et al. 2005). Women business owners often have their legitimacy questioned, and they feel the need to prove their abilities more frequently than men. Also, they feel that they actually have to be better at what they do than their male counterparts. Female entrepreneurship is viewed by some as a threat to society because the idea of a wealthy independent woman is unacceptable.

Nonetheless, Aidis et al. (2005) emphasized the importance of female entrepreneurial ventures for several reasons. First, these businesses tend to employ other women. This helps to dampen the effect of women's economic disadvantage in the job market. Second, by offering women legitimate employment, these small enterprises help to cut down on the trafficking in women, an issue of great concern in many transition economies. Third, women business owners serve as role models for younger generations of women seeking employment opportunities. Finally, the encouragement of female entrepreneurship helps to move the transition process along toward more successful private sector development and innovative capacity.

Characteristics

In surveys of Lithuanian and Ukrainian women, Aidis et al. (2005) found that most female entrepreneurs fell into the 40-49 age range (44 percent in Lithuania, 37 percent in Ukraine) followed closely in both cases by the 30-39 age range (36 percent in Lithuania, 31 percent in Ukraine). In the 2005 Global Entrepreneurship Monitor report, researchers found that early stage entrepreneurship in middle income countries was most prevalent in the 25-34 age range. In established businesses in these same countries, the 35-44 age range was more frequent (Minniti et al. 2006).[3]

In both Lithuania and Ukraine, the aforementioned surveys found a majority of women entrepreneurs was university educated. Despite women's lead in educational degrees, as of 2003, the gender pay gap was 16.8 percent in the private sector and 24.8 percent in the public sector in Lithuania (Mackeviciute 2005, 45). In Lithuania in 2003, women were employed primarily in the sectors of health and social work (85.6 percent), education (79.3 percent), and hotels and restaurants (81.3 percent) (Mackeviciute 2005, 45). Lack of access to capital as well as taxation were cited by both groups as barriers to business development.

Support Structures

A number of organizations have emerged to assist entrepreneurs and women in particular with new business startups. For example, in 2002, SMEDA (Lithuanian Development Agency for Small and Medium Sized Enterprises) received a subsidy from the government to provide support to women's startup businesses (Aidis et al. 2005). Other organizations include Lithuanian Women in Business and Management Society, Women and Business in Lithuania, Centre of Innovations of Women's Activities and Siauliai Women in Business and Management Society.

In a variety of ways, each of these organizations seeks to support women in entrepreneurial endeavors. These ways include encouraging women to seek professional careers, developing relations with Lithuanian and foreign women in business and management organizations and facilitating participation in international projects. In addition to these organizations, several women's centers associated with SMEDA have emerged as vehicles for disseminating information, holding conferences and publishing information and research reports of interest to women, such as WIIC (Women's Issues Information Center), the Kaunas Women's Employment and Information Center, the Kretingos Women's Information and Training Center, and the Anyksciai Women's Club.

Voices of Women Entrepreneurs

The voices of female entrepreneurs themselves help to flesh out the picture of women's entrepreneurial activity in Lithuania. The UNECE (United Nations Economic Commission for Europe, n.d.) developed a portrait gallery of "excellent women entrepreneurs." Among the 150 portraits, six from Lithuania are included. In their visions of entrepreneurship, some of the women suggested the importance of creativity. A micro-enterprise bookseller said,

> The vision of my entrepreneurship is like the empty pages of the book, which need to be completed by new ideas and interesting activities to make this book attractive to read for many other people.

A taxi company owner pointed out that:

> As an entrepreneur you need to be creative and ready to develop the business idea, products and services continually. As a reward, you enjoy independence, realization of your ideas and the fruits of your job immediately.

Others shared their visions for their own companies:

Our future vision is to finish the building an ethnographic style of village, where we could provide with servicing for people residing in the village. My vision of company is to develop the publishing service not for only my local region but also Western-Lithuania-wide.

When asked how she became an entrepreneur, a woman newspaper publisher, was clear:

I decided to establish the newspaper business because of changed economic situation. As the private business has been developed in my country, in 1993, I created my local newspaper. It became my business.

Another entrepreneur demonstrated her enthusiastic commitment to her business:

As a mother of two cookeries it's still big part of my life. After traveling through Europe and North America I became interested in international culinary. Four years ago I decided to develop a new style of bar-restaurant with 50 different international dishes on our menu.

If these women are a representative example, it seems clear that a new pathway to economic independence has been forged. With a very positive outlook, the taxi company owner seemed poised for a bright future and hopeful about women's role in the 21st century economy:

The goals of women entrepreneurs in the 21st century have to be the following ones: striving for gender equality; changing society's patriarchal attitudes; adopting the position and role of women in the society; increasing women's self-confidence; acquisition of strong computer skills including using Internet at work; and establishing networking.

Commentary
Vytaute Smaizyte

When I first read Kay Keels's chapter, I found it difficult to wholeheartedly agree with her argument that "being a female entrepreneur in Lithuania as well as other transition countries is said to be more difficult." After all, our legal system was created to give equal opportunities for women and men. In fact, considering gender equality and legislation, Lithuania is considered to be one of the most egalitarian states among the new members of the EU (European Union). It is illegal to discriminate based on gender in labor markets in this country. Being born a female did not prevent me from achieving my professional goals.

However, I admit that in Lithuania there are difficulties related to women's participation in the business world in general and female entrepreneurship in particular. These issues are cultural. Even in companies led by young (thirty-something) managers with Western education who were raised after the fall of the Soviet system, beliefs that men are "better" managers, more creative and more energetic than women are quite popular. The belief that women are "less capable" in business is held not only by men, but also by women. "Men do things for themselves, but women do things for men"—this popular conviction illustrates the situation in Lithuania's business world (and the rest of society) today. Given the absence of public debates about women in the business world, this situation is unlikely to change any time soon.

Notes

1. Although Hessler (1998) traces the history of "illegal" entrepreneurial ventures, she does not indicate the extent to which women played a role in such enterprises.
2. Data for the Global Entrepreneurship Monitor report was drawn from 35 countries around the world, not all of which are transition economies.

Bibliography

Aidis, Ruta, Friederike Welter, David Smallbone, and Nina Isakova. 2005. Female entrepreneurship in transition economies: The case of Lithuania and Ukraine. London's Global University. http://www.ucl.ac.uk/~tjmsrai/aidis-welter-smallbone-isakova.pdf (accessed July 1, 2008).

Baumol, William J. 2004. Entrepreneurial cultures and countercultures. *Academy of Management Learning and Education* 3 (3): 316-326.

Bird, Barbara, and Candida Brush. 2002. A gendered perspective on organizational creation. *Entrepreneurship Theory and Practice* 26 (3): 41-65.

Bliss, Richard T, Lidija Polutnik, and Ewa Lisowska. 2003. Women business owners and managers in Poland. In *New perspectives on women entrepreneurs*, ed. John E. Butler, 225-241. Greenwich, CT: Information Age Publishing.

de Bruin, Anne, Candida G. Brush, and Friederike Welter. 2007. Introduction to the special issue: Towards building cumulative knowledge on women's entrepreneurship. *Entrepreneurship Theory and Practice* (March 12), http://www.allbusiness.com/business-planning-structures/starting-a-business/3900114-1.html (accessed June 29, 2008).

Godwin, Lindsey N., Christopher E. Stevens, and Nurete L. Brenner. 2006. Forced to play by the rules? Theorizing how mixed-sex founding teams benefit women entrepreneurs in male-dominated contexts. *Entrepreneurship Theory and Practice* (September 1), http://goliath.ecnext.com/coms2/gi_0199-5853558/Forced-to-play-by-the.html (accessed July 1, 2008).

Grennes, Thomas. 1994. The Lithuanian economy in transition. *Lituanus: Lithuanian Quarterly Journal of Arts and Sciences* 40 (2), http://www.lituanus.org/1994_2/94_2_03.htm (accessed July 1, 2008).

Hessler, Julie. 1998. A postwar Perestroika? Toward a history of private enterprise in the USSR. *Slavic Review* 57 (3): 516-542.

Kanopiene, Vida. 1998. Women and the economy. In *Women in transition: voices from Lithuania*, ed. Suzanne LaFont, 68-80. Albany, NY: State University of New York Press.

Lisowska, Ewa. 2002. Women's entrepreneurship: Trends, motivations and barriers. In *Women's Entrepreneurship in Eastern Europe and CIS Countries*, ed. Ewa Rumin-

ska-Zimny, 23-43. Geneva: United Nations Economic Commission for Europe. http://www.unece.org/ie/enterp/documents/wmp.pdf (accessed July 1, 2008).
Mackeviciute, Indre. 2005. Equal opportunities for women and men: Monitoring law and practice in Lithuania. Open Society Institute Network Women's Program. http://www.soros.org/initiatives/women/articles_publications/publications/equal_20 050502/eowmlithuania_2005.pdf (accessed July 1, 2008).
Minniti, Maria, I. Elaine Allen, and Nan Langowitz. 2006. Global entrepreneurship monitor (GEM) 2005 report on women and entrepreneurship. Center for Women's Leadership at Babson College. http://www3.babson.edu/CWL/research/GEM-Report-on-Women-and-Entrepreneurship.cfm (accessed July 1, 2008).
Misiunas, Romuald J., and Rein Taagepera. 1983. *The Baltic states: Years of dependence 1940-1990*. Berkeley and Los Angeles: University of California Press.
Peng, Michael W. 2000. *Business strategies in transition economies*. Thousand Oaks, CA: Sage Publications, Inc.
Ruminska-Zimny, Ewa. 2002. Women's entrepreneurship and economic trends in transition countries. In *Women's entrepreneurship in Eastern Europe and CIS countries*, ed. Ruminska-Zimny, 7-23. Geneva: United Nations Economic Commission for Europe. http://www.unece.org/ie/enterp/documents/wmp.pdf (accessed July 1, 2008).
UNECE (United Nations Economic Commission for Europe). n.d. Portrait Gallery of Excellent Women Entrepreneurs. UNECE. http://www.unece.org/operact/gallery/ (accessed July 1, 2008).
Welter, Friederike, David Smallbone, Elena Aculai, Nina Isakova, and Natalja Schakirova. 2003. Female entrepreneurship in post-Soviet countries. In *New perspectives on women entrepreneurs*, ed. John E. Butler, 243-69. Greenwich, CT: Information Age Publishing.

Part II
Living Trauma
and Empowerment:
Stories and Strategies

Chapter 7
Left Alone, the Widows of the War: Trauma Reframed through Community Empowerment in Guatemala
Lisa M. Vaughn and Gabriela de Cabrera

They killed my husband. I was left behind suffering like a little girl. I didn't know how to manage money or work nor did I know how to provide for the family. See, [this was] the life of a woman among men, and the life of a woman alone with children. I was left like a bird on dry branches (a widow from San Marcos).

Our sacred dream is to say our people are weavers—a people who have woven history with our hunger, sacrifice and blood (Menchu n.d.).

In this chapter we describe how, through community-based groups, Mayan widows of war have reframed the horrific trauma they experienced during the 36-year Guatemalan civil war into empowerment and healing.

Women make up one of the most marginalized sectors of Guatemalan society. This is especially true about Mayan women. There are high levels of poverty and violence. The level of education for women is abysmal, and therefore Mayan women have high illiteracy rates. Rural women are overworked, toiling as many as 18 hours per day; some without compensation. Mayan women have difficult access to healthcare, a lack of political representation and general ignorance of their rights (O'Kane 2000; Shea 2001). In recent years, Guatemalan women and girls from all walks of life have experienced an increase in physical assaults, rapes and murders. Amnesty International (2005) reported that the brutality of the murders represents the pervasiveness of extreme sexual violence, discrimination and hatred toward women in Guatemalan society. Compared with pre-democratic times, there are more Guatemalan women working, receiving higher education and expressing themselves. However, the increasing numbers of violent murders are evidence that the machismo ideals continue to be alive and well, and that women and girls are ultimately seen as disposable. This violence seems to be a backlash toward the upward mobility of women and girls (Bermudez 2005; Amnesty International 2005). For widows of Guatemala's long civil war, the situation has been far worse. In addition to the low status of women in general in Guatemala, the situation is compounded for the widows of the war because many are dealing with depression and PTSD (Post Traumatic Stress Disorder—an anxiety disorder that follows a traumatic experience) and the grief of lost family members.

In today's Latin America women are not exempted from violence and continue to be targets of the military and police officials. For example, women in CONAVIGUA (National Coordinating Committee of Guatemalan Widows) and GAM (Mutual Support Group), two women's groups who work for human rights in Guatemala, report constant harassment by the military, police and other government related officials (Tooley 1997).

Historical Background: Political Violence and the Experiences of Women

Since the times of colonial rule, Guatemala has been laced with violence and brutality. The indigenous Maya have suffered discrimination, attempted eradication and marginalization at the hands of the dominant non-Maya minority. In 1954, Colonel Carlos Castillo Armas became president. Armas began to persecute and outlaw Communists, and then he was assassinated. This led to a period of violence and unrest in Guatemala. Left-wing political efforts continued to be suppressed, and this went on for more than three decades. Many leftist organizers and non-political Maya were killed during this unstable time. In 1960, a group of junior military officers who were inspired by the Cuban revolution tried to overthrow the government but failed. This group became the foundation for the guerrilla movement against the Guatemalan government for the next 36 years. This period is usually referred to as the Civil War. The Peace Accords were signed in 1996.

The army became the dominant force in politics from 1978-1983. The fighting between the left-wing guerrillas and the right-wing U.S. supported army allied with the military government of Guatemala led to major violence and economic decline. The worst violence (numerous massacres) occurred when retired General Efrain Rios Montt served as the president. (Anckerman et al. 2005). He came into power in March 1982, following a coup d'etat. Montt implemented the scorched-earth policy and was responsible for a counter-insurgency campaign which resulted in the massacre of entire indigenous villages as search for guerrillas was conducted. In addition, there were attempts to eradicate any support the guerrillas might find in these villages. During the brief presidency of Montt, thousands of civilian deaths by mutilation, execution and torture occurred. Mostly unarmed Maya were murdered. Although there were other violent executions, torture and forced disappearances conducted by guerrillas and the right-wing groups, the majority of the human rights violations were conducted by the military supported by the government and the civilian defense patrols under the military's control. According to the Guatemalan Historical Clarification Commission (CEH 1999) and the Catholic Church's *Project for the Recovery of Historical Memory* (REMHI 1999), the government is responsible for approximately 93% of all human rights violations committed during that period. At the hands of the Guatemalan military, some 626 Mayan villages in the highlands of Guatemala were destroyed, and more than 200,000 deaths and 50,000 disappearances occurred. More than 100,000 people were exiled (many to Mexico where they still live today). Approximately one million of Guatemalans became displaced internally. The majority of these victims were unarmed indigenous Mayan Indians (REMHI 1999). Numerous Mayan women and girls were raped and murdered. This violent history has been termed by some "genocide" due to attempted eradication of the Mayan people. In 1996, the final peace accords were signed by the Guatemalan government and the URNG (Guatemalan National Revolutionary Unity Party) which ended 36 years of Civil War—the longest war in the modern history of the Americas (Benz 1996; Schlesinger and Kinzer 2005).

As a result of the violence and 36-year war, most of Mayan men were killed, leaving many widowed women behind with a very low social status. These women became both the breadwinners and leaders of their families (Tooley 1997). Another reported outcome of the war was *tristeza*, a psychological condition similar to depression and PTSD. Women were left to pick up the pieces emotionally. Men who remained alive turned to alcoholism and domestic violence.

There are many other deep emotional traces of the war, such as fear, uncertainty, guilt, grief, frustration and pain. Silence, social apathy and loss of social participation are commonplace for the Maya. The Maya have lost trust and hope because of the destruction of entire communities and the rupture of family life. People are polarized. There has been a general militarization of individuals, communities and the country (Anckerman et al. 2005).

Throughout this turbulent history, Mayan women have suffered immensely. Continuing to live in the shadow of the war, they suffer emotionally. They do not have political freedoms or civil rights. They continue to suffer a triple oppression of being a woman, being indigenous and being poor. Many Mayan women experience threat within their families (domestic violence is extremely common), society and organizations (Stern-Patterson 1998). Currently the repercussions from the war, coupled with the status of Mayan women in Guatemalan society, results in a situation where these women are trying to find voice and reframe their traumatic history into healing and empowerment.

Coping with Trauma: Personal Stories

In order to fully understand the lived experience and the extent of their trauma and oppression, we must hear personal narratives from Guatemalan women in their own voices. In 2005 we (the authors of this article) had conversations with ten Guatemalan women from different geographic areas of Guatemala. Some of them were famous, like congresswoman Nineth Montenegro (see *The Authentic Voices* section) and renowned journalist, Marielos Monzon. Other discussions were conducted with indigenous Mayan women from rural communities.

During the war, many Mayan women ran to the mountains. There they lived in groups in order to survive. Having spent as many as 10 to 14 years in the mountains, hiding, some decided to come out and face life again. Several women mentioned in this chapter had to take many different jobs and live in many different places (towns) in order to hide their identity. They are still afraid that the military could find them. Some of them attend group therapy with the other women who have gone through the same ordeals. However, most of them confess of not having forgotten anything of what they have experienced during those horrible years, especially during the most violent times in the 1980s.

Most widows describe the pain that they continue to experience in their hearts. They still don't sleep well. They still can remember the smell of the bullets. These women saw unbelievable atrocities. Here is one story: "The soldier stabbed my husband and my father in the stomach with a large knife. After they had fallen dead, the soldier put the knife near his mouth and licked it. He said, 'the chicken tastes good.'"

When sharing their stories, the women describe *unforgotten trauma* as a result of the war. Some of the women who were very young during the war described unthinkable traumas of rape, physical brutality and violation ("at least nine soldiers raped and hit me and my two younger sisters"). They witnessed the deaths of their family members. They describe haunting memories of torture:

> My brother and I came in the house and found one of the men lying on top of my mother with his trousers down. She had blood all over her face and her neck. Her arms looked like soft Raggedy Ann's arms, bent the wrong way. By the time the bad men took my father and brothers away, my mother was unconscious and seemed to be dead.
>
> The men brought my father down and then my brothers. They were hitting them. They got a coal from the fire where my mother was going to make tortillas for lunch and began to burn my brothers' skin. They made them take off their clothes and began to burn the delicate parts of their bodies. I can still hear Juan's screaming inside my ears, and I can still see the hate in the men's faces, mixed with the pleasure they seemed to feel by doing so much harm.
>
> My mother and the older ladies were raped by more men, approximately 30 different soldiers. And they made the girls like me and my sisters watch that.
>
> Our little house had a horrible smell I will never forget. It was sweat, urine, blood, tears, hate—all those aromas smelled like death to me.

Such trauma undoubtedly leads to *unresolved grief* over the lost loved ones and destroyed communities. This is another re-occurring theme throughout the conversations. The women describe lingering memories of losing their loved ones: "everyday, I re-live the moment when my husband disappeared." They describe their belief that if the bones of the disappeared aren't buried, then their memories can never be buried:

> My sister is lost or dead, and the rest of my family too. We couldn't bury anyone. We don't know where their bodies are. We don't have peace because we feel that their spirits are going around in circles and will not get to heaven until we bury their bodies.

Women from various villages describe reoccurring invasions of their communities that usually resulted in kidnappings and disappearances of those (usually men) thought to be involved with the guerillas:

> The army always came and shot at our town from the road, and sometimes they killed people by doing that. It was horrible. The military came into our homes. They looked for weapons or other evidence that we worked with the guerrillas.

> They burned my grandparents, my uncles and some nephews alive. They couldn't escape because the army was around all houses. Like our family, many families were kidnapped, murdered and disappeared. In my town, the soldiers put all the persons they killed inside a well. Many people abandoned their houses and belongings and went away—who knows where. The army burned the whole town, including our homes and our fields.

> We never found our men. We were so poor in the village. The soldiers took all they could and burnt all they couldn't take.

The women describe *re-occurring physical and psychological complaints* as a result of the trauma they experienced:

> I have headaches; my heart hurts; I dream bad things every night because the spirits of my dead ones visit me, and I can't sleep. I am getting tired, and feel like I'm 90 years old. I am only 66.

> Sometimes I forget parts of what happened, and I feel alive. But when I remember, I feel like I'm dying. The doctors say that I will never have children. The soldiers hurt me inside and I have a problem with my uterus. Sometimes I have pain or cramps that throw me down and I can't walk for a couple of days. My last menstruation was 8 years ago.

During the conversations, another theme was ongoing *resentment* fueled by strong sensory memories:

> The soldiers took the best part of me, of my life. I saw my father, my grandfa-

ther and one of my brothers killed. My uncle and my other brother were taken away on that truck. Every night I hear the firing at their bodies. Every night I dream of the truck. I can still smell the smoke that burnt our *rancho*, and I can still feel the smell of the dirty soldiers' bodies on top of me. I will never get married. I hate men.

Some women felt *frustration and guilt* because they were not able to stop the violence or protect their loved ones during the war:

That night I was really scared. I felt that the truck was coming again. I could even hear the engine and the men's voices. It was my fault that they had found my dad and brothers. I felt that I not worthy of living.

What had I done as a little girl? I thought my father would be able to help my mother. Therefore, I told the soldiers where my father and brothers were hiding.

Trauma as a Source of Empowerment

The unforgotten trauma, unresolved grief, physical/mental maladies, resentment, frustration and guilt compels the Guatemalan women who were affected by political violence to work toward peace and social justice. Marielos Monzon, a well-known journalist, recognized for her work in human rights (2005 Amnesty International Human Rights Journalism under Threat Award recipient) is a case in point. She told us that she does this work in memory of her father who was kidnapped and killed in the 1980s because he was a lawyer who denounced violations of human rights.

In spite of their turbulent past, the Guatemalan women still have optimistic thinking about the future. One woman reflected: "Indigenous women never lose hope. They say it's like the light at the end of a tunnel—you know that it's there, and you know that you're going to reach it sometime. I still hope for peace, even if it's far away."

Despite their lack of political power, Guatemalan women have become empowered by actively participating in community-based groups (Fischer and Brown 1996). Although there are many community-based political organizations supporting Guatemalan women (e.g., CONAVIGUA and GAM), some of them are less politically active. For example, there are numerous art cooperatives formed by Mayan women (often widows of the war) who are experts at weaving textiles and making other craft items that are sold mostly to tourists. One popular cooperative is the ASOTRAMA weaving cooperative (a.k.a. *Asociacion de Mujeres Tejedoras*, Spanish for "association of women weavers"). According to their website, the cooperative includes "350 backstrap loom weavers, 98 percent women, from five ethnic groups." The cooperative operates as a "free trade" organization with fair wages given to the craftspeople. ASOTRAMA's proclaimed goal is "becoming economically self sufficient while working with the materials and methods traditional to our communities." The women in the cooperative think of themselves as artisans who are able to express themselves through the art of weaving cloth.

Art cooperatives, like ASOTRAMA, have empowered women economically and provided them with social support from other women with similar fates. They share an artistic method by which they can express painful memories, and thus create an opportunity to emerge from a traumatic and troubled past. A helpful by-product of such community-based groups is that the women are concerned with self-improvement and often learn about their rights as women (Tooley 1997). Because they are already organized as a group, the women are able to strive toward better social, educational and political services in their communities. In addition, the indigenous Mayan culture and traditions are being preserved. In their own way, these women are acting as "agents of transformation, turning the conspiracy of silence and the intimacy of pain into social protest"(Tooley 1997, 95). This same transformative empowerment has been noted in other arts and crafts cooperatives and other community-based groups globally (for example, see Kate Wells's chapter in this book).

Some of the women with whom we met were involved in arts and crafts cooperatives. They offered testimonies of their experience. Amparo has worked for ASOTRAMA weaving cooperative for 12 years. She told us that "step by step and thanks to the association we have come ahead."

Mariana, who is involved in a small village-based basket making business with other women, explained:

> This making of baskets is making us come out of all of the trauma and painful memories. Sometimes I forget parts of what happened, and then I feel alive. The pain often returns—the soldiers took the best part of me and my life. I will help other women not to suffer.

> We, women of the community, needed to make some money. Therefore, we created an association. Thanks to my sister who works in CENAT (Textile Handicraft Center) we learned to sell things better.

> Thank God here we are with ASOTRAMA, fighting to bring a better life to our homes.

Anckerman et al. (2005) highlighted the importance of creating hope and reconciliation within the context of community healing and participatory democratic community development. They argued that such context is particularly important in societies where there are large numbers of traumatized people. This is the case in post-conflict Guatemala. Women's traumas in Guatemala cannot be solely examined at the individual level but must include the psychosocial (community, historical, social) context. Martin-Baro (1994) indicated that the social structure of the community had to be addressed to alleviate suffering. The trauma affecting Guatemalan women is deeply embedded in the society (and for many in their identity as Mayan women); therefore, community-based empowerment must be there for true healing to occur. As Berliner et al. pointed out, such strategies work by actively rebuilding interpersonal relationships which strengthens local community resources for "psychosocial support, community empowerment and participation in development issues in the community" (2006, 73). During this process, new social structures are created. These structures help to achieve social transformation and prevent future violence (ibid.). Through such efforts, Mayan women find their voice, heal themselves and forge a new vision of empowerment.

Commentary
Kate Wells

This paper explains the shocking circumstances of Guatemala's 36-year war and the dramatic impact it has had on the surviving female population in this country.

There are far too many similarities and far too many dangerous congruencies for marginalized and poverty stricken women who live in South Africa and Guatemala. Whilst in Guatemala it has been a traumatic war of horrendous and atrocious proportions, here in South Africa it is a war called AIDS which silently and relentlessly moves into communities, killing many more women than men, mostly indiscriminately. In many ways the HIV virus can be seen to be perpetually looking for new host groups and new communities to conquer and infiltrate in order to sustain itself as it wages its deathly war in Southern Africa.

When reading the paper, I was struck by the sheer resilience of the Guatemalan women (the Mayan widows) and their indeterminable hope for reaching the "light at the end of the tunnel." This attitude resonates so closely with their sisters in KwaZulu-Natal who have often reported on what their wishes and hopes are for the future beyond the AIDS pandemic. Remembering Fischer and Brown's (1996) claim that despite their lack of political power, the Guatemalan women have become empowered by actively participating in women-centered community groups, one can immediately see the benefit of these "less politicized community-based art coalitions" coming together to encourage the sharing of stories, experiences and building on traditional expert craft making abilities. These projects and cooperatives have a unique and most powerful function which affords women a degree of economic individuality and freedom. This, in turn, breeds both confidence and integrity. If, at the same time, traditional skills are being nurtured and preserved, then "transformative empowerment" has surely been attained. The benefits are broad and meaningful.

As Suzanne Leclerc-Madlala explains in her commentary on Pilinkaite-Sotirovic's chapter, "these tragedies force us to think about the complexities of the challenges involved in the advancement of women's human rights." This is a very important statement as it "forces" us to unravel, dissect and develop important and appropriate empowerment strategies which raise women's awareness of women's issues. Ultimately, I believe, this is how women will find closure to some of the traumas that they have experienced, and continue to suffer from.

The women themselves will find the answers to the questions on how to deal with painful experiences. They will undoubtedly find ways to succeed and achieve the healing they so dearly desire. Maybe then being "left alone" to get on with their expert weaving of memories might be just the right remedy for the Guatemalan widows and their KwaZulu-Natal sisters after all.

Bibliography

Amnesty International. 2005. Guatemala: No protection, no justice. Killings of women in Guatemala. Amnesty International. http://www.amnesty.org/en/library/info/AMR34/017/2005 (accessed July 4, 2008).

Anckerman, Sonia, Manuel Dominguez, Norma Soto, Finn Kjaerulf, Peter Berliner, and Elizabeth Naima Mikkelsen. 2005. Psycho-social support to large numbers of traumatized people in post-conflict societies: An approach to community development in Guatemala. *Journal of Community and Applied Social Psychology* 15 (2): 136-152.

Benz, Stephen Connely. 1996. *Guatemalan journey*. Austin, TX: University of Texas Press.

Berliner, Peter, Manuel Dominguez, Finn Kjaerulf, and Elizabeth Naima Mikkelsen. 2006. What can be learned from 'crazy' psychologists? A community approach to psychological support in post-conflict Guatemala. *Intervention* 4 (1):67-73.

Bermudez, Manuel. 2005. Guatemala: Violence against women unchecked and unpunished. *Interpress News Service News Agency*, November 25, http://ipsnews.net/news.asp?idnews=31192 (accessed July 4, 2008).

CEH. 1999. Guatemala: Memory of silence. CEH. http://shr.aaas.org/guatemala/ceh/report/english/toc.html (accessed July 4, 2008).

Fischer, Edward F., and R. McKenna Brown. 1996. *Maya cultural activism in Guatemala*. Austin, TX: University of Texas Press.

Martin-Baro, Ignacio. 1994. *Writings for a liberation psychology*, ed. Adrianne Aron and Shawn Corne. Cambridge: Belknap.

Menchu, Rigoberta. n.d. Quoted in Megan McKenna. 1992. Beyond this place, there will be dragons. *Spirituality Today* 44 (1), http://www.spiritualitytoday.org/spir2day/92441mckenna.html (accessed July 7, 2008).

O'Kane, Trish. 2000. *Guatemala in focus: A guide to the people, politics and culture*. New York: Interlink Books.

REMHI. 1999. *Guatemala—never again*. Maryknoll, NY: Orbis Books.

Schlesinger, Stephen C., and Stephen Kinzer. 2005. *Bitter fruit: The story of the American coup in Guatemala*. Cambridge, MS: Harvard University Press.

Shea, Maureen E. 2001. *Culture and customs of Guatemala*. Westport, CT: Greenwood Press.

Stern-Patterson, Maria. 1998. Reading Mayan women's insecurity. *The International Journal of Peace Studies* 3 (2), http://www.gmu.edu/academic/ijps/vol3_2/Petterson.htm (accessed July 4, 2008).

Tooley, Michelle. 1997. *Voices of the voiceless: Women, justice and human rights in Guatemala*. Scottdale, PA: Herald Press.

Chapter 8
Dolls with Jobs: A Compelling Response by Traditional KwaZulu-Natal Craftswomen in an Era of HIV/AIDS
Kate Wells

This chapter describes how a small group of rural traditional craftswomen from KwaZulu-Natal have attempted to circumvent some of the prescribed societal and cultural requisites with regard to respectable behavior for Zulu women. The chapter details how the traditional craftswomen employed their own narrative and traditional medium of expression (beaded cloth doll and tableau making) to exercise their rights as women and to "speak" openly about sensitive, traumatic and taboo topics.

The *Siyazama* (Zulu for "we are trying") Project's beaded collection, which has been collected and archived since 1999, contains numerous artifacts which provide three dimensional evidence of the prevalence of rape in their communities, their opinion on virginity testing, the role of *sangomas* (Zulu for "traditional healers") and the serious, life-threatening dilemma facing the *makoti* (Zulu for "married woman") in an era of AIDS.

The *Siyazama* Project, through linking visual communication with health education, has for the past decade led to enhancing and building a link between art and anthropology, cultural affirmation, confidence building and a degree of economic empowerment on behalf of the craftswomen and their rural families and communities.

Background

When I was invited to work alongside the small group of rural traditional craftswomen in 1996, my agenda, set by the African Art Center, a well-known outlet for rural crafts in Durban, South Africa, was to understand the new aesthetic requirements of tourists and to propose new and necessary changes within the two dimensional and three dimensional beaded cloth dolls and structures. This was to make them more saleable. The fact that the small group of traditional craftswomen, amounting to no more than sixteen women, was facing further economic hardship should no solution to their poor craft quality be found was a most powerful motivating force. My initial research revealed that most lived in very poor circumstances and few, if any, had electricity, piped running water or toilet facilities. Their beadwork skill offered the best way to improve their circumstances.

In 1996-1997 I organized a series of workshops to provide the bead workers with technical construction skills and quality materials. The response was immediate and gratifying with the quality of their work improving markedly to such an extent that their crafts were soon once more in demand.

The vast majority of rural traditional craftspeople in KwaZulu-Natal are women, the majority of whom have an impressive ability and skill in beadwork acquired matrilineally, from mother to daughter. With the passage of time I became familiar with beadwork details created by individual craftswomen in the project with regard to distinctive design, form, structure and color of their beadwork. Each producer displayed her own highly distinctive and recognizable idiosyncratic style. Similarly, observing their nuances of construction techniques and how they easily strung beads together on a needle, I had never once seen them outwardly adding or counting. Yet their beadwork and three dimensional constructions reflected a high level of knowledge about geometry, mathematics, balance and rhythm.

A major objective and motivator for the initial intervention was to identify crucial strategies that would alleviate poverty and improve the quality of life of the rural craftswomen: the all-human side of craft making. Collaborating and creating partnerships with craftswomen, as well as linking rural groups with marketing outlets and craft centers were important components of this early work. My initial involvement focused upon the augmenting and enhancement of their crafts and supported the development of new opportunities for income generation. None of us were prepared for what the AIDS pandemic was about to usher in.

The *Siyazama* Project Workshops

During the lively and interactive *Siyazama* Project workshops (the name given to the project by the craftswomen in 1999) they discussed the problems that they were encountering in their lives. For example, many spoke at length of the neglected health, social and economic environment in which they live. This "small talk" was highly significant as much of it revolved around the illness of so many people in the community: HIV/AIDS. Descriptions of their social environment, homesteads, communities and villages seemed to reflect a high degree of suspicion, uncertainty and fear. It was clear that these craftswomen felt acutely vulnerable to HIV/AIDS and that their unique abilities and cultural heritage were at severe risk.

By the close of the 1990s, the local HIV/AIDS epidemic had matured into an epidemic of highly visible physical debility and death (Leclerc-Madlala 2002). Yet there remained a great silence around the topic. In consultation with the groups of craftswomen that I was working with at the time, I felt a moral obligation to broach the highly sensitive subject of AIDS. It was decided that, together as women, AIDS education would be welcomed as part of the craft innovation workshops which began in earnest in 1999. Of equal concern was the fact that the small group of women appeared largely ignorant about the basic facts of AIDS. This overwhelming and prevailing ill-preparedness to deal with HIV/AIDS was revealed to me immediately after the very first workshop:

> I took the condoms home which I had received at the *Siyazama* workshop and gave these to my husband. He grabbed my hair and pulled me down the front steps of my house. He shouted at me and kicked me in front of my neighbors. He was very angry. I was very worried (workshop participant).

This was evidence enough that a very slow and considerate approach was deemed necessary. Although safe and secure in the workshops in Durban, it was clear that the rural women had been placed in a dangerous and threatening position once they returned home armed with the new sexual behavioral information.

At this stage it was also apparent that the few marketing outlets in Durban and Johannesburg that marketed the beaded crafts profitably, were in no way able, nor interested, in making sure that these traditional craftswomen were AIDS literate or able to manage the AIDS epidemic that was creating havoc in their communities. When I floated the idea of the workshops in AIDS awareness with outlets in Durban, I received two very telling responses: "Why? Do not bother—there are thousands of them!" and "What's AIDS got to do with crafts?" I then took it upon myself to seek ways to address the growing life-threatening concern that affected these vulnerable women and to help bridge the communication gaps that existed in their lives. Information gathered on literacy levels revealed that few could read or write in Zulu and the vast majority of the women had no proficiency in English at all. It was clear that the message had to be conveyed in ways other than through literacy to be of any real benefit.

Women and AIDS in South Africa

There is no doubt that the black female population in South Africa is the most severely affected by the HIV/AIDS epidemic. Gow and Desmond attempt to explain one of the reasons for this as being a "cultural difference in sex behavior" and the way "dry sex" is favored and practiced among the black population, leaving women more physically vulnerable to infection (2002, 26). Citing other implicating factors which can be attributed, they list extremely low income, social affects of forced removals, the migrant labor system and the breakdown of traditional society all leading to the disintegration of sexual mores and the erosion of traditional values. Compounding this is the fact that rural women occupy a lower social position than men and their inability to insist on safer sex practices seemingly makes them all the more susceptible to infection.

Yet statistics measuring the urban-rural differentials in an early study by McAnerney in 1994 show that prevalence was generally lower in rural communities than in the urban areas at that time. "The explanation for the low prevalence levels in rural areas may lie in the limited scope for sexual networking in isolated communities, as well as the greater influence of traditional practices" (Johnson and Budlender 2002, 33). Unfortunately, more recent sentinel studies conducted by Wilkinson, Connolly and Rotchford (1999) have shown that within the HIV/AIDS prevalence statistics the rural and urban areas have mostly caught up with each other due, in part, to the increasingly superior transport system and migrant labor practices which link rural communities with the work laden cities in South Africa. Circumstantially this division of labor creates a contested hot house situation for both genders which supports the growth of relationship infidelity and multiple sexual partnerships, whilst endorsing strong masculine behavior as perfectly acceptable. In Zulu culture *hlonipha* is the mode of behavioral conduct which a female is expected to adhere to at all times, and it is within this mode of conduct that she is exposed to some of the most dangerous sexual behavioral mores. According to Raum (1973), in Zulu society *hlonipha* ("respectful restraint") is a sociological phenomenon of powerful practical importance which talks of the avoidances and taboos imbedded in the culture. These prescriptions still largely apply today.

In a unique and important study, Raum (1973) shows that the list of *hlonipha* rules and regulations is an expression of the pyramid of respect upon which the Zulu ethos is raised. The rules link in each instance an inferior to a superior status in traditional forms of expressing deference, the link not being without some reciprocity. This system of restraints is felt by many Zulu to be an essential identifying marker of Zulu culture and its preservation viewed as vital to the maintenance of ethnicity.

The rural women display highly respectful and polite character traits in accordance with the *hlonipha* practice which describes the code of conduct to which most traditional rural communities in KwaZulu-Natal subscribe. For them, it is behavioral mores which clearly list both respectable and disrespectable behavior. According to the participants in my study *hlonipha* may be detrimental in some respects as it could directly result in one's inability and impotence to discuss matters of intimacy with one's husband or partner. One respondent described *hlonipha* as making her inferior and servile to her male counterpart and claimed it enforces the requirement that she pleases her husband by saying "yes" to everything. This situation can be made far worse if one's partner is "Head of the house," wants skin-on-skin sex and refuses to use condoms even if one suspects infidelity.

A high level of discontent emerged in the study with regard to the gender inequality that women suffer daily, and the extreme extent of this can be seen as an insurmountable barrier to survival. Accordingly, their social realm is ripped apart by the notion that "women must be respectful at all times and the men don't have to listen to women." Women must "get married as an unmarried woman is not respected if she is not married," and, once married, "she must respect her husband and nothing else."

The mass production of the beaded cloth dolls representing married and unmarried women, showing their status through their dress and beadwork accessorizing, lent further credence to this serious predicament and has visually demonstrated that the marriage ritual may require reification. The dolls have given rise and voice to a wide range and complex array of emotions; mostly of confusion and contradiction.

Marriage is, in a time of AIDS, provoking a great fear amid the female population. The risk of infidelity in relationships in KwaZulu-Natal runs high, and is most especially prevalent amongst the young men who desire to be considered as *isoka*. This term describes young men who are praised for having more than one partner.

Amongst the most significant ethnographic studies undertaken in South Africa are those by researchers Leclerc-Madlala (2002) and Wojcicki (2002). Their research describes the unacceptably high level of sexual violence against women. Claiming this situation to be "endemic" and one in which rape is sometimes considered "a normal recreational activity," these researchers clearly make the point that any intervention which aims to promote behavior change must look into the sexual culture of the community or society under study.

Although the rural male partners are not directly involved in the training and educational *Siyazama* Project workshops, they are not only the direct recipients of the information but are also, importantly, beneficiaries of the most welcome financial income which their partners are bringing into the homestead on a fairly regular basis. This augmented cash earning, I believe, is a singularly powerful force for all who live in poverty stricken rural areas and has led to the men of *Siyazama* showing support for their partners' attendance in the workshops.

For example, becoming "informed" about the importance of sexual fidelity and AIDS awareness may have a different meaning and impact when it means extra cash resources. "Informed" in this case means that the information has been duly received, but may not be fully articulated nor deemed appropriate to apply, due to other social pressures, such as the need to prove manliness or simply rejecting any (sexual) advice from a woman. On the other hand, the growing sexual economy of transactional sex, according to Leclerc-Madlala (2002), an outcome of the post-apartheid political economy, shows that women's sexual behavior is most definitely a product of economic circumstances. This author is also of the opinion that interventions at the level of individual behavior and sexual culture seem unlikely to be very successful. Concerned with this and addressing the ramifications of this notion, this chapter also lends support to the argument that poverty must be addressed as a major component in any strategy to combat HIV/AIDS effectively and efficiently, and it is the women themselves who must be empowered.

The submersion and the silence which surrounds any form of kinship conflict is typical of African families and this is often characterized by submission

106 Chapter Eight

to one's husband or male partner regardless of character, behavior or personality (Kayongo-Male and Onyango 1984). In many African groupings conflict avoidance within the rural household is common and verbal arguments between males and females are rare. Any form of open discussion and direct confrontation between the conflicting parties are frowned upon. According to Kayongo-Male and Onyango (1984), the preferred method of serious conflict resolution is witchcraft or sorcery, or at best to send the "argumentative offender," mostly female, away.

African sociologists such as Kayongo-Male and Onyango attest to the underlying tension which is created, not only by unequal opportunities between kinship members, but by the African family ethic of reciprocity (1984, 98). In other words, those who advance must help those who have been less fortunate. Opportunities for advancement are seldom similar for all family members; therefore, family goals may often result in conflict. The inequalities of role allocation among the household members often result in wife-beating, fighting among the children or depression of members, especially the women. Exacerbating this conflict is the well-meaning role of developmental programs which often favor one sex over the other creating further tension and conflict.

The *Siyazama* Women "Speak" through Their Beadwork

Images of dolls created by workshop participants are available from the project website www.siyazamaproject.co.za. One of the most impressive artifacts in our collection (its image is available on this site) is *Unsafe Sex A*, a beaded cloth sculpture made by Gabi Gabi Nzama. The use of black, white and red beads is typical of this regional style, as is the accessorizing of multi-colored linear stranded loops of the small glass beads. The two figures, each with tightly bound encircled strands of beadwork at the waistline, are tightly intertwined sexually, physically and emotionally. On closer inspection the intimate details of the male genitalia are vividly evident.

To Gabi Gabi this is a personal reflection of her own life and how she avoided becoming an AIDS victim through the timely death of her husband, who was a practicing *isangoma* (Zulu word for "traditional healer"). The tableau reflects "where everything began. My husband had an affair. He was sleeping with his mistress in my own house. Although he had AIDS, he did not tell anybody." According to Gabi Gabi, she was "given a second chance" after his passing, when his brother who wanted to have her as his rightful wife, also died from AIDS soon afterwards.

This most unusual and explicit tableau that was presented to me in the early stages of the *Siyazama* workshop schedules certainly defined for all participants the reality of the alarming and life threatening problems which most rural women face in KwaZulu-Natal: in a time of HIV/AIDS.

Conclusion

The collection grew with each particular series of informational programs and creative interactions between 1999 and 2005, and became of its own accord a three dimensional record of the craftswomen's feelings and reactions to the new information, as they received it, on HIV/AIDS. As their awareness around HIV/AIDS increased, so did their creative reactions. As a collection of sculptural beadwork, it is viewed by many as being stirring and thought-provoking whilst also, at times, unusually sexually explicit and highly detailed in its rendering. Most importantly, it became a vehicle through which the Zulu craftswomen spoke of their beliefs and culture as it relates to HIV/AIDS and as it exists today. The opportunity to create this collection offered the rural women an environment in which to express their thoughts and feelings, often disturbing in nature, whilst exploring the boundaries of their roles as women. As posited by the craftswomen, it enabled them "to push the boundaries" of their culture.

An understanding of gender and power relations in rural KwaZulu-Natal is crucial as this can provide a more culturally sensitive basis for designing and implementing meaningful developmental approaches which will ultimately empower women to have greater control over their lives, physically and financially. In closing, I believe that this study has provided a reliable and effective method of messaging on AIDS which links anthropology, art and health and could be implemented more widely as a developmental strategy.[1]

Commentary
Dovile Rukaite

To most Lithuanians, South Africa remains a distant and exotic land. By and large, HIV/AIDS, the main problem mentioned in this chapter, is not discussed much in the public, although it is a huge issue in neighboring Russia. The feminist community in Lithuania is primarily concerned about the traumas resulting from domestic violence.

Nevertheless, I found the practices used to heal and empower women in South Africa very impressive. My first reaction to the chapter was that I really could not identify any reasons why similar practices could not be applied to other cultural contexts. However, the more I thought about whether similar projects could work in Lithuania, the more skeptical I became about the universality of community-based empowerment strategies.

Currently there is a trend in Lithuania to experiment with different techniques to heal and empower women. Group work is one of them. In 2006, a group of law students who had internships with our center (WIIC, Women's Issues Information Center) experimented with women's support groups meant to help women understand their legal rights and thus avoid domestic violence. The students placed advertisements in the leading newspapers, magazines and streets. The response rate was very disappointing since no one came to the first meeting of the support group.

However, this does not mean that women in Lithuania are not seeking legal advice. During the same year, more than 260 women came to our center to get free legal advice related to domestic violence, but they did it individually. Why weren't these women interested in forming a community to achieve empowerment? One possible explanation is that domestic violence is still seen as a "family problem" in Lithuania, and "family problems" are seen as a very private matter, not to be discussed in public. In fact, the victims of domestic violence are likely to do everything to hide their experiences from a public view. This is why I can only admire the communal aspect of the *Dolls with Jobs* empowerment project.

On a more positive note, after ten years of efforts to raise the issue of domestic violence to the public consciousness, more and more Lithuanian women have started to speak out about this problem, although this is not easy. There are still unwritten social taboos related to open discussion of sexual violence, sexuality and sexual behavior, and many women find it difficult to discuss domestic violence in a group, even though other members in the group have likely had similar problems. Therefore, I find it difficult to imagine that a group of women engaged in an arts and crafts group would start sharing their private life stories in the Lithuanian context. Honestly, I cannot see a Lithuanian woman stating openly in front of a group of women that her work reflects "where everything began. My husband had an affair. He was sleeping with his mistress in my own house," like Gabi Gabi of *Dolls with Jobs* did.

Public reactions toward *The Vagina Monologues* broadcasted by the Lithuanian radio in 2003 are a good example of how difficult it is to discuss anything related to sexuality openly. During that year, WIIC (Women's Issues Information Center) presented the translated Monologues as a radio show. This was the first time that *The Vagina Monologues* and V-Day campaign took place in Lithuania. Brave and open sexual expression in *The Vagina Monologues* shocked the Lithuanian women. Many thought that the author of the play was "too crude" and "too open." One female listener commented that "only the Americans can speak so openly about private matters." Having read *Dolls with Jobs*, I know that art can be a powerful incentive to start an open discussion about women's issues. I hope that numerous initiatives pursued by WIIC and other women's rights organizations will help to make a cultural change in Lithuania.

Notes

1. In October 2006 a funding bid put to the United Kingdom's Department of International Development under the EAP (England and Africa Project) fund was approved. This bid, totaling R1.5m, was designed by three Universities under the leadership of Jackie Guille (United Kingdom), Kate Wells and Ian Sutherland (South Africa), Bruno Sserenkuumo and Venny Nakazibwe (Uganda). The intention of this EAP is to link three

Universities: the Durban University of Technology, Durban, South Africa, the University of Newcastle/Northumbria, United Kingdom, and Makerere University, Kampala, Uganda.

Bibliography

Gow, Jeff, and Chris Desmond. 2002. *Impacts and interventions: The HIV/AIDS epidemic and the children of South Africa*. Pietermaritzburg: University of Natal Press.

Johnson, Leigh, and Debbie Budlender. 2002. *HIV risk factors: A review of the demographic, socioeconomic, biomedical and behavioral determinants of HIV prevalence in South Africa*. Rondebosch: University of Cape Town.

Kayongo-Male, Diane and Philista Onyango. 1984. *The sociology of the African family*. London: Longman.

Leclerc-Madlala, Suzanne. 2002. On the virgin cleansing myth: Gendered bodies, AIDS and ethnomedicine. *African Journal of AIDS Research* 1: 87-95.

McAnerney, J. 1994. HIV seroprevalence in TB patients. *AIDS Bulletin* 3 (3): 14-15. Quoted in Johnson, Leigh, and Debbie Budlender. 2002. *HIV risk factors: A review of the demographic, socioeconomic, biomedical and behavioral determinants of HIV prevalence in South Africa*. Rondebosch: University of Cape Town, 26.

Raum, Otto Friedrich. 1973. *The social functions of avoidances and taboos among the Zulu*. Berlin: de Gruyter.

Wilkinson, D., C. Connoly and K. Rotchford. 1999. Continued explosive rise in HIV prevalence among pregnant women in rural South Africa. *AIDS* 13: 740. Quoted in Leigh Johnson and Debbie Budlender. 2002. *HIV risk factors: A review of the demographic, socioeconomic, biomedical and behavioral determinants of HIV prevalence in South Africa*. Rondebosch: University of Cape Town, 24.

Wojcicki, Janet Maia. 2002. Commercial sex work or Ukuphanda? Sex-for-money exchange in Soweto and Hammanskraal area, South Africa. *Culture, Medicine and Psychiatry* 26: 339-370.

Chapter 9
Confined Space: The Simultaneous Installation of Art and the De-Installation of a Relationship
Mary Beth Looney

The only way for a woman, as for a man, to find herself, to know herself as a person, is by creative work of her own. There is no other way (Friedan 1963, 344).

In 2004, the Art and Design department of Brenau University in Georgia offered an unusual course for upper-level students. The course was entitled *Sculpture Topics: Jewelry/ Metalsmithing and Installation Art*. Co-taught by metalsmith artist Nisa Blackmon and artist Mary Beth Looney, the semester was divided into two eight-week segments. The first segment involved instruction in small-scale work in metals and stones, yielding both semi-conventional jewelry and sculpted objects. The acquisition of basic techniques of assemblage and fabrication enabled students to embark upon the second segment of the course, which forced them to eventually work on a much larger scale in the realm of installation. An art form employed by artists in various formats since the early 20th century, installation is best described as holistic, encompassing the entirety of a given space. By utilizing an extraordinarily wide variety of media and approaches, the installation artist's objective is to completely manipulate a typically contained environment, engaging the viewer in a total art experience.

In the planning stages of this completely new course, instructors Blackmon and Looney faced the dilemma of finding an appropriate space that students could occupy for several weeks' time. Brenau University's campus, which hosts approximately 750 students in the women's college and around 70 students in the only all-girls boarding school for grades 9-12, measures less than a mile in any given direction. Despite these comparatively small numbers, there is a perpetual need for space. A 1905 Queen Anne-style house adjacent to campus and recently acquired by Brenau beckoned to the instructors. It possessed large rooms with hardwood floors, a grand staircase and early 20th-century stained glass windows (possibly designed by the studios of Louis Comfort Tiffany), suggesting historic days of Southern grandeur.

The previous owner, by whose name the house was called in casual conversation, was Maude Martin. She had lived there with her African-American housekeeper into old age, and had passed away in the house some weeks before Brenau officially acquired it. The Martin House deserved restoration and renovation, but Brenau needed a major donor for the work. As one had not yet been secured, the house sat unoccupied. Instructors Blackmon and Looney obtained permission to use the house for a significant duration, and brought eight future installation artists to visit it for the first time.

After exploring two stories of large and small rooms, exclaiming over the historic architectural detailing and fixtures—as well as the rather disconcerting state of the house and how it had been kept—students were instructed to sit on the floor and write about their first impressions of the space. They were told of Maude Martin and her black housekeeper, and Maude's drug-addicted grandson who had lived in an upper bedroom for some time. Writing samples from that evening's class repeatedly alluded to ghost-like presence, to the sadness of a lapse in the lives of a young man, an elderly woman and her house. Initially, students seemed fixated on these facts, but their eventual, resulting installations in the spaces evolved to address both women of history and the contemporary era. One of these installations, *Confined Space*, spoke to the women of Brenau in many ways. It also spoke *of* two Brenau women: two of the four artists who created the installation, reflecting and possibly effecting powerful changes in the lives of its makers. Just as higher education in art practice and theory directly impacts the art student, it sometimes also indirectly impacts her personal relationships, sometimes empowering her with new strength and even occasionally altering the path of her life.

The traditional education of an art or design student at Brenau entails foundation courses in the elements and principles of art, where considerations are given to basic premises, fundamentally universal components and resulting compositional arrangements. Built upon those foundations are more specialized subjects in fields ranging from interior design to studio art. Most of these specialized subjects center on the production of art forms that are discrete, portable and eligible for display or use in a typical gallery space or a design firm. In contrast, installation art rejects the discrete and traditional work of art in favor of the complete manipulation of a space. The creative process forces the artist to consider all the ramifications of something that has to appear permanent yet is actually temporary. It must be pervasive and exhaustive in consideration. Thus, great amounts of physical labor couple with comprehensive concerns with content. This requirement for successful installation art translated to work that most students did not anticipate or envision for themselves. Successful alteration of their allocated spaces required the deconstruction of unwanted elements, such as the removal of wall-to-wall carpeting, tall window drapes and nails imbedded in walls. Related tools borrowed from fathers, husbands and brothers appeared in the work sites. Tall ladders assisted with the painting of walls and a stair rail, or the installation of enlarged pieces of text on window glass and other walls. Trucks and otherwise large vehicles hauled in a range of unexpected items liberated from a host of sources: piles of college textbooks, a human skeleton, an overwhelming number of pottery pieces and piles of paper scraps. This broadened range of media and expansion of tasks were the first means to artistic empowerment for these eight Brenau students. Developed concepts for the installations, most particularly *Confined Space*, related heavily to the lives and/or histories of two of its four creators.

Confined Space was conceived as an exploration of the idea of entrapment, first imagined for Maude, the elderly owner of the house, and her housekeeper, who was employed in the racially disempowering manner that the Southeastern region of the United States has struggled for decades to overcome. The 99 year-old house, with its historical accoutrements of details, finishes and fixtures, further influenced this feeling of being "stuck" in time. The team of four students working on this project therefore painted the walls and carpeted floor of the front parlor gold, thereby alluding to a sense of preciousness—and the overprotected, domestically prescribed "gilded cage" that women of history often occupied. Other objects such as a woman's corset, an obvious symbol of confinement and also painted gold, was stretched taut between two posts at the base of the staircase. This was but the beginning suggestion of an overriding sense of tension, prompted by the inclusion of piles of broken pottery strewn about the floor, implying forcible destruction. Something had gone horribly wrong and the result was wreckage. Among the pottery shards, strategically placed newspaper clippings of 1960s and 70s-era wedding and engagement announcements—while certainly germane to the theme of the installation—also pointed more directly to the lives of two students on the creative team.

Senior studio art major Amanda* had begun the fall of her senior year with a new boyfriend who very quickly became a fiancé. By December, everyone was aware of the upcoming nuptials scheduled to occur just one month after May graduation. Amanda came from a small Southern town peppered with antebellum homes and trees hung with Spanish moss, located three hours' drive away from campus. Her betrothed managed a large retail chain within this same town. Amanda's parents welcomed this young man into the family, and since she was busy finishing her senior year in college, wedding plans were largely undertaken by her mother and older sister. On the surface, everything appeared to be perfect: A studio art graduate has little hope of making a substantial salary upon graduation, and any rare opportunities for such might take her elsewhere, beyond the parameters of home. With plans for a marriage to a gainfully employed resident of her hometown, Amanda was "taken care of."

Or was she? Over the course of the eight weeks of installation class, Amanda seemed to progressively withdraw from creative consultations with classmates and instructors. She later grew almost combative in the face of criticism. She appeared fatigued and traumatized. She often stepped outside on the veranda of the house during our work sessions to take phone calls. Finally, she spoke to the author of this essay about how yes, the wedding plans were coming along, but there were problems with the betrothed. He phoned often, complaining when she didn't answer or rapidly return calls. He interrogated her about her whereabouts, wanting to know which friends she'd been out with. Had she really been in class? Had she seen a former boyfriend recently? He "yelled," she said, and she did not enjoy it.

Private consultations initiated by other team members and classmates—one of whom, a future bridesmaid in the planned wedding—revealed a great deal of concern for Amanda. One teammate, an older student, tried to advise Amanda from the standpoint of personal experience: a prior relationship in which she was so abused that a hospital stay was required had forced her to be particularly wary of similar behavior elicited by Amanda's fiancé. All counseling amounted to nothing, it seemed, despite repeated mentions of very real statistics supporting the probable progression from verbal to physical abuse and violence. It was clear that there was mounting discord between the warm, familiar acceptance on behalf of Amanda's family and the true personality of the individual who was enjoying such acceptance. Clearer still was Amanda's inability to extricate herself from her own sense of confinement, instead demonstrating Simone de Beauvoir's repeated use of the existentialist "bad faith" concept in *The Second Sex* (de Beauvoir 1953). Despite the social and political advancements of her gender by the 21st century, Amanda persisted in self-denial, resisting her own autonomy and personal empowerment. After all, the wedding plans were fixed: dresses purchased and altered, church and reception spaces rented, photographer employed, invitations mailed. Those plans seemed to have carried Amanda away with them. There was no way out.

Meanwhile, as the installation of *Confined Space* developed, other contributing elements were introduced. A "golden" hammer was strung from a nail, accompanied by safety goggles, situated in a corner allocated for what can only be surmised as a locus for venting frustrations. Nearby were unbroken pottery pieces, cute figurines of angels and small animals, awaiting destruction by that hammer. A piece of signage, warning "Danger: Confined Space" hung in the parlor. A borrowed parakeet in its cage was placed in another corner with video footage of that same bird projected onto an opposing wall. Just before our opening event in which we staged a public reception, the last piece was inserted underneath the pottery debris, barely visible to the casual observer: the freshly cut newspaper announcement of Amanda's engagement and future wedding.

The opening reception was well attended by Brenau and the neighboring community. To our surprise, many students, staff, faculty and even some students' families formed a line in the *Confined Space* installation in order to don the safety goggles and take several whacks at pottery pieces with the golden hammer. The already debris-strewn floor gained a fresh layer of broken pieces of angels and animals. Later, some of the installation artists reported talking to one or two young women who absolutely refused to take up that hammer: they did not like the connotation of violence. Signers of the guestbook at the entrance to the installation appeared to in some cases understand the totality of the message, which was posted as an artist statement outside the space:

This installation seeks to inspire a sense of confinement. Emotions associated with tension and entrapment are targeted by this experience. The audience may enjoy that there are many manifestations of cages in our lives that are not as palpable as this one. Absence is presence in this parlor as the testament to the struggle between physical surroundings and captive(s) remain on the walls, floor and sparse furniture. So it seems that many seek stability and security in their job, relationships, community and other aspects of life. But at what point does security become captivity? Following this question, our installation warns, "Danger: Confined Space."

Other signers of the guestbook merely indicated their general feelings of gratitude for the chance to vent a wide variety of frustrations during exam week. The eight students enrolled in the class were pleasantly surprised at the visitor turnout as well as the overwhelming engagement of the crowd. After much work in both physical and conceptual terms, they had succeeded in transforming spaces into total, artistic experiences. At the close of the reception, they lingered, perhaps because they had truly commanded those rooms, and upon receiving visitors' commentaries and reactions, they took that last chance to reconsider the depth and breadth of what they had achieved. Everyone parted company that evening with a dual sense of success and wonder.

Amanda's mood had improved by that night. She clearly enjoyed the experiences of both the work and the outcome. While several students' family members attended the reception, Amanda's fiancé did not. Given the pall that his actions and sentiments had cast upon his fiancé, her classmates and their creative activities, he was not missed.

Shortly after that event, word traveled that Amanda had enacted her own private (and public) form of liberation. Driven to finally speak honestly with her parents, she learned that they would support her choices despite the loss of deposit monies and the changes effected within a small town community. They assured her that they "wanted her happiness," and the nuptials were officially cancelled. Three years later, she is happily married to a warm and gentle man who lives in the Gainesville community. They have a young son and the loving network of two united families. She continues her artistic pursuits and has exhibited in an alumni exhibition at Brenau University Galleries.

While the conceptual development and creation of *Confined Space* cannot necessarily be considered as the source for Amanda's eleventh-hour radical change in plans for her future, the parallels between art and life nonetheless assert themselves. The question of security as captivity posed by the creators of that installation inspired many answers, amidst the strewn debris of smashed pottery and wedding announcement clippings within an historic, gilded cage. The best and most hopeful answer—the freedom of expression and the empowerment that art can provide and inspire elsewhere—lives on in a young artist who chose a more liberated path.

*For the sake of confidentiality, the name of the individual has been changed.

Commentary
Dovile Rukaite

All over the world, there are numerous women trying to address their personal issues in their own complicated private spaces. Most are less fortunate than Amanda who was able to explore her own personal life in a spacious Victorian house.

Although not every woman is a talented artist, we all can be creative in our own ways. Creativity is a very powerful healing force. Art therapy is the power of creativity that helped Amanda to be brave. In my opinion, one of the most important lessons from Amanda's story which is applicable to any cultural context is that creativity heals and empowers.

Amanda's story has a happy ending. She garnered a lot of support from her family and friends. She confronted her personal problems in a caring, supportive environment. What would have happened to Amanda in Lithuania?

I do not think that Amanda's story would receive a warm welcome in my country. People do not like to discuss their private matters (and especially domestic violence) in public. Her story would be seen as a personal, private matter. Thus, I do not think that a "Lithuanian Amanda" would have received the same level of support from her peers and the professor. In fact, she probably would not have even attempted to discuss her problems with this particular group. Of course, she may have tried to obtain professional help (counseling) or advice from her friends who may have experienced something similar. But the context in which the story would have been told would be different.

Having read this story, I remembered another story involving an art student here in Lithuania. She was defending a project focusing on violence against women as a social issue. Her professors were old and well respected in academia. They told the student that violence against women is simply not a pertinent social problem in Lithuania, and gave her a failing grade.

To conclude, a "Lithuanian Amanda" would have to confront a different academic culture (which offers less support to women than a liberal arts women's college abroad) and less social support. It seems to me that she would have to be braver and stronger than Amanda in America's South.

Bibliography

de Beauvoir, Simone. 1953. *The second sex*, New York: Alfred A. Knopf.
Friedan, Betty. 1963. *The feminine mystique*, New York: W.W. Norton.

Part III
Authentic Voices:
Nothing Lost in Translation!

Chapter 10
Were All Women Born to Suffer? Understanding Resistance to Empowerment: A Lithuanian NGO Activist's Perspective
Dovile Rukaite

Today I visited several doctors to get a routine health check required in Lithuania for anyone who works with computers. Having spent hours in line, I finally was lucky to spend several minutes with a pleasant female physician to get my blood checked. Trying to keep my attention away from the needle, she asked me about my workplace, WIIC (Women's Issues Information Center). "Is this a place for unhappy women to get help? A place where physically abused wives can hide from their husbands?" she wondered. "Not necessarily," I answered. "We work with many different women, and we pursue many different initiatives, including consultations about legal matters, usually related to divorce." The doctor then remarked that "all women were born to suffer," and that their "fate" is to deal with their "bad luck" throughout their lives. I concluded our conversation by saying that not all women choose to suffer. Some of them choose to fight for a better life. Then I left the room, but the thoughts about this conversation lingered in my head. I can't say that I was surprised by the beliefs about the inferiority of women. What surprised me most was that these ideas were voiced by someone so well educated and holding such a respectable social status. I have always thought that educated people were less likely to believe in women's inferiority. Obviously, I was wrong—at least in this case.

This experience inspired me to rethink the projects pursued in Lithuania that are meant to empower women. Could similar beliefs explain why some of the projects, pursued by the local women's groups and international actors, are not as effective as the women's rights activists would like them to be? To gain insight into this question, this essay will focus on the initiatives to address two traumatic issues—domestic violence and trafficking of women. Each section will describe the issue and analyze the ways to address it. The goal of these two in Lithuania and other post-transitional societies. The first section of this essay briefly describes the main agent behind the empowerment of women in Lithuania—the NGO movement.

Women's Empowerment through Lithuania's NGO Movement

Lithuania's women's movement currently unites many NGOs promoting women's rights. There are more than 100 women groups registered in this country of approximately 3.4 million people. Approximately half of these organizations actively promote equal rights for women and men and therefore can be described as "feminist." Although most of these organizations are located in the urban areas, there are women activists in smaller towns as well. Approximately 25 NGOs offer help to victims of domestic violence by providing shelter (OSI 2007, 36). Thus, especially in comparison with the other two Baltic states, it is fair to say that Lithuania's women's movement is relatively strong. During its infancy in early 1990s, the movement received support from international donor organizations from the United States, the World Bank, the UNDP (United Nations Development Programme) and the EU (European Union). The Scandinavian countries played an important role in this movement as well—through trainings, raising awareness and helping to develop networking strategies. WIIC, my current workplace, is an integral part of Lithuania's women's movement.

WIIC was created in 1996. It received financial support from the UNDP and inspiration from a group of active and determined women. During this decade, it became an umbrella organization for different women's groups active in Lithuania. WIIC and several other organizations associated with Lithuania's women's movement are not afraid to use the term "feminist" to describe what we do and what we stand for. At the same time, we realize that many women in Lithuania tend to embrace feminist ideas, such as equality of women, without using the label "feminist," probably because the label is associated with radicalism and something too foreign to traditional Lithuanian way of life. Unfortunately, similar attitudes are still popular in other post-communist countries as well.

This resistance to the "feminist" label has not prevented Lithuania's women's movement, including WIIC, to focus on women's issues that matter to feminists in countries such as South Africa or Armenia—countries that are perceived as very distant culturally and geographically from Lithuania. Domestic violence and human trafficking are cases in point. Our organization defines domestic violence and trafficking in women and children as the most pressing issues.

To address these issues, WIIC works together with different women's organizations, including *Caritas* (associated with the Catholic Church) and the Center for Equality Advancement which openly supports gay and lesbian rights. Although ideologically these two organizations are very different, we are able to work with them because we are united by our desire to help women and address practical, pressing issues related to violence against women.

Fighting Domestic Violence

There are approximately thirty women's organizations in Lithuania who are trying to help women suffering from domestic violence. There are several functioning hotlines and some government support for our initiatives. However, social attitudes toward domestic violence are difficult to overcome. There is a saying in Lithuania, "If he beats you, it means that he loves you." It summarizes very well the attitude that many men and women still hold towards domestic violence. Furthermore, economic dependence of women on their husbands is another problem contributing to the prevalence of domestic violence.

The relationship between economic dependence, prevalent social attitudes and continued domestic violence is illustrated by a story from Alytus, a small Lithuanian town. One forty-something year old woman who lives in a rural area close to Alytus was beaten up severely by her husband. She walked eight kilometers (approximately five miles) to the Women's Crisis Center which operates from a small apartment twenty-four hours every day. The victim had to walk because she was ashamed to take a bus. She wanted to spend one night in a safe environment, but she knew that she would have to come back to live with her husband, two kids and his parents. Apparently, her husband controlled her every step and wanted to know what she was doing every minute of her life. She spent seventeen years with her husband, and she did not see a way out of this relationship because she felt that she will never be able to get a job which would pay her rent if she moved out. The Crisis Center gave a note to the woman stating that she had spent the night there so that she could show this note to her controlling husband. The woman came to the Crisis Center one more time. This time, she did not seek shelter. Instead, she was unhappy about an anonymous story related to domestic violence published by the local newspaper. The victim thought that the Crisis Center shared her story with the journalists. Having expressed her dissatisfaction with the fact that domestic abuse became public knowledge, she left the Center. She never returned.

Although the victim suffered greatly from her husband, she did not want the issue to become public. Similar attitudes are held by many. To change such dangerous attitudes, our NGO pursues mass media campaigns and tries to get the attention of the newspapers. Despite the widespread resistance, we believe that it is necessary to raise the awareness about this issue and introduce a "zero tolerance" approach. It would be great to have more politicians or people who have a high social status speak out against domestic violence. In addition, we believe that changes in legislation could make our struggle against domestic violence more effective.

Lithuania's legal system still views domestic violence against women as a "private matter." Several years ago, the laws were amended to make the perpetrators leave the house in which the victim(s) live. However, it is difficult to implement this law because the police officers do not know where to put the violent men (and they are unwilling to jail the offenders). Furthermore, the house is likely to be the property of the abuser which can't be easily taken away from him. Thus, in most cases, the perpetrators and the victims continue to live under the same roof.

Given these difficult circumstances, it would be logical if the victims of domestic violence could unite into some kind of an organized movement to address the issue. Unfortunately, many victims, just like the woman from the Alytus area, are unwilling to make the first step to address the problem. A national representative study conducted by WIIC in 1997-1998 helps to understand the mentality of the victims. According to this study, one reason explaining why the female respondents subject to domestic violence did not seek help was that they did not see "any sense" in doing this (Purvaneckiene 1998).[1] In fact, 36 percent of respondents identified this reason. 23 percent of the respondents told the interviewers that they were "ashamed" to seek help. Some did not know where to get help. Overall, however, only 22 percent of all respondents who did not get help told the interviewers that they did not want or did not need any assistance.

Although the study was conducted a decade ago, unfortunately, the situation has not changed drastically since then. The institutions that should be ready to provide help for the victims of domestic violence (such as crisis centers) need to become more visible and more accessible to the victims.

Furthermore, the results of this study help to shed light on the main reason why domestic violence is prevalent. 65 percent of the victims reported that the perpetrator was drunk. Given the high rates of alcohol consumption, it is not surprising that the rates of domestic violence are quite high in Lithuania. According to our estimates, 63.3 percent of women (older than sixteen) have experienced male physical, sexual violence or threats. This number is significantly higher than in Finland (40 percent) and Canada (51 percent). According to Purvaneckiene (1998), similar studies were conducted in Finland and Canada during the same time. This comparison suggests that the level of economic development and other socioeconomic characteristics of Lithuania can influence the levels of domestic violence as well as the severity of incidents.

Unfortunately, as of 2008, there is a shortage of reliable statistical information about domestic violence against women in Lithuania. The NGOs do not collect data about violence against women on a regular basis. In 2000-2005, with the support from international donors, several research centers and NGOs in Lithuania completed a series of studies about different forms of violence. Their research suggested that approximately 35 percent of women experience physical violence regularly. Like ten years ago, most women distrust public assistance, and silence is still the most common response to domestic violence. Consequences of having experienced domestic violence include job loss and economic disempowerment (OSI 2007, 54-55). It is still very difficult for women to find well paying jobs and start profitable businesses in Lithuania. Therefore, economic empowerment of women is a powerful tool in our fight against domestic violence.

Attempts at Economic Empowerment

It seems to me that the fact that some women are compelled to stay at home contributes to the persistence of domestic violence. In the past, there was a widespread belief that "staying at home" is a Western-type privilege, enjoyed by rich women, and it is "good for children" if their mother can afford to stay at home with them. After the disintegration of the Soviet regime, there was another problem. The childcare system, developed during the Soviet times, disintegrated, and many women with children had no other choice but to stay at home. This led to psychological and economic problems as it became increasingly difficult for women to go back to the labor market after staying several years with their children.

To empower women economically, in 2005, WIIC started a new project involving the kindergartens. We made sure that three kindergartens were open two hours longer than regular work hours. This project attempted to test a model created for young parents who are trying to balance their family responsibilities and their careers. Single mothers working in low paid jobs with long hours were the most active participants of this project. Additional services, such as professional training, were offered to the participants.

Although it appears to be a simple project, we had to overcome quite a few obstacles: The kindergarten staff members were unwilling to come up with all necessary documentation required for two extra hours of work. In the end, I believe that this initiative will contribute to the economic empowerment of twelve most active participants of the project, allowing them to make at least one more step towards their career goals. The project was partially funded by the ESF (European Social Fund) for two and a half years. Now we are trying to make sure that the kindergartens find ways to continue this project even without international support.

In addition to receiving financial help for similar small scale projects, many of our projects have an international dimension. We have close contacts with women's rights organizations abroad. From our international contacts we found out that domestic violence is an issue of growing importance in the countries that are much better developed than Lithuania. Even though Lithuania's economy is growing, domestic violence is not likely to disappear any time soon.

Trafficking of Women

Initiatives at economic empowerment are crucial to address another issue experienced by Lithuania—the trafficking of women. Lithuania is a transit country and a sending country. Approximately 1,000-1,200 young women are trafficked from Lithuania each year (OSI 2007, 60). This is the highest number in the Baltic states. Not only Lithuania's women's rights organizations (approximately twenty NGOs), but also the US State Department, the EU and numerous women's rights organizations from abroad are interested in fighting this problem. Admittedly, sexual trafficking receives more attention internationally and locally than domestic violence. In this case, there is robust government support. Since 2003, the Social Security and Labor Ministry of Lithuania has supported the NGO initiatives to stop sexual trafficking. Some government funds are awarded to smaller NGOs located in smaller towns and villages. These NGOs help the victims of trafficking by renting one or two rooms and providing for their basic needs. Yet despite all these attempts to address sexual trafficking, this issue still presents a major challenge.

Most victims of sexual trafficking are young women and girls with no social and economic skills. They usually come from single parent families, many of whom suffer from problems such as alcoholism. Each year, younger and younger women and girls are recruited by sexual traffickers.

In 2005, to raise awareness about sexual trafficking and prostitution, our organization started a campaign called "It is Shameful to Buy a Woman."[2] One of the goals of this campaign was to inform the public about the law punishing "the buyer." Huge posters showing a male figure with a piece of his shirt sticking out from his pants were placed in public areas of thirteen Lithuanian towns. The posters stayed in the public areas for more than a year. This was a revolutionary approach to sexual trafficking because it challenged the demand side.

During the same year, the Lithuanian government introduced an amendment to Administrative Violations Code of the Republic of Lithuania, Article 182-1. According to this amendment, "the same responsibility for rendering prostitution services and for purchase of such services is foreseen." Minors, the victims of physical violence, psychological pressure or deceit, or victims of trafficking in human beings are not held responsible. In 2007, this amendment became part of the law. Since then, both the buyer and the prostitute (not only the prostitute) should be punished in Lithuania. (A similar approach is practiced in Sweden.) Unfortunately, this law is not often applied in practice. Since 2005, this law was applied in only three cases, and all of these cases were covered in mass media as "strange" incidents. Consequently, legal measures alone cannot be totally effective in reducing the flows of sexual trafficking. More education and public awareness campaigns are necessary.

One of the most dangerous popular beliefs related to sexual trafficking and prostitution is that "these women do it voluntarily." WIIC's position is that teenagers (especially fifteen and sixteen year old girls) who are engaged in prostitution were most likely *forced* into it, especially if they came from abusive environment and did not have many other choices in their career. Many women who are drawn into prostitution come from rural areas where economic growth is still much slower than in the cities. Furthermore, many victims are seduced and poisoned with drugs before being forcefully taken to brothels. Thus, our goal is to develop a sense of compassion instead of outright condemnation for the victims of sexual trafficking.

Concluding Thoughts

In post-transitional Lithuania, there are numerous NGO and government-supported projects created to address women's issues. However, changing public attitudes towards domestic violence still remains a Herculean task. This needs to be done—as soon as possible.

On a more positive note, globalization and transition to democracy and capitalism has made transnational women's groups' cooperation easier. My experience with working with the projects related to women's economic empowerment, trafficking of women, and domestic violence suggests that the Lithuanian women's rights are important to people outside Lithuania. As a result of these concerted efforts, more and more women (and men!) in Lithuania realize that women were not "born to suffer." It seems to me that there is an international language against gender violence spoken widely already. Learning it and sharing it with others is a source of my individual empowerment.

Commentary
Randall Scott

In reflecting on the possible cross-cultural implications of the programs the author discussed in this chapter, I was somewhat intrigued by the story of the woman who visited the crisis center. This story raises the issue of individual empowerment vs. community empowerment as well as the how to address issues of cross-cultural communication and creating a space for subject-to-subject communication, rather than subject-to-object communication. The innovative approaches to the social problems of domestic violence and the trafficking of women discussed in this chapter confront these particular problems in ways that I am sure could be utilized by other social activists/feminists in various cultural contexts. In the United States, social service agencies also deal with issues related to economic empowerment. However, American culture tends to respect economic independence. Therefore, public policies tend to treat economic empowerment and economic independence as two completely separate issues.

Even though trafficking in women is without doubt directly related to economic issues, domestic violence is not in any way exclusively an economic problem. Still, I would like to discuss the proposition that economic stability is central to empowerment in more detail. I am especially interested in whether this proposition could be applicable to the United States.

While there is a great deal to be learned by a truly democratic sharing of empowerment approaches to particular women's issues and to understanding trauma as community issue, we cannot lose sight of those individuals who have directly suffered the actual physical and emotional bruises of domestic violence and human trafficking. Dovile Rukaite argues that it is a problem when public officials blame the victim. This is a problem that the U.S. shares with Lithuania. This shared issue is compounded by the issue of internal shame (felt by the victims) and blaming oneself for the abuse. Treatment strategies necessarily include empowering individuals who have suffered from domestic violence to overcome the fear of public humiliation and self blame. Social and political approaches are interconnected, but social programs intended to empower come with their own inherent risks.

This brings me back to "the forty-something years old woman who lives in a rural area close to Alytus" and a general unease that I encounter in myself when I think about issues in general as social rather than individual. Unease, in this case, does not in any way mean that I do not agree that these issues should be addressed by empowering communities. In fact I do, but we must always be cognizant of how our social/community solutions to issues such as violence toward women risk becoming institutionalized in ways in which these well-meaning and loving solutions take on somewhat of an oppressive nature in-and-of themselves.

There is no indication that the shelter in Alytus was anything but supportive to the "victim" in this case, but my experience tells me (I did emergency psycho-social interviews and mental health outreach in domestic violence shelters for a few years) that the social response to a problem inherently implies a structure of empowerment on to the individual "victim." The interaction of the individual, who seeks some sort of comfort and/or relief and the institution established to help, is inherently a helper-victim/subject-object interaction, which, in the context of this book, brings to mind the same sort of communication that occurs between Western feminist and "non-Western" women.

"Helping" institutions that emerge with the intention to empower are still institutions, which in the relationship to the individual assuredly risks treating the individual as an object. Domestic violence centers are historically based on the value of personal empowerment, but at the same time, are forced to act to as bureaucracies in order to operate. Women entering domestic violence shelters are "empowered" to understand their situation in a particular way, much like the Western-feminist approach to "empowering" their sisters in non-Western cultures. Institutional responses to social problems always run the risk of objectifying the individual as victim.

This does not mean that institutions should be condemned and/or criticized as oppressive, but it does seem to imply that a consistent reflection on the nature of communication between helper/victim and/or subject/object should always cast a critical eye toward the marginalizing possibilities inherent in the helping relationship.

Notes

1. 1,010 women (ages 18-74) were interviewed.
2. A copy of the poster is available from http://www.lygus.lt/ITC/news.php?id=772 (accessed July 2, 2008).

Bibliography

OSI (Open Society Institute). 2007. *Violence against women: Does the government care in Lithuania?* Budapest: Open Society Institute.

Purvaneckiene, Giedre. 1998. Short overview of research on violence against women in Lithuania. WIIC. http://www.lygus.lt/ITC/files_smurtas/giedre1.doc (accessed July 1, 2008).

Chapter 11
Women and Empowerment in Armenia: Traditions, Transitions and Current Politics
Svetlana Aslanyan

Can traditional societies, often described as patriarchal, be women-friendly? The case of Armenia suggests that they can. Even though traditional Armenian society was patriarchal and hierarchical, with specific gender roles, ancient Armenian codes and legal regulations provide evidence that in some spheres men and women were at times considered to be equal members of society. For instance, the Code of Shahapivan (5th century B.C.E.) had a rule which provided women the right to possess family property in case a husband deserted his wife without cause. The Code also allowed such a woman to bring a new husband into her home (Zeitlian 1992, 24). Mxit'ar Gosh's *The Book of Conviction* (12th century), a famous collection of laws and regulations, specified that men and women had equal rights and were equally responsible for the welfare of the family (Thomson 2000). The book banned violence against women, prohibited forced marriages and provided for the equal sharing of property. Men and women were free in their own spheres of activities—men as family providers and protectors, women as household and family organizers as well as transmitters of customs, traditions, moral values and national aspirations.

During the 19th and early 20th centuries feminist ideas about gender equality were embraced not only in the West. During the late 19th century, two famous Armenian women crafted a *Declaration of Women's Rights*. This document embraced feminist ideals, such as gender equality and women's rights to fully participate in social affairs.[1] Some of these ideals were implemented by the First Republic of Armenia (1918-1920), which became one of the first nations to give women the right to vote. It also appointed Diana Abgar (Abgaryan), the first female ambassador in the world, to represent Armenia in Japan. These developments suggest that women's progress is possible in traditional societies such as Armenia.

Sovietization: "Women's Liberation" and the "Women's Question"

The Soviet system challenged traditional norms by proclaiming gender equality. In 1920, when the Soviet power was established in Armenia, a decree was issued which proclaimed equal rights for men and women. The so-called "Women's Councils" and "Women's Departments" were established to pursue this goal and address women's issues. These institutions were a failure. The vast majority of women in Armenia (and elsewhere in the USSR) were not ready for radical gender "equality" enforced from the top down. They were not interested in working outside their homes. This is why words like "emancipation," "activism" and "feminism" acquired negative meanings. However, there were some Soviet women who fell for this ideology, although soon it was challenged by a different set of beliefs.

During the 1950s, the time of the Khrushchev "thaw," when the "iron curtain" was slightly raised, the Western image of "feminine glamour" was introduced to Soviet women. An image of a gloomy woman worker wearing a masculine dark suit was "replaced" by a feminine woman in a bright-colored dress and high-heeled pumps. This is when the concept of equal workers' rights became widely questioned. In everyday life women saw that they were forced to carry a "double burden" that was not commonly carried by women in the West. The Armenian women cooked and cleaned, did laundry, cared for their old mothers and stood in long lines for food on their way home from work. At that point, many women throughout the USSR thought that it might be better to withdraw from the workforce, focus on home and thus escape the "double burden." This was exactly the opposite of what Western feminists were advocating. Thus, paradoxically, the Soviet legislation which proclaimed gender equality resulted in disempowerment of women and (as some have argued recently) included elements of gender discrimination.

Perestroika

Political democratization did not translate into support for feminism and the women's movement. During the time of Perestroika, Mikhail Gorbachev (a reformist Communist leader) suggested that restructuring should allow women to return to their traditional female roles, including housework and children's upbringing (Gorbachev 1987). This did not happen.

Having traveled abroad, Gorbachev saw the achievements of the women's movement in the West. Thus, he decided to revive the Women's Councils. However, instead of promoting full gender equality, these institutions were based on the top-down, Moscow-centered model developed during Soviet times. Even today, the President of the Women's Council in Armenia is a political appointee. She is "given" a high salary, nice office and a "free" car. She has little if any contact with the grassroots women's movements and in reality does not promote gender equality.

During the time of Perestroika (late 1980s), even former women dissidents (who fought against the Soviet regime) supported the traditional family model, according to which a woman is expected to stay at home and take care of her family, while her husband is making money. During this period, the strength of this model was clearly seen as people voiced their belief that women's equality is bad for women's well-being because equality results in a "double burden" for women. In the words of one 62 year-old woman, Anaid Khachatryan, from the town of Ashtarak: "Equality? Why equality? Equality for what reason? Equality for working 24 hours as a donkey in factory and home? No, I prefer to stay at home and take care of my family."

The massive backlash in Perestroika times against the verbiage and many of the ideas of the Western women's movement, which may at first seem self-contradictory in the context of long-awaited democratic reforms, was rooted in the belief (prevalent during the Soviet times) that gender equality is bad for women's well-being. Gender equality was commonly equated with equal rights to employment, and this was believed to be the main cause of the so-called "double burden."

Empowerment after Perestroika?

According to the current constitution of Armenia, women and men enjoy equal rights in political life, workplace and family. Legislative norms in Armenia mostly correspond to major international standards; however, there are no corresponding mechanisms to ensure the proper implementation of this legislation. The result is discrimination against women in all spheres, including political participation.

The downfall of the USSR and the loss of government protection took Armenian women by surprise. They had no experience of fighting for their rights; rather, their Soviet mentality made them expect the government to support them. They had only vague ideas about democracy and the role of NGOs in civil society. Even today many Armenian women consider that democratization was responsible for the grave decline in their economic condition and their expulsion from the political arena. This mindset creates nostalgia for the "good old days" of the Soviet Union. Even women who fought hard to gain independence from the USSR feel similarly.

This feeling of hopelessness means that many women embrace a subservient status in their own families, serving as supporters for men, who are considered to be the "heads of the families." Women live in the shadow and do not use their professional skills. The situation is unlikely to change in the future because there is little public support for the women's movement.

Currently Armenian society has a negative attitude towards women activists and the women's movement. My personal experience is a case in point. Several years ago, when I was negotiating the terms of publication of my book *The Role of Women in Democratic Society*, an important person (a man) who had the power to publish the book, told me (referring to my argument): "What are you talking about? There is no problem with women's rights in Armenia. There is no discrimination. For example, look at yourself. Who discriminates against you? You are better educated than most men. You are a university professor. You have many publications. You speak four languages. What else do you want?" He concluded by saying that "There is no problem of women's rights in Armenia!" Such beliefs are very common. Therefore, understandably, Armenian women activists prefer to act as feminists without calling themselves "feminists" in order to avoid negative consequences.

Like elsewhere in the former USSR, Armenian women's rights activists have to deal with many problems. For example, domestic violence is widespread, but it is little discussed and not perceived as a serious problem. Many argue that it is shameful to discuss "intimate" problems (such as domestic violence) in public. Our NGO conducted research on violence against women, and we found that the vast majority of the Armenian population has no knowledge about international norms against gender violence (such as the CEDAW, Convention on the Elimination of All Forms of Discrimination against Women, and the Beijing Platform for Action). Both women and men try to conceal domestic violence. Many women simply keep silent. These findings suggest that there is a need for special legislation against domestic violence in our country.

Unfortunately, there is no real women's movement to push for these changes. Sovietization interrupted what was started in the 19th and early 20th centuries. The Soviet system killed community volunteerism, "grassroots" discussions, individual initiative, citizen participation and private advocacy of public policies. These civil society concepts remain largely misunderstood and distrusted, although there are many (approximately 65) women's organizations in Armenia today. Almost all these groups were formed in the beginning of the transition period, i.e., in the early 1990s. Their activities are largely focused on humanitarian aid and the environment. Many do important and useful work with elderly women, children, refugees, mentally disabled and other disadvantaged groups. However, these organizations do not focus on improving women's leadership skills, women's rights and advocacy. Younger women are not actively involved in the women's movement. The average age of leaders in women's organizations is 49-50 years (NGO Strengthening Program and World Learning 2001, 67).

In addition, although there are many registered NGOs, not all of them are active. Even active NGOs have trouble getting engaged in a dialogue with the government. They are not readily accepted by the Armenian society and seen as the agents of Western influence.

The NGOs have trouble creating a coherent force to oppose government policies; in fact, some of them have developed a cozy relationship with the government. It is especially troublesome that recently some authorities and ruling political parties started to create their own NGOs in order to secure funding and even launder money. However, such NGOs do not last long.

To survive, the NGOs need to try to please their donors. Almost 90 percent of NGOs in Armenia do not have sustainable funding. Given this situation, it is difficult to expect the NGOs to be active proponents of women's rights. There is hope, however, because many people (including women) employed in this sector are highly educated and sincerely interested in charitable work.

Concluding Thoughts

Unfortunately, there is no coherent national policy addressing women's issues in Armenia today. The declared state of gender equality, inherited from the Soviet system, continues to contain elements of gender discrimination. Few attempts are being made to change the situation. Male-oriented and male-dominated political elites do not take women's issues into account. Many believe that the "women's question" was "solved" during the Soviet times, and there is no gender discrimination in Armenia. This is why civil society must be empowered.

Women of Armenia, we must unite! Our education in the post-Soviet school of hard knocks and practical experience have helped us to appreciate the essence of democracy and begin to understand the importance of activism to address "hidden discrimination." Now we must network, cooperate, be open, engage and inform the public and unite to develop better mechanisms for legislation and implementation of the existing laws protecting our human and women's rights. Only then can we truly begin to solve the "women's question" and achieve real equality.

The institutions of civil society can serve as the mechanism which will bring about the equal participation of women in the social, political and economic life of our nation. By exploring what civil society is and what the tenets of democracy are, women will be able to abolish the information vacuum that exists today around these subjects. Then women will be able to achieve personal development and empowerment. A better society will follow, which will provide a better life for families.

Commentary
Anna M. Rulska

In the December 2007 issue of *Wprost*, one of the leading Polish magazines, I read an article maintaining that the current government is *the most feminized* one in the history of Poland (Nowicka and Dzierzanowski 2007). Not being sure about the exact ratio of male to female ministers, the headline baffled me. Surely Prime Minister Donald Tusk must have appointed more women than men to the ministerial posts to have evoked such a radical statement. Imagine my surprise when I looked at the numbers: 25 percent of the current government consists of women, compared to 4 percent under the first government; 0 percent in the second and third governments; and roughly 4-5 percent in the next three governments. First in 1997, under Prime Minister Jerzy Buzek, the percentage of women in the ministerial posts started reaching double digits, culminating at 22 percent under the current President's twin brother's government.

These statistics, compared with the argument posed in the preceding chapter, are troubling for so many reasons, most of them indicative of the situation of women in Poland—in many respects akin to trends prevalent in Armenia, as discussed by Svetlana Aslanyan. Similar to the experience of Armenian women, Polish women had an equalized role in the work field during Communism, which drastically conflicted with their continuing, traditional roles of wives and mothers at home. In the post-Cold War transition, however, there has been a somewhat more effective establishment of a non-discriminatory environment for women. This is not to say that women in Poland enjoy full equality, be it professionally, traditionally or privately, that results in the same scope of opportunities as men have.

As in Armenia, tradition and current reality represent and interact as two opposite and contradictory forces. On one hand, women have been expected to share the responsibility as bread winners. On the other hand, the patriarchal traditions are prevalent in Polish society, reinforced by the strong role of the Catholic Church. These conditions have effectively prevented gender equality from taking hold. (According to the CIA *World Factbook*, in 2002, 89.8 percent of Poles considered themselves Catholic and approximately 75 percent were actively practicing their religion.) This traditional and religious trajectory has thwarted the generational communication among women about issues specific to their gender and perpetuated the educational stereotyping of men as more intellectually capable. Those problems are further exacerbated by differences in social standing, financial position, education, age and rural versus urban settings. In effect, while Polish women enjoy a reasonably unlimited access to high-profile well-paid professional opportunities, at the same time the law in Poland imposes very moderate punishments for domestic violence and rape, and virtually no support exists for unwed mothers or teenage pregnancy. And again, as in Armenia, that Polish society is not ready to address the gender inequality issues is very aptly revealed by the supposition that 25 percent of government ministers being female constitutes "feminization."

Where do we start looking for solutions? How do we address the issues without a feeling of futility? Svetlana Aslanyan points to the role of education. I could not agree with her more; however, I would like to also add the power of trans-generational communication—maybe even more empowering than education and definitely more intimate. Mothers talking to their daughters, who then chat with their offspring of both genders, seem to carry the vast potential for change. The question, then, remains: How to impact the initial maternal base to spur this trend of communication? Here, the developments of globalization, sharing of information, insights into other societies, openness of communication, which then in turn impact the traditional and religious values, serve as natural, already hard-at-work tools of empowerment of women.

Notes

1. The main principles of this declaration are listed in Gulnara Shahinian's essay *Armenian Women's Rights throughout History*, http://www.isar.org/pubs/ST/ARwomrights481.html (accessed June 29, 2008).

Bibliography

CIA. 2008. The World Factbook: Poland. CIA. https://www.cia.gov/library/publications/the-world-factbook/geos/pl.html#People (accessed on June 29, 2008).

Gorbachev, Mikhail. 1987. Mikhail Gorbachev on women and the family. *Population and Development Review* 13 (December): 757-759.

NGO Strengthening Program and World Learning (Armenia). 2001. *Hayastani HK sectori gnahatum* (Armenian for "Armenia NGO sector assessment"). Yerevan: NSP/USAID.

Nowicka, Katarzyna, and Marcin Dzierzanowski. 2007. Damski naped Tuska (Polish for "women are the driving force in Tusk's cabinet"). *Wprost*, December 26.

Thomson, Robert W. 2000. *The lawcode [Datastanagirk'] of Mxit'ar Gosh* (translated with commentary and indices). Amsterdam: Rodopi.

Zeitlian, Sona. 1992. *Hay knoj dare hay heghapokhagan sharjman mej* (Armenian for "the role of women in the Armenian revolutionary movement"). 2nd ed. Brentwood, CA.: Hrastan Sarkis Zeitlian Publication.

Chapter 12
Zara's Travail: A Life Story
Azniv Eyramjyants

During all her life she has been tortured by one question: What would her life have been like if her parents, whom she could not remember, were alive? She has always tried to block this distressing question from her mind. Even now, when most of her life is already gone, thoughts about the childhood that she never experienced continue to haunt her.

Zara was born in 1939 in a small town in Russia to an Armenian father and a Russian mother. Therefore, she has always felt both Russian and Armenian, which has meant belonging to two worlds at the same time. Sometimes these worlds have merged into one, but sometimes they have clashed, which has been exciting and made learning two languages incredibly easy.

The year 1939 could have been the beginning of a happy life, but Zara does not remember it. Two years later, in 1941, war between Germany and the Soviet Union broke out. Hitler became her personal enemy. She blamed him for the loss of what mattered most to her—her parents and her childhood. At first, her father sent his wife, a four year old son and Zara, two years old, to Yerevan, where his sister (Zara's aunt) lived. Then he went to the battlefields. In Yerevan, Zara's mother worked in a factory, became ill with typhoid fever and died. Fortunately, the father's sister and brother did not abandon the children. Zara's brother went to Tbilisi to live with his uncle, and she stayed in Yerevan to live with her aunt. Zara was separated from her brother for many years, which built an invisible wall between them.

When the war was over, her father came back home ill with cancer—without a job, homeless, without a wife and without any hopes for a better life in the future. He did try to get married again, but it was already too late, and he died, leaving his children alone once again; this time forever. *Oh, damned war, what have you done to our lives?!* The reader may ask: Couldn't the orphans expect the government to help them? Of course there were state-supported orphanages, but it was a disaster to live in them. Living there ruined children psychologically. In addition, orphanages were not an option because the unwritten moral code of Armenians did not permit giving children away to orphanages, if they had relatives who were still alive, no matter whether those relatives were good or bad. Consequently, the only solution was to separate the children one more time and take them back to their uncle in Tbilisi and aunt in Yerevan. The children were horrified by this separation. But who cared what they thought? It happened in 1948.

The children had little if any contact with each other, and the distance between them grew every day. Their troubles continued. Soon the uncle in Tbilisi, and later the aunt in Yerevan died. Zara found herself in a house where nobody needed her, and they kept her only because she had no other place to go. She had to endure this for ten years! Until today she does not want to remember those years. She was humiliated many times. Her so-called relatives would go away, leaving her without a key to the house. She would sit in front of the door and wait for them to come back so that she could get into the house and go to sleep.

Her "caretakers"—her uncle and his son, and later the wife of his son—focused on their own lives. They treated Zara not as a human being, but as part of the house. They forgot that this "part" was alive. She constantly felt surrounded by emptiness. Her shabby clothes or having no personal space did not cause her much pain. What hurt most was the fact that she was remembered only when she had to do chores. Nobody from that house ever said a nice thing to her; nobody gave her a hug or a kiss, although she needed them badly. It was not her home. It was a place of residence.

Can the reader feel how much pain there is in these words? This story is being told for the first time. The heroine has decided to share her personal story only with the readers who do not know her personally. Those who know her probably have no idea how many little and huge traumas still live within her, although she now appears to be very self confident, having earned the love of the people who are around her, especially her students at the university. But this is now. Back then she yearned to grow up as soon as possible, so that she could leave the house and start a real life.

Zara was always a good student. She loved to learn, and she has never lost her curiosity. She graduated from high school with high honors and entered the University of Yerevan without having to take the entrance exams. There she could never study enough. On one wonderful day she went through a Cinderella-like experience. A letter from Paris written by one of her uncles reached her relatives. The Armenians are a traumatized nation, living with the memory of genocide in Turkey. In 1915, the whole family of Zara's father ran away from the massacres. Most ended up in Russia, only the oldest son (her uncle) went with his family to Paris. During the times of Stalin, it was forbidden to keep in touch with relatives who lived abroad. This is why no one talked about the uncle in Paris. When Zara's family had to fill out different questionnaires, they wrote that they had no relatives abroad. God forbid, if someone found out that there were relatives in foreign countries! That could have been a reason for deportation to Siberia or Solovki (a prison, a prototypical Gulag).

Fortunately, Stalin died, and Zara's uncle decided to look for his beloved sister, Zara's aunt, not knowing that she had died a long time earlier. He sent a letter to his sister's old address. Zara's relatives were all excited about this letter, but no one wanted to take the risk of answering it. Therefore, they (Zara's uncle and three cousins) decided that Zara had to answer the letter. And she did. Her uncle from Paris learned about the deaths of Zara's immediate family. He started mailing parcels with clothes and shoes to her. Life became better. She started having nice things. A shabby Cinderella became a well-dressed princess. Only then was Zara not ashamed to go out, even though she still did not have cash. She gave her stipend (which was very modest, like now) to her caretakers who let her stay in their house. To be more exact, the inhabitants took her stipend from her. It was understandable: It was really difficult for common people to survive back then, and her "relatives" had a very hard time getting by.

Having nice clothes and feeling a little more self-confident, Zara realized that she could be attractive to men. She decided to marry as soon as possible and run away from the house where she was unwanted. She did. However, the traumas experienced in her childhood made her believe that she could never be happy. She has never experienced happiness in her personal life, although she has tried, having married twice. Zara wanted a lot of love, so much that she would forget about her childhood, but men could not understand her. They wanted love only for themselves.

If a heart is hurt during childhood, it does not heal. It can heal only when it stops. Is it possible to convey this feeling to others? Furthermore, who wants to listen to such stories in a troubled poor country? So Zara has remained silent about her traumatic experiences, bottling up her childhood and youthful memories.

One of her husbands had many traumas as well. During Stalin's times, his father was accused of anti-Soviet activities and deported to a camp where he died. Zara's husband's life was affected by what happened to his father. This made him concentrate on his own problems, leaving him incapable of understanding his own wife. Probably this was his coping mechanism. He did accept her the way she was, but at the same time he refused to care about anyone or anything except himself.

Zara has never been able to find a human being who has wanted to listen to her and understand her. Only now, for the first time in 67 years, is she letting her story out. The people who are close to her will not be able to hear it, which makes telling it easier.

A difficult life can turn us either into scoundrels or into caring human beings who want to treat others in the way in which they want to be treated. Zara has been lucky because she has learned not to blame the whole world for her problems. She does have the right to be angry because she has experienced a lot of pain. Fortunately, there have been some positive changes in the country in which she continues to live. She wishes that there were places in which every person, even a child, could find help without fearing ridicule and rejection, and without being taken advantage of. All of her life, Zara has dreamed about working in such a place. She does like her current job of teaching Russian at a university. She can earn a living, travel and write textbooks with a lot of love for the whole world and her many children—her students.

Maxim Gorky, the Russian writer, wrote that people are created by the ways in which they resist the outside world. Zara has found this out through her life experiences. The most important thing is to never give up. Where there is a will, there is a way.

Why is it so important to me, Zara, the author of this story, that my voice be heard? Look at the world we live in. There are many wars going on: big and small, wars to spread democracy (although this is impossible to do), terrorism... Innocent people, including many children, are suffering. If a child is orphaned, she may have been better off perishing with her parents. If she remains alive, she may be doomed to a painful and lonely life. Psychological traumas do not heal; they can only turn into scars. Let the children keep their parents, and there will be fewer problems in this world.

Commentary
Ingrida Vegelyte

My first impression was that the essay *Zara's Travail: A Life Story* was full of internal contradictions and silences. It appeared that the author deliberately wanted her "real" life story to be unintelligible and left outside the public discourse. As a reader, I was not presented with any reliable empirical information. As I was reading the story, I was trying to analyze its internal logic and the use of language.

The story does involve a real person, a girl named Zara, and is not an anonymous confession. It comes directly from the person who has experienced it, first hand. However, it is presented in the third person, with a narrator telling the story. The Narrator has the power to participate in the story. She has the power to voice her own opinion, interpret, summarize and even influence the flow of events.

The story is structured in such a way that Zara (the main character) and the Narrator often speak using the same voice. Sometimes it becomes unclear when and why Zara is transformed into the Narrator. At one point in the story, the Narrator starts to identify herself with Zara and her pain, tries to find logical arguments to explain Zara's experiences and ways to represent Zara's interests. The Narrator starts asking for justice, thus expressing her (the Narrator's) own positions and values.

Clearly, the Narrator is much more sophisticated than the girl Zara. She (the Narrator) indirectly interacts with Zara. She also tries to address the reader directly. In the end of the story, the Narrator starts addressing someone else, someone more powerful—perhaps the world powers responsible for initiating the wars, important actors who can affect the outcome of world history and maybe even God. The last sentence in the story, demanding that children have their parents, exposes the Narrator as an ardent defender of children's rights.

The main character (Zara) is going through an enormous internal struggle. She is trying to understand why she was born to go through so much suffering.

The girl cannot answer this question. As the story is told, the heroine simply stops pursuing this query. The story (and life) goes on. Zara exhibits interests and desires (such as looking for truth, finding answers to important questions, understanding the meaning of life, etc.), but she does not have enough power and expertise to pursue these interests. Throughout the story (and life), Zara is struggling with an enormous tension between desire and impotence.

Trying to address this internal conflict the heroine starts to look for answers in the outside world. She starts analyzing her relations with other people. This is understandable. Anyone who has lost his or her parents is likely to do the same—try to reach out to other people instead of becoming introspective. However, the heroine fails to find a solution to her internal conflict by engaging with others. She abruptly terminates her relations with the others. As a consequence, she continues to have trouble expressing herself as an adult woman.

The heroine is much more successful when it comes to her professional relations. She interacts with students, whom she describes as her "children." Thus, her professional activities become a bridge between the inner self of the heroine (Zara) and outside world (the other "children"—the students). But this is not entirely satisfactory. The story implies that the heroine could solve her internal conflict by directly communicating with the unhappy children in special "institutions." She would love to help the suffering children, but there are no such "institutions" in her country. This desire, like many others, remains an unfulfilled dream.

Let's try to focus on the crucial relationship between Zara and the Narrator. The main character (Zara) was never presented to us as an independent actor. She always needs someone to help her to tell her story. (The Narrator plays this role.) Having listened to (and communicated) the "confession" of Zara, the Narrator suddenly becomes an empowering agent, giving Zara a voice to address the entire world! Not only does the Narrator declare boldly that somewhere in the world there is a little girl living in the soul of the sixty-seven year old woman, but she pronounces that the girl is describing a problem of global significance. The Narrator demands that the reader pay attention to lonely, unhappy children everywhere and take action.

To understand the relationship between a powerless girl and the empowering Narrator, we need to engage two philosophical categories—"experience" and "expression." Essentially this is a story about private feelings (experiences) and finding ways to express them. A pure "feeling" (experience) is something very private. It is a puzzle that cannot be understood unless it is somehow communicated to other actors. In this case, we are faced with language (story-telling) as a form of expression. Confession of the Girl and the interpretation of the Narrator make the experience tangible and accessible to us, the readers.

This insight can help us to gain insight into the merciless question in the end of the story: Would the children have been better off if they died together with their parents? Zara has experienced enormous pain, and she found a way to express it through this story; therefore, the expression of this pain started to acquire meanings accessible to others. Thus, the story has attempted to become part of world history, universal memory. This individual story attempts to prove its relevance to many other individual stories of suffering and demands radical changes to stop it. Having understood this, should we still be asking whether it was better for the Armenian Girl to survive and tell her story, instead of perishing with her parents?

Chapter 13
Gender In/Equality in Egypt and Armenia
Isabella Manassarian

This chapter seeks to examine cultural and legal norms that affect the status of women in Egypt and Armenia. Although seemingly poles apart, the two countries have some commonalities. Both are situated at the junctures between different "civilizations." Both have deeply-rooted, although different, religious traditions. Egypt claims to be the intellectual center of the contemporary Muslim world. Armenia, proud to consider itself the very first Christian nations, claims that Christianity became the state religion in the 4th century. Moreover, both have traditional patriarchal cultures that are widely supported by societies and political elites.

However, legal and social positions of women are radically different. On the one hand, Egypt's constitution institutionalizes discrimination against women. In addition, one can observe constant discrimination against women in everyday life. On the other hand, Armenia's "liberal-Western" legal framework promotes gender equality and tries to prevent discrimination, even if it does not fully eliminate it on the popular level. Armenia's deeply rooted patriarchy does incorporate a relatively high level of respect towards women.

Legal Frameworks

On the surface, the Egyptian legal system is one of the most progressive in the Middle East when it comes to women's rights, especially after the enactment of the right to *khula* (separation) in 2000. Previously a woman could file for divorce only if she could prove physical harm. The amendment granted women the right for divorce on the grounds of incompatibility provided that she returns the dowry and renounces all financial claims.

The system still has many loopholes, which are used and abused to institutionalize gender disparities (Human Rights Watch 2005). The government is often reluctant to act on behalf of women, and frequently those that have suffered mistreatment are hesitant to approach the authorities. The gap between the law on paper and its implementation is huge. The legal system does not promote gender equality, and it does not challenge society's traditional patriarchal notions, including the supremacy of Sharia.

Article 40 of the Constitution of Egypt stipulates that "all citizens are equal before the law, [and] they have equal public rights and duties without discrimination due to sex, ethnic origin, language, religion or creed" (Egyptian government n.d.). However, the Constitution as a whole does not challenge traditional norms and gender inequality, especially in the private sphere. Several other articles (in particular, 9 and 11) were written to protect the nature of the Egyptian family, with its deeply rooted patriarchal notions and traditions, women are effectively subordinated to men.

Discrimination against women is strongly supported by the Egyptian Penal Code (UNDP 2005, 188). According to this Code, if the husband catches the wife in an act of adultery and kills her, his punishment will be limited to imprisonment for a maximum of seven years. In similar circumstances the wife will receive a death sentence, life imprisonment or hard labor for life. The Penal Code does not clearly define adultery. It is also noteworthy that marital rape is not considered a criminal act. This is the result of a deeply rooted belief that the wife has no right to refuse her husband sexual pleasure.

Egypt has ratified, with extensive reservations, a number of international conventions regarding the protection of human rights and women's rights. The most important reservations pertain to the supremacy of Sharia and the principle that none of the conventions should contravene the principles of Islamic jurisprudence. In the case of the CEDAW (Convention on the Elimination of all Forms of Discrimination against Women), according to the Division for the Advancement of Women (n.d.), the Egyptian delegation made reservations to two core provisions of the treaty—Articles 2 and 16, condemning discrimination against women in "all its forms" (Article 2) and "taking all appropriate measures to eliminate discrimination against women in all matters relating to marriage and family relations" (Article 16). Thus, the ultimate purpose and meaning of the CEDAW was undermined and subjected to the institutionalized discrimination within the Egyptian legislation.

In contrast, when compared with Egypt, the legislation related to women in Armenia is almost heavenly. From a legal perspective, men and women have equal rights, since the current legal framework of Armenia was designed using the Western "role model." The Armenian Constitution stipulates the equality of all citizens. None of the articles in the Constitution are gender-specific unless they address privileges given to females due to their biological ability to bring new life. Otherwise, both men and women have equal rights in marriage, divorce and with regard to children.

However, there are several weaknesses in Armenian (and Egyptian) laws affecting women. First, there is no specific definition of gender discrimination or sexual harassment, and second, there are limitations on adoption. Unmarried people cannot adopt a child together. This legal provision is closely intertwined with societal attitudes towards the sanctity of marriage in both cultures.

In terms of international treaties and conventions, Armenia is clearly ahead of Egypt. Armenia ratified more than fifty conventions and other legal documents written to promote gender equality (Ministry of Territorial Administration of the Republic of Armenia and UNDP 2007). The CEDAW was ratified without reservations, along with other major human rights treaties. The CEDAW Committee has acknowledged significant Armenian progress, which perhaps can be attributed to Armenia's commitment to democratize and its heavy dependence on the EU's (European Union) financial assistance (DESA 1997). In 2006, the EU-Armenia Action Plan included a reference to the government commitment to ensure gender equality (Ministry of Territorial Administration of the Republic of Armenia and UNDP 2007).

Despite the fact that both countries have patriarchal traditions, their trajectories are very different. While the Egyptian society is moving towards stronger conservatism and patriarchy, the Armenian society is gradually opening up to more liberal norms and international influences. Generally speaking, in terms of popular attitudes, women in Armenia are treated better and have stronger leverage in societal affairs. Their rights are not restricted legally and notions of equality are more embedded in the Armenian society than in the Egyptian one.

Social Norms: Discrimination and Violence against Women in Egypt

Some eight years ago, my family moved from Armenia to Egypt when my father was sent to Cairo for diplomatic service. Although in Armenia the traditional patriarchal culture impedes the legal notions of gender equality, Egypt left me flabbergasted. Male authority and dominance in both the public and private domains of life were unquestionable. The discrimination of women was widespread and provoked no public outcry. It was strongly felt in such daily routine as grocery shopping and personal interactions. When my parents left Cairo and I stayed to finish my B.A. degree, my encounters with discrimination against women increased rapidly. Now, even after living outside of Egypt for quite some time, I carry some bitterness about the way in which I and virtually every other woman in Egypt was perceived on a popular level, regardless of social standing or age. She is firstly an object of sexual satisfaction if she is not a wife; she is a child bearer and a maid if she is married. Only afterwards she is a human being with a personality of her own. It is even more difficult for foreign women because there is a widespread belief that "Western women are easier to get."

The discriminatory provisions contained in the national legislation are exacerbated by societal beliefs in the inferiority of women and by the traditional roles assumed by women within the household. Male dominance is tolerated and even accepted to varying degrees by women themselves. As an example, my maid in Egypt came to my home with a big bruise on her arm. When I asked, she smiled and told me that her husband got mad at her. I was surprised and tried to explain that she did not have to tolerate it. But she disagreed: "It was my fault: I refused him." She later explained to me that if he hits her at times, it is fine as long as he "does not cross the accepted boundaries." This sort of attitude that domestic violence is permissible under certain circumstances is widespread among Egyptian women, especially the less educated ones. When domestic violence becomes intolerable or when the woman does not want to accept it anymore, in most instances, she does not go to the police. Reasons behind such decisions are numerous. Observers cite embarrassment, fear and lack of confidence in the police, among others.

Too often, the police officers themselves are responsible for gender discrimination and sexual violence against females. The ECWR (Egyptian Center for Women's Rights) recorded numerous cases of sexual harassment used as a tool of political pressure by the security forces during the times of elections. I saw how the security forces that are meant to protect the citizens and the inhabitants of Egypt sexually harass them. During the demonstrations against the war in Iraq, police officers groped and assaulted female participants. Similarly, I was harassed by a man in his 20s in downtown Cairo. I called for help. The police officer who was standing nearby, instead of helping me and stopping the man, himself tried to touch me.

Much of the time, Egyptian society blames the woman in cases of sexual harassment. A question like "What were you wearing when you got harassed?" is frequently asked not only by the police, but by the members of the society as well. The traumatic impact of such behavior still needs to be assessed. In 2006, horrifying statistics from a report prepared by the Research Center for Women and Children were published in a daily newspaper (ECWR n.d.). This report claimed that 68 percent of female employees reported sexual harassment by their superiors. Unless immediate actions are taken by both the national and international communities, women in Egypt will be subjected to severe discrimination, sexual harassment and abuse.

"Diminishing" Morality and the West

In both societies, there is strong resistance to Western "immoral" ideas and influence. Objects and places related to sex are seen as "immoral" Western influence. In 2005, when a sex shop opened in Yerevan, the country was on the verge of public mayhem. Virtually all the newspapers had a full coverage of "diminishing Armenian morality." At first the public debates centered on whether the owner would be able to control minors entering the shop. Then deliberations took another direction: Does our "moral" Armenian society need a sex shop? Why do we need to imitate the West? Weren't we living comfortably without it?

In Egypt there was a similar reaction when video clips of Ruby, a pop-singer, appeared on TV in 2003. In one video clip, she was wandering around Prague, dressed as a belly dancer. In another, she was wearing tight athletic clothes and riding a bicycle, thus revealing her sexuality. Many called it "soft porn." There were calls to ban the clip and to prohibit her from touring in the country. Many parents feared that their daughters would try to imitate Ruby, while their sons would develop "perverse" Western notions of sexuality. Both societies feel somehow comfortable in their conservative daily routine and are hesitant to change. However, Armenia is more open to international influences, at least at the governmental level.

Influenced by society and its conservative cultural norms, the Egyptian government has to make many reservations on international treaties. Armenia embraces them fully. Egypt, through its attachment to Sharia, hurts women's rights. Armenia's constitution and laws advocate equality. Armenia's NGOs dealing with women's rights do not face the same legal problems that their counterparts in Egypt experience. The Egyptian authorities hinder the work of such organizations with limited funding and a prohibition on receiving funds from abroad.

Conclusion

Women's rights in Armenia are strongly protected by the law. The same cannot be said about Egypt. On the popular level Armenian women are treated with more respect than their Egyptian counterparts. At the same time, some similarities can be observed. First, both societies are strongly opposed to any substantial changes related to the status of women. In both cases, proposals for a gradual opening and introduction of "Western notions of sexuality" were met by a huge public outcry and opposition.

Unless positive discrimination is implemented from above on a large scale in both societies, change is not likely to occur any time soon. Harsher quota laws (in politics) and stricter sanctions for non-compliance with legislation promoting gender equality are needed. It is important to incorporate sexual education in the school curriculum and conduct workshops on gender equality among the students. Similar workshops are needed for professionals and media representatives to avoid gender bias. The appearance of genuine local feminist voices will be important to achieving gender equality. Only then women who are speaking out will not be perceived as Western "implants."

At the same time, we must be aware that there are limits to legal empowerment. The legal framework in Armenia is egalitarian, but societal attitudes are not. Unless change occurs at a grassroot level and in people's minds, gender equality will remain a distant dream.

Commentary
Ellen Rafshoon

Isabella Manassarian's move from Armenia to Egypt as a teenage girl in a diplomatic family was clearly a traumatizing event for her. In Armenia, one gathers, this child of the elite was taken seriously as a student and suffered no untoward mistreatment because of her sex. But when she lived in Cairo during her college years, she was the victim of sexual harassment (by a police officer among others) and came to understand that brutality against women and the denial of basic civil rights were common occurrences. Long since gone from Egypt, she still carries the "bitterness about the way that I and virtually every woman in Egypt were perceived"—as sex objects, maids or child bearers—without a unique identity.

This experience moved Manassarian to try to document the laws and traditions that account for the differences she perceived in the status of women in Armenia and Egypt. She argues that while Armenia is making progress in granting basic citizenship and political rights to women in law and attitudes, Egypt is turning back the clock. The reason for the disparity, she suggests, is that Egypt has turned to Muslim Sharia law, which upholds rigorous notions of patriarchy.

Unfortunately, her comparison is highly uneven—as she delves into the hated Egyptian system with much more depth (and despair) than the Armenian one. And her investigation is too heavily influenced by her personal encounters as an elite Westernized woman, someone not at all representative of the typical poor Egyptian or Armenian.

This is not to say that Manassarian's intuitive perceptions are not accurate. But we don't know if the disparity in treatment she recounts might not have been influenced by her own status as a foreigner. Had she paid at least some attention to the experiences and opinions of Egyptian and Armenian women, we might have learned much more about what conditions are really like. For example, she describes the situation for women in Armenia as "heavenly" compared to Egypt. Because she doesn't interview women in either country or use any other measures of public opinion, we are left wondering whether it is simply better to be a young Westernized female in Armenia than one in Egypt.

The lack of attention to authentic voices also is problematic in considering whether women of either nation accept or reject their plight. Manassarian mentions that there is "no popular outcry" against sex discrimination in Egypt. If this is indeed the case—and I say "if" because it's unclear what she considers a form of resistance—we need to hear from the women themselves as to why they remain silent. Is it that the women accept Sharia because they perceive a benefit we Westerners don't understand or is the level of coercion so high that women fear for their lives should they protest their situation?

Bibliography

DESA (UN Department of Economic and Social Affairs). 1997. Committee on the Elimination of Discrimination against Women, 17th session. http://www.un.org/documents/ga/cedaw/17/country/Armenia/cedawc-arm1corr1en.htm (accessed on June 30, 2008).

Division for the Advancement of Women. n.d. UN Convention on the Elimination of All Forms of Discrimination against Women. http://www.un.org/womenwatch/daw/cedaw/reservations-country.htm (accessed on June 30, 2008).

ECWR (Egyptian Center for Women's Rights). n.d. Scientific study proves the scandal. ECWR. http://www.ecwronline.org/english/sexual%20harassment/article.htm (accessed on June 30, 2008).

Egyptian government. n.d. Egypt Constitution, chapter three: Public freedoms, rights and duties. Egyptian government. http://www.egypt.gov.eg/english/laws/Constitution/chp_three/part_one.asp (accessed on June 30, 2008).

Human Rights Watch. 2005. Women's status in Egypt. Human Rights Watch. http://www.hrw.org/reports/2004/egypt1204/2.htm (accessed on June 30, 2008).

Ministry of Territorial Administration of the Republic of Armenia and UNDP. 2007. *Promoting equal rights and equal opportunities in Armenia*, http://europeandcis.undp.org/uploads/public/file/gender/Armenia%20EREO%20Pro%20doc.doc (accessed on June 30, 2008).

UNDP (United Nations Development Programme). 2005. *The Arab human development report: Towards the rise of women in the Arab world*. Palo Alto, CA: Stanford University Press.

Chapter 14
Addressing Trauma through Political Action: Nineth Montenegro's Story
Gabriela de Cabrera

Nineth Montenegro is one of the most famous women politicians and human rights activists in Guatemala. She is known for her devotion to social justice. Currently she is very worried about what she calls "social violence" (discrimination and poverty) plaguing Guatemala. Which events in her life led her to become politically active and care about the whole nation?

Nineth was raised by her grandmother, a strong woman and a community leader. She was not afraid to fight for her rights. Nineth believes that she inherited her inner strength from her grandmother.

In 1973-74, when Nineth was a high school student, there was a teachers' strike in which her grandmother and aunt participated. Nineth believes that during this time she understood the government's role in oppressing Guatemala's teachers by not raising their wages and denying benefits.

When she was 22, Nineth got married to Fernando Garcia, a community activist. Fernando was a counselor at the School of Union Orientation and studied to become an engineer. Nineth motivated Garcia to form a group called GAM (*Grupo de Apoyo Mutuo,* Spanish for "a mutual support group") which protested in the streets and demanded the government to investigate assassinations that were happening at the time. On February 18, 1984, Garcia was abducted by government forces. At 26 years of age, Nineth was left alone (likely a widow) with a two year old daughter. However, she always held a glimmer of hope that her husband might still be alive.

This was a very traumatic experience which filled her life with fear, distress and rage. She carried all these negative feelings inside of her, especially when she thought of her two year old daughter who was to grow up without a father. However, Nineth did not want to remain quiet when travesties like this were happening in her Guatemala—kidnappings and killings of innocent people whose only "crime" was a different point of view.

In spite of experiencing all these powerful emotions, Nineth decided to suppress her pain, fear, war and worries. She kept on living. Her daughter was affected by trauma enormously. Nineth had the dual responsibility of serving the roles of both a mother and a father for her daughter. Nineth continued to support the struggle in the streets, dividing her time as an activist there and a mother at home. Sometimes in private Nineth shared her frustrations and uncertainty with her daughter. However, in the streets, Nineth had to be a strong woman. Nineth's political activism became a way of self-healing. It gave her an opportunity to process her traumatic history and turn her rage into something productive which (she hoped) could help the other innocent Guatemalans.

There were other women activists who experienced similar dual empowerment and suffering through street action. Working for AVANSCO (*Asociación para el Avance de las Ciencias Sociales*, Spanish for "investigation center for the advancement of social sciences") was Myrna Mack, a writer. She was assassinated in 1990 by government forces. Then there was Marielos Monzon, a young journalist, whose father had been killed in the same way. Marielos received death threats from Guatemala's secret services, but she denounced the military before the CIDH (*Comision Interamericana de Derechos Humanos*, Spanish for "interamerican commission of human rights"). Knowing that such women were putting themselves out into the public sphere to make a difference helped Montenegro to feel indirect support for her own efforts.

After her husband's disappearance, Nineth began a public activity to demand information about her husband's fate. In 1985, with the help of the GAM, her efforts finally became fruitful. The President of Guatemala formed a commission to investigate the disappearances. However, on March 30, 1985, one of the leaders of the GAM, an activist who was very close to Montenegro, Hector Gomez Calito, was kidnapped. In 1986, Montenegro and members of the GAM occupied the President's palace to demand that the commission proposed by the president be created immediately. This demand was heard, and the president authorized a commission to investigate the disappearances and assassinations.

Even though Nineth's efforts to investigate her husband's disappearance yielded some results (she found out that her husband was murdered by a death squad), the woman believed that this pursuit was preventing her from spending time with her daughter. She had to make a decision—whether to continue political fight or university studies. She quit the university for a couple of years. In early 1990s, when her daughter was already a teenager, she decided to finish her college education. Nineth's daughter was the impulse that kept her going. In addition, she dreamed of becoming a Congresswoman who could stand up for her beliefs.

In 1996 Nineth was elected for the first time to Congress, and since then she has always won the re-election. In 2004 Nineth has formed her own political party called *Encuentro Por Guatemala* (Spanish for "encounter for Guatemala"). She told me that she was willing to compete in Guatemala's presidential elections in 2011.

Living in a country which has been ruled by men for centuries, Nineth wants to make her voice heard by operating in the political sphere, voicing demands and creating social organizations. Because of Nineth's devotion to human rights and social justice, she has received numerous death threats. Nineth confesses that amidst all the suffering, fear, weaknesses and worries, she feels satisfied with all the work and effort she has put into her public and private life. Her daughter has always been an excellent student, and now she is a great lawyer. Nineth says she is fueled by the support from fellow Guatemalans who have suffered as much or more than she has. During our conversation, Nineth expressed a desire that other women should never feel defeated by pain. Everyone at some time in life suffers, but the important thing is to get up, to have faith and a lot of discipline. Nineth believes that in childhood everyone has a right to hear about God or a Supreme Being. Her grandmother prayed with her every night and took her to church to light a candle every Sunday. She stood on her knees and stared into space, never knowing what to say. But as Nineth grew up, she began to ask for wisdom and strength. Now she strongly believes that God has always been with her, providing support and strength. Nineth's suffering was transformed into faith and empowerment.

Commentary
Ligia Gomez

Nineth Montenegro's story moved me because of the strong parallels that I see in her life and in the lives of immigrant women from many developing countries. Leaving a transitional country to move to the wealthiest and most powerful country presents challenges that those of us who have lived our entire lives in relative comfort can barely comprehend.

Crossing the border to the United States is an incredibly traumatic experience. Women are subject to physical and sexual abuse on this journey. Frequently they walk for miles without food or water through the desert. Many are raped, but they don't want to talk about these traumas after they move to the new country.

In Cincinnati, we, immigrant women with children, organized a group called *Grupo de Madres* (Spanish for "a mothers' group"). This group meets at least once a month at a local pediatric clinic. For five years, fifteen women have attended the meetings regularly. Many others show up sporadically. This group empowers women by creating a forum in which women who have experienced difficult times (such as economic difficulties, domestic violence, or even making an appointment to see a doctor—a challenging task for someone from rural Latin America) can share information with others who are suffering.

Nineth's daughter was the impulse that kept her going. Similarly, children give strength to the members of *Grupo de Madres* to keep them going. One woman, originally from Guatemala, once shared with me that her husband was arrested and about to be deported. "I love him. I may never see him again. But I can't follow him back to Guatemala. I have to stay here for my children. Here they will have free education, a better future, and they will have healthcare. In Guatemala they would have live in poverty, deal with hunger and violence. I will miss him, but I have to stay."

Nineth believes that God has always been with her and gave her strength. Religion is very important for the *Grupo de Madres*. When one of our mothers lost a baby to illness, in spite of her personal agony, she calmly accepted the God's will: "Lo que Dios quiera" (Spanish for "whatever God wants"). She also said: "Mi angelito esta con Dios" (Spanish for "my little angel is with God").

Immigrant women are inspired by their children's education. They are strengthened by community groups that provide them with a sense of belonging and reassurance that their hopes and dreams are possible to obtain.

Conclusion:
A Conversation among the Editors
Dovile Budryte, Lisa M. Vaughn and Natalya T. Riegg

Dovile Budryte (DB): The book is an interdisciplinary endeavor. It includes perspectives from political science, international studies, social psychology and even art appreciation, to mention a few. How has openness to other disciplines enriched our understanding of empowerment? The importance of trauma? Democracy and democratization?

DB: I'd like to discuss some insights from political science and international studies—the two disciplines in which I have received formal graduate training. In both disciplines, power is the central concept. One of the most important contributions of feminist writers was to introduce the definition of power as "the human ability to act in concert, or action which is taken in connection with others who share similar concerns" (Tickner 1989, 434). As discussed in *The Introduction*, feminist definitions of "empowerment" also mention collective action to achieve progressive changes, including the well-being of women. Transnational movement to address violence against women is an example of transnational feminist project to empower women. Democratization enables more civil society activity (allows non-governmental groups to act); thus, logically, the processes of democratic consolidation should help the well-being of women in post-transitional societies because it allows for more transnational cooperation between different groups, both nationally and internationally. However, as the case studies suggest, there are many obstacles to transnational cooperation and democratic values, such as gender equality, which are seen as crucial to eradicate violence against women.

Openness to insights from the other disciplines helped me to understand these obstacles better. Specifically, Eyramjyants's, Aslayan's, Vaughn and de Cabrera's, Wells's, Leclerc-Madlala's, de Cabrera's, Pilinkaite-Sotirovic's and Rukaite's contributions point to the importance of local networks, local connections and traditional beliefs, especially for those women who have experienced trauma. This is when social psychology can provide useful insights on which strategies can prove to be most successful at the individual and community levels. Former victims are primarily interested in creating security networks, even if they have to put ideas about gender equality on the "backburner." *Living*

Trauma and Empowerment and *The Authentic Voices* section made me think about Amitai Etzioni's thesis put forward in his recent book *Security First*, in which he wrote: "At its core (new "Security First" foreign policy) is the recognition that all people have an interest in and the right to security, understood to include freedom from deadly violence, maiming and torture. . . . This right is more fundamental than all others, including legal-political and socioeconomic rights" (2007, 1).

Natalya T. Riegg (NTR): It seems to me that openness to other disciplines constitutes a major (if not the major) strength of the book. And I mean this "openness" in a very broad sense. In addition to going beyond political science and international relations toward social psychology, the book has reached into less formally organized areas of knowledge that go beyond theoretical analyses and move toward "genealogical narratives." The important narrative feature of this book serves as a successful forum for cross-cultural communication. In this regard, some narratives from *The Authentic Voices* and *Living Trauma and Empowerment* sections, in particular the works by Eyramjyants, Vaughn and de Cabrera, as well as the one by de Cabrera and Looney, seem to be real contributions to the promotion and improvement of cross-cultural understanding which, in its turn, seems to be almost a prerequisite for effective transnational cooperation.

Those narratives of trauma and empowerment are rooted in the paradoxical mixture of the universality, contingency and subjectivity of human experience. In a certain sense, pain and humiliation speak a universal language, with which one can rather easily identify, i.e. imagine oneself in a similar situation. Presented in a form of narratives, as less "scholarly" rigorous, simpler, more subjective and socially/historically contingent tales of (traumatic) experiences, these stories of trauma and empowerment may become exceedingly salient sources of human (and feminine) solidarity and understanding, in comparison with complex, professionally written academic papers. As Richard Rorty put it, human solidarity is "the ability to see more and more traditional differences (of tribe, religion, race, customs and the like) as unimportant when compared with similarities with respect to pain and humiliation—the ability to think of people wildly different from ourselves as included in the range of 'us' " (1989, 192). After all, everyone can understand and relate to pain or humiliation!

These observations bring us to an even heightened understanding of the importance of the eradication of violence against women—as a crucial transnational security issue. A number of chapters reflect on the issues of violence against women in different contexts and from different perspectives (in particular, the chapters by Rukaite, Vaughn and de Cabrera, Pilinkaite-Sotirovic and Leclerc-Madlala). The resulting variety of insights is quite remarkable. "Security first"—I agree with the statement of Amitai Etzioni quoted by you, Dovile! I agree that eradication of violence (i.e., promotion of security) and the consequent reduction of suffering caused by violence are more important (if apparently connected) concerns than legal-political and socio-economic rights. In other words, security concerns are more important than the concerns of democracy and democratization. Therefore, I will address democracy and democratization in my answers to later questions.

Lisa M. Vaughn (LMV): Due to the interdisciplinarity of the contributors to this book, I have learned to see trauma, empowerment and the effects on women with a more "macro" lens and thus as a much more global and political issue. I agree with Dovile and Natalya that part of the success of this project is that, in the truest sense of participatory action research, we welcomed participation from women actually living trauma and empowerment rather than only including perspectives from the academic tower of privilege. Part of the reason we agreed to use participatory action research and the communicative action format was to give voice to women within their own political, social and cultural contexts. Very many attempts at empowerment are well-intentioned but end up being paternalistic and perhaps even repackaged in colonialism because they ignore the local ways of knowing and coping with traumas. This can occur especially at the academic level because the local indigenous practices and individual voices may be suppressed in favor of what Fisher and McKenna described as the "elixir of empowerment" offered by more powerful and resourceful agents, such as community development academicians and governmental agencies (1996, 4). In order to establish a constructive dialogue (a communicative action) of people "in the trenches" and academics from the "ivory tower," we solicited an exchange of views and perspectives through conversations about women, trauma and empowerment at various levels. In dialogical communication, a construction of awareness occurs whereby both actor and "intervener" can be called to participate collaboratively in community action (Campbell and Jovchelovitch 2000).

LMV: *The title of our book includes a reference to feminism. However, not all of our contributors would like to be called "feminists," even though they are clearly interested in helping women to address their "real" problems. Should we continue to use this word? Does it really help or hinder transnational feminist/women's conversations?*

DB: Many feminists, especially those who study women's movements in post-colonial settings, tried to dissect the feminine/feminist dichotomy. I could not agree more with some arguments put forward by the "post-colonial" feminists. Women's interests are not the same everywhere. The norms associated with the privileged middle-class Western model of feminism should not be applicable universally. Feminist agendas should be formulated with a specific cultural context in mind.

At the same time, I find a distinction between women's movements that are "feminine" and "feminist" useful. As explained by Shireen Hassim, both feminine and feminist movements try to mobilize women on the basis of their gender identity, making references to the roles traditionally prescribed to them (2006, 7). However, feminist movements promote gender equality and try to challenge hierarchies of power that promote women's oppression, while "feminine" (women's) movements try to address immediate issues affecting women.

Thus, it is helpful to draw a distinction between "strategic gender interests" and "practical gender needs." "Strategic gender interests" are associated with feminist ideology. They imply a desire to challenge hierarchies supporting gender inequalities. "Practical gender needs" refer to everyday responsibilities and worries of women. Some of these issues, however, result from unequal gender relations (Hassim 2006, 5).

Several contributions in our book successfully challenge the dichotomy between the "strategic gender interests" and "practical gender needs." Specifically, the articles by Leclerc-Madlala and Wells suggest that we need get rid of this dichotomy. In South Africa, women are burdened by HIV/AIDS, domestic violence, oppressive traditions. These issues cannot be successfully addressed without fully embracing gender equality (a feminist belief). Thus, I agree with the following insight put forward by Hassim: "Feminist ideology is pivotal in women's movements, as its relative strength determines the extent to which collective action is directed to democratic ends" (2006, 8). This implies that we (women's rights activists and feminist scholars) should not be afraid to continue to use the word "feminism"—as long as there is sincere interest in democratic values, such as equality, inclusiveness, collective action and participation.

NTR: Well, feminist ideology is pivotal in women's movements if by democratic ends we primarily understand the ends of *gender* equality. However, feminist ideology (as opposed to feminine concerns or practical gender needs) is not necessarily pivotal in women's movements if by "democratic ends" we understand participatory equality of diverse women, even those who seem to be uncomfortably suspicious of the feminist ideology, or suspicious even of democracy itself. It seems to me that it could be to the common benefit of women's movements if feminism (in which I as well as you believe strongly) was able to move toward a reinvention of itself as a large (the largest?) subculture within the women's movements and a large (the largest?) if still historically and socially contingent discourse on women's issues. It seems to me that some moderation of the ideological rigidity of feminism's promotion of the "generic" discourse of gender power disparities, in response to diverse gender issues (even if this ultimate discourse is being adjusted to different cultural contexts) could have both "pragmatic" and "philosophical" benefits.

In pragmatic terms, such a moderation of the claims of feminism, it could be instrumental in promotion of more truly grass-roots international cooperation among women aimed at some practical improvements in women's lives without getting into nominal preaching; in philosophical terms, some moderation of the all-encompassing, ideological claims of feminism could be more conductive to the philosophy of tolerance and pluralism which encompasses a truly liberal-democratic culture. That said, the issues of pressing concern like violence against women or women's trafficking, are really in need of immediate transnational cooperation, but these seem to be related more to basic security than to ideological differences within the women's movements.

Moreover, it even seems to me that eradication of violence against women is only relatively relevant to the feminist meta-project of promotion of gender equality. After all, in order to eliminate violence against women one does not really need to believe in their equality with men. (Examples supporting this argument can stretch across many traditional cultures, from the chevalier culture of medieval knights to the behavior codes of Victorian gentlemen.) As a matter of fact, acceptance of gender equality per se under some circumstances may even result in increased violence against women, unless the development of the belief in gender equality is somehow accompanied by the development of a belief in equal physical strength of both sexes. All I am trying to say is that eradication of violence against women and eradication of patriarchy are different issues, and they should not necessarily be lumped together.

In the spirit of the recent book of Amitai Etzioni, quoted above, one can say that the provision of "basic" protection of women from violence should probably be the aim of many feminist interventions. Nonetheless, the "oppressive" or other traditions of particular societies should probably be left to the participants of those societies to judge and negotiate among themselves, rather than us (the "outsiders") assessing those traditions for them. In the words of Etzioni, "Liberal democracy is a delicate plant that grows only slowly under favorable conditions; it needs to be cultivated carefully by those who aim to live under it rather than by those who wish it for them" (2007, 3). To sum up, my answer to the question of whether we should even continue to use the word "feminism" is yes, we should use it as long as the word reflects our beliefs. I only wish that we could somehow stop treating those beliefs as revealed universal truth!

LMV: I absolutely agree with both of you that the term "feminist" should continue to be used by people involved in both political and practical efforts affecting women. In such efforts, the feminist ideology can become empowerment in and of itself for women who have traditionally relegated their needs to the non-political arenas. In other words, I would argue, like many early Western feminists, that every issue related to women is both personal and political. Historically, empowerment theory has emphasized individual political *power over* (competition and conflict) rather than "traditionally feminine concerns" like cooperation and personal empowerment (*power to*) (Riger 1993; Yoder and Kahn 1992). This suggests that while women may be more focused on the "relational" aspects (connection, community, relatedness, etc.) of empowerment, especially perhaps after a trauma. They may de-emphasize the more political and thus power-related aspects of empowerment. However, an understanding of empowerment in a more "aggressive," feminist manner and exposing the oppressive power structures behind traditional social arrangements may help to challenge the structural sources of women's powerlessness. In such a fashion, feminist ideology may create a welcomed balance in women's empowerment by contextualizing women's personal needs and issues within the existing patriarchal political and environmental structures without minimizing women's relational nature and practical concerns.

NTR: *It appears that democratization helps to increase openness to the international women's movement. In turn, this leads to the introduction of gender violence as an important social issue. But is that all? What do international feminist interventions do? How do they really help to empower women? What are the broader and unintended consequences of international interventions?*

DB: It seems to me that international feminist interventions can achieve two major goals. On one hand, they can attempt to redefine the norms of prevalent political discourse. This is done by drawing attention to important global issues, such as violence against women and "normalizing" certain norms, such as condemnation of domestic violence. Rukaite's contribution includes descriptions of the activities pursued by WIIC (Women's Issues Information Center) in Vilnius, Lithuania. Many of them, including national campaigns against sexual trafficking, were inspired and at least partially financed by international actors. Other examples include the attempts at "normalization" of paternity leave in Lithuania and other post-transitional societies. This is a good example of how "Europeanization" (that is, acceptance of norms and laws associated with the European Union) and interpretation of the "European" norms by the local actors may challenge the patriarchal norms. Specifically, I am referring to an international project *Modern Men in Enlarged Europe: Developing Innovative Gender Equality Strategies* which was sponsored by the European Union Community Framework Strategy on Gender Equality and Lithuania's government (Tereskinas 2005). This project tried to encourage men to take paternity leave to empower women to succeed in their chosen careers.

On the other hand, international interventions (feminist or not) may define the terms of democratic transitions. This was especially true during the early nineties, when Lithuania and other countries in post-communist Europe were trying to enter the European Union. The aspiring member-states were asked to revise their legislation to incorporate protection for women's rights. This is an example of how international actors can push for broad democratic values, thus creating a democratic milieu which is a necessary condition for feminist/women's movements to succeed.

I understand that I have outlined a very optimistic picture. However, having read the "non-European" contributions to our volume (perhaps with partial exception of Armenia as described in Manassarian's essay), I could not detect the same transformative impact of international actors in other post-transitional societies. In this case, is post-communist "Europeanized" Europe an exception?

NTR: It appears that international actors as well as local authorities can play quite positive roles in the reduction of gender power disparities. I do not think that this positive role is restricted exclusively to the European context. It can happen in other regions as well. As Mala Hatun (2000) has argued, in Latin America, for example, the ratification by a number of countries of the CEDAW (Convention on Elimination of Discrimination against Women), as well as adoption of the Inter-American Convention on Violence against Women has brought positive changes in the gender profile of the region. She also showed that some civil code reforms adopted by a number of Latin American countries within the last sixty years also contributed to relative empowerment of women in their societies.

At the same time, the interactions among international actors, local elites and broader local populations are complex processes that require subtlety. In the last few years, as I have watched international interventions aimed at democratization of targeted societies (including the promotion of gender equality), I could not help but remember an ancient idea that goes back to Plato. Politics, as well as medicine, should be guided by some sort of Hippocratic oath: First of all, do not do harm. In the process of intervention in different cultural contexts, do not do harm to the local people, particularly women whom you are trying to help, but also do not do harm to the causes of democracy in general and gender equality in particular...

Let me explain. As discussed in *The Introduction*, democracy (including gender equality) is a product of the historical development of Western social and political traditions, and as such it is contextual and contingent. "Feminism-ization" of other traditions, as a subset of their "democratization," is a very different process. Accordingly, the global, cross-cultural export of the feminist system of beliefs or feminist ideology can be considered to be a subset of the process of international democratization. As such, this process is subject to a variation of the generic "aporia of democratization" discussed in *The Introduction*, which might be called the "aporia of feminism-ization." As it was mentioned earlier, even several contributors to our volume do not wish to be called "feminists." The promotion of greater gender equality in their societies is almost a side-effect of their work.

As a number of contributors to this volume have shown, in different parts of the world, time and again, the establishment of "gender-sensitive" institutions (as well as the establishment of democratic institutions in general) does not automatically entail the establishment of a culture of gender equality (or a liberal-democratic political culture in general). Very often the situation in post-transitional societies can be described by the words of Guatemalan sociologist Bernardo Arevalo, who said about his country, "We have the hardware of democracy but the software of authoritarianism" (Harrison 2000, xxx). In a similar vein, Pilinkaite-Sotirovic's chapter (among others) has shown that post-transitional societies often have the hardware of gender equality, but the software of patriarchy.

If international approaches to date have too often been insufficient to achieve the hoped-for levels of democracy and gender equality, has our work on this book helped us to conceive of modified approaches? Perhaps it has. Could international interventions for democracy and gender equality, for example, try to focus more on bringing to the surface, humanizing and developing those already-present "universal" elements of local cultural traditions? Would it help were international actors more open to learning something from the local traditions themselves (what Habermas (1985a, b) would call a "subject-to-subject" approach)? Would such interventions have a better chance to succeed than those that try to fight the "backward" local traditions and replace them with more "progressive" ones (thus constituting the "subject-to-object" approach)? In the case of Lithuania, mentioned by you, Dovile, as in almost all cases related to the European Union, could it be that the EU is only dealing with other European, largely like-minded post-transitional societies (including Lithuania) and that this quality facilitates different aspects of democratization, including gender aspects?

All this brings us to the question the role of local elites, NGOs as élite groups, and whether the NGO leaders represent the local women, among other things. As you, Dovile, have noted earlier, previous literature on feminist movements in emerging democracies (as well as my chapter, Manassarian's narrative and Aslanyan's chapter) suggest that there is a gap between the women's rights NGOs (promoting gender equality) and the "other" local women in post-transitional societies. You wrote that *The Authentic Voices* section and analysis presented in the case studies (Lithuania and Armenia) suggest that women's rights' NGOs are currently much less likely to use feminist rhetoric. You then asked if the lessened use of such rhetoric indicates a trend and if these non-governmental organizations are more likely to promote social change. Personally, I hope that the diminished use of distracting feminist rhetoric (in local contexts) is a lasting trend. The development of more "locally-defined" NGOs could be much more instrumental in addressing real, hands-on needs of local women than some "generic" approaches based on the ideology of "global sisterhood." However, I do not feel very optimistic about this trend. It seems to me that as long as local NGOs have to seek funding from foreign ("Western") sources, their financial dependency will translate into attempts to use the "language" and address the issues that the potential sponsors consider more important or appropriate, even if this language and these issues are not very reflective of local realities and needs. That is why it seems to me that it is important for us on the "Western/First world" end to adjust the dominant language of our gender discourse and to make it more inclusive and tolerant toward other (gender) discourses.

DB: *Depret and Fiske (1993) came up with a thought-provoking definition of "empowerment"—being a subject rather than object of others' actions. This may involve a perception that your own social context has changed. It appears that some NGOs, as described by Natalya, fail to achieve this important goal—making women feel as subjects rather than objects of others' actions. This observation suggests the following question: What does it take to make someone (especially a former victim) feel like a "subject"? Drawing on the case studies presented in the book, could we identify the most important insights about empowerment as a process?*

LMV: Even more importantly (than feeling like a "subject" in political life), it is essential that former victims feel like "participants" in their healing, which is the essence of empowerment understood from a participatory action-oriented psychological point of view. This distinction is important because long lasting empowerment for those women who have experienced traumas is impossible without their active participation in communal projects. For example, if we look at the involvement of women in creative modalities like arts and crafts (Wells's chapter) or weaving cooperatives (my and de Cabrera's chapter on Guatemalan widows), we can see the healing involved via participation in social communities with a purpose. In fact, having some type of an "external container" (art or semiotic structure) in which a woman can hold emotions, beliefs and attitudes toward collective events of the past may allow for both individual participation and a sociopolitical expression of the societal trauma (Igartua and Paez 1997, 99). It seems to me this is how a transition from the individual level to the collective level is made.

I believe as do Anckerman et al. who focus on community development efforts in Guatemala that "people are capable of changing their life situation if they have access to resources and space for maneuver" (2005, 138). Participation in small scale projects is the first step to political and economic empowerment which may lead to significant influence in a country's political life.

As mentioned in *The Introduction*, we turn to Rappaport's (1987) notion of empowerment with women becoming empowered through participation in order to change their social and political realities. In psychology, most literature exploring empowerment after traumatic experiences tends to neglect the "macro" outcomes (community, society) and instead analyze trauma at the individual level, emphasizing the symptoms associated with the PTSD (Post Traumatic Stress Disorder). These symptoms include repeated re-living of traumatic memories, avoiding the reminders of trauma and difficulty pursuing "normal" life (APA 2000). Lykes (1997) and Martin-Baro (1994) argued that Western psychological theories have viewed violence and trauma as an "intrapsychic" (internal, individual) matter. According to Martin-Baro, this tendency "shares the problem inherent in the medical model, of abstracting socio-historical realities and insisting on locating disorders in the individual" (1994, 124). Through a *social* psychological lens, empowerment can be viewed as "learned hopefulness," to borrow Zimmerman's phrase (1995, 73). "Learned hopefulness" can be contrasted with "learned helplessness," which refers to a condition when a person feels helpless, without control and thinks that any action is futile (Seligman 1992). Empowerment as "learned hopefulness" represents "a process by which people gain control over their lives, democratic participation in the life of their community, and a critical understanding of their environment" (Perkins and Zimmerman 1995, 570). Several aspects of this definition are noteworthy, given the conversations in this volume. First, for women to be empowered, they must feel some sense of control. Second, the socio-cultural context and environment are intimately connected to empowerment. Third, empowerment is more likely to occur when women are involved and participating in the outcome. Fourth, reducing alienation and increasing support from and identification with a group contributes directly to women's empowerment.

As a psychologist and counselor, I believe that this individualistic approach (described above) can be helpful in understanding the biological and intrapsychic (internal) nature of trauma, I admit that recognition of trauma as a collective or communal phenomena embedded in the "social fabric of the community" (Martin-Baro's term) is lacking. As such, empowerment interventions, especially those from the Western world, have tended to focus on the individual level with limited success. Such interventions have left "devastated communities and even societies unattended" (Lykes et al. 2003, 80). Empowerment is a complex process; thus, efficient and effective empowerment strategies have to address different issues (economic, social, political, cultural and communal) that affect the status of women.

The chapters in our book are good examples of the so-called "non-traditional" approaches to empowerment that are becoming more and more accepted in psychology. These approaches highlight the importance of sharing the memories about traumatic experience socially, making them public, thus "normalizing" the experience and avoiding stigmatization. It is very important that the former victims see themselves as speakers rather than silent victims. Zara's testimony about her childhood is a good case in point.

NTR: Yes, Zara's narrative is a very good example of a woman moving from victimization to empowerment. I couldn't agree more with Lisa's explanation of empowerment. In the light of this understanding, I believe that Zara's writing of her narrative was an empowering experience for her. When narrating her story, Zara assumed the role of an active subject (rather than an "objectified" victim) of the dramatic events described by her.

NTR: *Research suggests that collective action may lead to positive feelings of empowerment when the participants of this action become aware of their social identity "against the power of dominant forces" (Drury et al. 2005, 305). It seems to me that some may feel powerless if they have to go against "the dominant forces." How can women make empowerment a source of positive feelings?*

LMV: When something incomprehensible occurs, one way to preserve our identities both at an individual and cultural level is to construct personal narratives. Those narratives can be passed from generation to generation, made public and thus meaningful and empowering (Halbwachs 1992, 43). If they get social recognition, narratives about traumas experienced in the past allow for a redefinition, modification and continued questioning of the existing power relations. This is when the "power of the dominant forces" may become obvious.

This is why usually only the most vocal and most powerful actors are able to make sure that their voices are heard and acknowledged. This insight applies to women's groups as well. My fieldwork in Guatemala suggests that women with the loudest voices and best domestic and international connections are able to make sure that their narrative is recorded. For many reasons, including historical memory, the Mayan women in Guatemala do not trust the "outsiders" (people outside of their community). They are reluctant to share their stories. Therefore, it is difficult for them to connect with the other women who may have had similar experiences. In this particular case, I am sure that the Mayan women remember and fear "the power of dominant forces." Therefore, they choose silence. Paying attention to "local" realities and systems of thinking is essential to giving voice and establishing effective dialogue between what "we" know and what "they" know (Campbell and Jovchelovitch 2000).

At the same time, I believe that it is necessary to try to make sure that less powerful groups of traumatized women are heard and their attempts to survive are recorded. Why is this important? This is part of participatory democratic community development, which is necessary for the creation of a fully functioning, long lasting and inclusive social and political order. If the former victims are ever going to regain self-esteem, they need to be able to see themselves as spokespersons and be able to connect with similar groups. In addition, we (feminist practitioners and scholars) need to listen. Ogundipe-Leslie, a feminist scholar, pointed out that the problem is not that women are voiceless but that we (the more powerful, the more privileged) fail to *listen* to their voices in places where women speak—kitchens, watering sites, kinship gatherings and political communal spaces (1994, 10). If the "outsiders" agree to listen, then there is hope that a new, "healthier" narrative is created, which will bring voice to the internal trauma.

Creating spaces for conversations—locally, nationally, or even internationally—helps to redefine individual identities, thus making empowerment (associated with group activities) a source of positive feelings. Because individual identity is so closely linked to and derived from group identity, "everything that colors the history of the group may color an individual's sense of identity" (Frijda 1997, 109). Communal efforts to address trauma help to "normalize" emotions associated with the painful past. This is clearly seen in the chapters discussing empowerment efforts in Guatemala and South Africa. Ultimately empowerment means "social recognition and dignity, just as, most of all, it means space to speak, act, and live with joy and responsibility" (Ogundipe-Leslie 1994, ix).

DB: I could not agree more with the argument about the need to be heard. This is probably one of the greatest needs of women living in what we have described as "post-transitional societies" where women experience many social pressures associated with structural changes and a shortage of institutions offering help. According to Dalia Puidokiene, the Director and Founder of Social and Psychological Services Center in Klaipeda (Lithuania), it is necessary to approach women who have experienced violence (she was referring to the victims of trafficking) "from a perspective of absolute love," keeping in mind that "what happened to these girls could happen to any one of us" (Vince 2008, 22). To me, this is an example of a "universal language" of understanding described by Natalya in her previous comment. Our volume suggests that the ability to listen and emphasize with those who have experienced violence and trauma is impossible without respect for numerous differences—cultural, social, economic, age and so on. This "universal language" consists of numerous dialects.

Troutner and Smith concluded in their book on empowerment of women in Asia and Latin America that all forms of empowerment for women should be celebrated, and that women should continue "to pursue power with all its dissonant modifiers—*within*, *with*, *to*, and even *over*" (2004, 28). Cross-cultural understanding becomes crucially important in such pursuits. Our contributions suggest a similar conclusion. In addition, we would like to highlight the importance of less tangible aspects of empowerment, such the need to reinterpret popular misogynistic myths, challenge traditions and create new identities. We would also like to emphasize the importance of local community participatory efforts. Perhaps this is one way to confront the "dominant forces" hurting women and avoid the "aporia of democratization" described in *The Introduction*.

Bibliography

APA (American Psychiatric Association). 2000. *Diagnostic and statistical manual of mental disorders.* Washington, D.C.: American Psychiatric Association.

Anckerman, Sonia, Manuel Dominguez, Norma Soto, Finn Kjaerulf, Peter Berliner, and Elizabeth Naima Mikkelsen. 2005. Psycho-social support to large numbers of traumatized people in post-conflict societies: An approach to community development in Guatemala. *Journal of Community and Applied Social Psychology* 15 (2): 136-152.

Campbell, Catherine, and Sandra Jovchelovitch. 2000. Health, community and development: Towards a social psychology of participation. *Journal of Community and Applied Social Psychology* 10 (4): 255-270.

Depret, Eric, and Susan T. Fiske. 1993. Social cognition and power: Some cognitive consequences of social structure as a source of control deprivation. In *Control motivation and social cognition,* ed. Gifford Weary, Faith Gleicher, and Kerry L. Marsch, 176-202. New York: Springer-Verlag.

Drury, John, Christopher Cocking, Joseph Beale, Charlotte Hanson, and Faye Rapley. 2005. The phenomenology of empowerment in collective action. *British Journal of Social Psychology* 44 (2005): 309-328.

Etzioni, Amitai. 2007. *Security first: For a muscular, moral foreign policy.* New Haven: Yale University Press.

Fischer, Edward F., and R. McKenna Brown. 1996. Introduction: Maya cultural activism in Guatemala. In *Maya cultural activism in Guatemala,* ed. Edward F. Fischer and R. McKenna Brown, 1-18. Austin, TX: University of Texas Press.

Frijda, Nico H. 1997. Commemorating. In *Collective memory of political events: Social psychological perspectives*, ed. by James W. Pennebaker, Dario Paez, and Bernard Rime, 103-130. Mahwah, NJ: Lawrence Erlbaum.

Habermas, Jurgen. 1985a. *The theory of communicative action. Volume I: Reason and rationalization of society.* Boston: Beacon Press.

———. 1985b. *The theory of communicative action. Volume II: Life world and systems. A critique of functionalist reason.* Boston: Beacon Press.

Halbwachs, Maurice. 1992. *On collective memory,* ed. Lewis A. Coser. Chicago: University of Chicago Press.

Harrison, Lawrence E. 2000. Introduction: Why culture matters. In *Culture matters: How values shape human progress,* ed. Lawrence E. Harrison and Samuel P. Huntington, xvii-1. New York: Basic Books.

Hassim, Shireen. 2006. *Women's organizations and democracy in South Africa: Contesting authority.* Madison: University of Wisconsin Press.

Htun, Mala. 2000. "Culture, Institutions, and Gender Equality in Latin America." In *Culture Matters*, edited by Lawrence E. Harrison and Samuel P. Huntington. New York: Basic Books.

Igartua, Juanjo, and Dario Paez. 1997. Art and remembering traumatic collective events: The case of the Spanish Civil War. In *Collective memory of political events: Social Psychological Perspectives*, ed. by James W. Pennebaker, Dario Paez, and Bernard Rime, 79-103. Mahwah, NJ: Lawrence Erlbaum.

Lykes, M. Brinton. 1997. Activist participatory research among the Maya of Guatemala: Constructing meanings from situated knowledge. *Journal of Social Issues* 53 (4): 725-746.

Lykes, M. Brinton, Martin Terre Blanche, and Brandon Hamber. 2003. Narrating survival and change in Guatemala and South Africa: The politics of representation and a liberatory community psychology. *American Journal of Community Psychology* 31 (1-2): 79-90.

Martin-Baro, Ignacio. 1994. *Writings for a liberation psychology*, ed. Adrianne Aron and Shawn Corne. Cambridge: Belknap.

Ogundipe-Leslie, Molara. 1994. *Re-creating ourselves: African women and critical transformations*. Trenton, NJ: Africa World Press.

Perkins, Douglas D., and M.A. Zimmerman. 1995. Empowerment, theory, research and application. *American Journal of Community Psychology* 23 (5): 569-581.

Rappoport, Julian. 1987. Terms of empowerment/exemplars of prevention: Toward a theory for community psychology. *American Journal of Community Psychology* 15(2): 121-148.

Riger, Stephanie. 1993. What's wrong with empowerment? *American Journal of Community Psychology* 21 (3): 279-292.

Rorty, Richard. 1989. *Contingency, irony, and solidarity*. Cambridge: Cambridge University Press.

Seligman, Martin E. P. 1975. *Helplessness: On depression, development, and death*. New York : W. H. Freeman.

Tereskinas, Arturas. 2005. Men on paternity leave in Lithuania: Between hegemonic and hybrid masculinities. In *Men and fatherhood: New forms of masculinity in Europe*, ed. Arturas Tereskinas and Jolanta Reingardiene, 11-37. Vilnius: Eugrimas.

Tickner, J. Ann. 1988. Hans Morgenthau's principles of political realism: A feminist reformulation. In *A Selection from Millennium* (a special issue distributed during the International Studies Association Annual Meeting in San Francisco, 2008), 429-440. Quoting Hannah Arendt (1969), *On violence*. New York: Harcourt, 44.

Troutner, Jennifer L., and Peter H. Smith. 2004. Empowering women: agency, structure, and comparative perspective. In *Promises of empowerment: Women in Asia and Latin America*, ed. Peter H. Smith, Jennifer L. Troutner, and Christine Hunefeldt, 1-30. Lanham, MD: Rowman and Littlefield Publishers.

Vince, Laima. 2008. Healing with love: Exceptional women make a difference in social work. *Lithuania in the World* 16 (2): 22-27.

Yoder, Janice D., and Arnold S. Kahn. 1992. Toward a feminist understanding of women and power. *Psychology of Women Quarterly* 16 (4): 381-388.

Zimmerman, Marc A. 1995. Psychological empowerment: Issues and illustrations. *American Journal of Community Psychology* 23 (5): 581-599.

Index

abortion, 27, 41, 46
agriculture, 53, 75–78, 80n1
Amnesty International, 40, 79, 91, 96
apartheid, 60, 63, 65–67, 69, 105
Armenia, xviii, 3-4, 6, 8, 9n1, 15-16, 23, 33-38, 41–45, 82, 129, 129–34, 135n1, 137–38, 142–48, 160, 162
ASOTRAMA, 7, 96, 97

Beijing Declaration and the Platform for Action, 34, 39, 41, 132
Beijing Conference on Women, 33, 38
Butler, Judith, 17, 23

capitalism, vii, 25, 54, 78, 82, 125. *See also* market economy
CEDAW. *See* Convention of the Elimination of All Forms of Discrimination against Women
Center for Equality Advancement, 37n2, 61, 120
children, 36–37, 46, 54, 57–58, 63–64, 66, 73–75, 82, 91, 95, 106, 120, 123, 130, 132, 137–41, 144, 146, 153–54
civil society, 8, 23–24, 33, 36, 40, 45, 55, 60, 69–70, 132–33, 155
CoE (Council of Europe), 33, 39–41, 61n1
colonialism, 65, 75, 157
communication, 9–10n1, 27, 101, 103, 126, 134, 157; cross-cultural, 22, 27–28, 125, 156; subject-to-subject, 5–6, 9–10n4, 18, 125, 161. *See also* Habermas, Jurgen
communicative approach, viii, 6, 21–23, 27–28, 157. *See also* Habermas, Jurgen

Communism, 9n3, 15, 20, 25–27, 34, 82, 134
CONAVIGUA. *See* National Coordinating Committee of Guatemalan Widows
Convention of the Elimination of All Forms of Discrimination against Women, 34, 39, 132, 144–45, 160
Côte d'Ivoire, 9n1, 79
counseling, 42, 114, 116
crime, 37, 51, 66, 68, 63–66, 69–70, 151
crisis, 8, 64, 66–67, 79; centers, 121–22, 125
cultural norms, 52, 54, 60, 82, 148. *See also* patriarchy

de Beauvoir, Simone, 16, 18, 25, 115
democracy, 1–3, 5, 7, 9n1, 9–10n4, 20, 22, 25, 29, 34, 38, 55, 60–61, 64, 66–67, 70, 78, 125, 131, 133, 140, 155, 157–59, 161; consolidation of, 3, 9n1, 70, 155
democratization, 1–3, 5–6, 9, 9n1, 16–17, 19, 25, 28, 130–31, 151, 157, 160–62, 166; aporia of, 2, 9, 161, 166
disempowerment, 5, 123, 130

Egypt, 8, 9n1, 17, 143–48
Einhorn, Barbara, 25–27, 40, 52
emancipation, 24–25, 68, 130
empowerment, vii, 5–9, 19–23, 27–29, 34, 39, 45, 54, 61, 75, 91, 93, 96–98, 101, 107–108, 113–5, 119–20, 122–23, 125–26, 129, 131, 133–34, 147, 152–57, 159, 160, 162–65; commu-

170   Index

nity-based, 7, 27, 33,54, 70, 91, 96–98, 105, 107–8, 114–5, 125–6, 154–55, 157, 159, 164–66; economic, 81–85, 96–98, 101, 103, 105, 122–25, 163; strategies of, 3–4, 6, 22, 28, 41, 61, 65, 71, 75, 98–99, 103, 108, 121, 127, 156, 161, 165
entrepreneurship, 7, 81, 83–85, 87n2
equal opportunities, 40, 51, 59, 61n1, 86
Etzioni, Amitai, 156, 159
EU (European Union), 34–35, 38–40, 44, 55, 59, 82, 86, 120, 124, 145, 160–61

feminism, vii, 15, 17–19, 23, 26–29, 68, 97, 130, 157–59, 161. *See also* Social movements
Foucault, Michel, 21
Friedan, Betty, 18, 24–25, 112

GAM. See Mutual Support Group
gender discrimination, 3,5, 33–35, 40–41, 51, 53, 75–76, 83, 91, 130–33, 143–48, 160
gender equality, 1–3, 5–7, 16, 22, 24, 29, 34–35, 39–41, 47, 51–52, 55–61, 65–67, 69–70, 82, 86, 121–22, 130–32, 134–35, 144–46, 148, 156, 158–63
gender neutrality, 56, 60
globalization, 77, 126, 135
Guatemala, viii, 7–8, 9n1, 91–99, 151–54, 161–65

Habermas, Jurgen, viii, 9, 9–10n4, 18, 21, 22, 27, 161
Hassim, Shireen, 66, 157–58
Havelkova, Hana, 23, 35
healing, 4, 91, 93, 97, 99, 116, 152, 162–63
HIV/AIDS, 7, 64–70, 101–7, 158
human rights, 1, 5, 8, 33–34, 39–40, 12–61, 92–93, 96, 98, 143–45, 152–54

IMF (International Monetary Fund), 77, 79
interdisciplinary, 5, 19, 157

international norms, 6–7, 33–34, 36–38, 42, 44–46, 132
international community, 3, 33, 39, 45, 47, 59
Iraq, 2–3, 17, 146

Keck, Margaret E., 5, 36

Lithuania, vii, 3, 6–8, 9n1, 28, 33–46, 47n2, 51–60, 81–87, 107–108, 116, 119–126, 160–62, 165

market economy, 76, 82. *See also* capitalism
Marxism, 24, 26
memory, 93, 96, 138, 142, 164
misogyny, 69, 58, 165. *See also* gender discrimination
Mutual Support Group (*Grupo de Apoyo Mutuo*), 92, 96, 151–52
myth, 39, 64, 165

National Coordinating Committee of Guatemalan Widows (*Coordinadora Nacional de Viudas de Guatemala*), 92, 96
NGOs (non-governmental organizations), 4, 28, 35–38, 40–42, 44–46, 54–55, 60–61, 61n1, 70, 78, 120, 122–24, 131–33, 147, 162
PAR (Participatory Action Research), viii, 6, 9n4, 157
patriarchy, 4, 7–8, 17, 24, 28, 36, 43, 51–52, 60, 67–71, 143–45, 148, 159–61
Perestroika, 23, 25, 47n1, 130–31
Poland, 4, 9n1, 82, 133–34
political culture, 3, 161
polygamy, 65, 71
post-colonialism, 19, 66, 75–76, 157
post-communism, viii, 1, 25–28, 34, 36, 45–46, 52, 55, 57, 59, 120, 160
poverty, 7, 53, 65, 67, 73, 82–83, 91, 98, 102, 105, 151, 154
privatization, 77–79, 80n2, 83
prostitution, 38, 124–25
PTSD (Post Traumatic Stress Disorder), 92–93, 163
proverb, 37, 52

rape, 37, 39, 58, 63–69, 74, 79, 91, 93–94, 101, 105, 134, 144, 153
Rorty, Richard, 17–18, 21, 156

security, 7, 25, 73, 75, 77–78, 115, 146, 155–56, 158
sexual harassment, 52, 58–61, 144, 146, 148
Sharia, 132, 135–36
shelter (for abused women), 38–42, 44, 55, 58, 120–21, 126
Sikkink, Kathryn, 5, 36
Siyazama project, 70, 101–3, 105–6
social movements, 1, 5, 8–9, 17, 23, 28, 33–34, 40–44, 57, 60, 66–67, 69, 120, 122, 130–32, 155, 157–58, 160; feminist, 8, 28, 44, 157, 161; women's, 1, 3, 5–6, 9, 17, 40, 67, 69, 120, 130–32, 157–58, 160
social transformation, 1, 3, 5, 98. *See also* democratization
Socialism, 17, 24, 27, 52–53, 55, 60, 75–76, 78
South Africa, viii, 7, 9n1, 60, 63–70, 98, 101–7, 120, 158, 165

Tanzania, 7, 9n1, 73–79
trafficking of women, 4, 38, 41, 42, 45, 61n1, 84, 119, 120–21, 124–26, 159, 161, 166
trauma, vii, 1, 4–9, 15, 25, 63, 69–70, 73, 79, 91, 93–98, 107, 113, 119, 125, 138, 139, 140, 146–47, 151, 153, 155–57, 159, 162–65

transition: economic, 1, 3–4, 6–7, 16, 25, 81–83, 86, 87n2; political, vii, 2–4, 9n1, 15–17, 25, 34, 55, 64, 69–70, 125, 132, 134, 160; social, vii, 1–5, 9n1, 25, 34
UN (United Nations), 33–38, 40–41, 55, 85, 120; Development Programme, 37, 40, 120, 144–45
unemployment, 9n3, 35, 53, 65, 82–83
USA (United States of America), vii, 9n1, 113, 120, 125, 153
USSR (Soviet Union), viii, 4, 8, 9n1, 15, 23, 24, 36, 39, 130–32, 137

violence: against women, vii, 5, 33–34, 36–42, 46, 47n4, 51, 53, 56, 59–60, 61n1, 65, 69–70, 105, 116, 121–122, 129, 132, 145, 155–56, 158–60; domestic, 4, 8, 34, 37–45, 47n4, 51, 53–60, 67, 93, 107–8, 116, 119–26, 132, 134, 146, 153, 158, 160; gender, vii, 5–6, 33, 36–40, 42–44, 61, 125, 132, 160; political, 92, 96

WIIC (Women's Issues Information Center), xi, 41–42, 46, 85, 106–7, 119–20, 122–24, 160
WNC (Women's National Coalition), 66–67
women's rights, 28, 34–36, 38–46, 51–52, 54–55, 67–68, 70, 73, 79, 108, 119–20, 123–25, 129, 132–33, 143–44, 146–47, 158, 160, 162
World Bank, 77, 120

Yuval-Davis, Nira, 51, 66

About the Editors and Contributors

Editors

Dovile Budryte is an Associate Professor of Political Science at Georgia Gwinnett College in Lawrenceville, Georgia. She has been interested in women's issues since 1994, when she took her first graduate college class dealing with international security and read Ann Tickner's critique of Hans Morgenthau's ideas. In 2005, together with Lisa M. Vaughn and Natalya T. Riegg, Dovile started this project to contribute to a broader understanding of security which she believes should include the experiences of women. Dovile is a native of Lithuania and has published articles on democratization in the Baltic states and the book *Taming Nationalism? Political Community Building in the Post-Soviet Baltic States* (Ashgate, 2005). Her primary interests within political science include democratization and nationalism.

Natalya T. Riegg is a Professor of Political Science and Global Studies at the University of Saint Mary in Leavenworth, Kansas. Her fields of specialization include political philosophy, cross-cultural communication and international women's issues. She is the author of dozens of articles and a book, *The Social Philosophy of Alvin Toffler* (in Russian). A member of the Russian International Academy of Humanitarian Sciences, a former Fellow at the Maison des Sciences de l'Homme in Paris and a professor and NGO leader in her native Armenia, Natalya originally came to the United States in 1998 as a Senior Fulbright Scholar. Natalya has been interested in women's issues since 1992, when she worked with others to build a dialogue of peace and reconciliation between Armenian and Azerbaijani women during their countries' war over Nagorno-Karabakh. Having a life path similar to Dovile Budryte's, as well as sharing academic interests with her and Lisa M. Vaughn, Natalya saw the utility and potential power of the ideas that could be conveyed through this project.

Lisa M. Vaughn is currently an Associate Professor of Pediatrics at the University of Cincinnati, College of Medicine and Cincinnati Children's Hospital Medical Center in Ohio. She is formally trained as a social psychologist and counselor and has concentrated on issues relevant to women throughout her career. Her primary research interests are socio-cultural issues affecting the health and well-being of families, especially immigrant and minority populations in the United States. With a life-long interest in other cultures, Lisa has worked with universities and communities around the world, including Guatemala, South Africa, Denmark and the Dominican Republic. A strong advocate of interdisciplinary and international collaboration, she believes strongly that marginalized and disenfranchised people should have a voice. This belief is the main reason why she undertook this project with Dovile and Natalya.

Contributors

Svetlana Aslanyan is the Head of the Research Group in Yerevan, Armenia, and the Scientific Secretary on International Relations at the Institute of Linguistics of Armenia's National Academy of Sciences. She has been active in civil and women's issues for nearly two decades. The founder and President of the Center for the Development of Civil Society in Yerevan, she attended the Fourth Women's Congress in Beijing in 1995. The Congress deeply impressed her and helped her to realize that there was covert discrimination against women during the Soviet period. Since 1996, Dr. Aslanyan has researched issues faced by Armenian women. She has conducted many workshops, organized several programs to help and train women and taught a gender studies course at the university level. She compiled a comprehensive reader for this course. In 1997, Dr. Aslanyan got an IREX Fellowship for study in the United States. In 1999-2000, she was a Fulbright Senior Scholar, and in 2005, she received an EU Tempus-Erasmus Mundus Individual Mobility Grant. Svetlana joined this project because she sees it as one more step toward women's rights and real equality.

Eric J. Boos is an Associate Professor of Philosophy at the University of Wisconsin in Fond du Lac. He remains active in the administration of a conflict resolution center at the Salvatorian Institute in Morogoro, Tanzania, which deals with land-tenure issues for small-holder farmers, pastoralists and women. Eric regularly involves students from the USA in various human development projects in Tanzania which involve micro-financing (women's) cooperatives. Dr. Boos's interest in women's issues stems from his participation in social development projects in Tanzania since 1995. He was awarded a Fulbright Scholarship in 2003 to teach and research land tenure issues in Tanzania. He published a book on the impact of land tenure laws on women and pastoralists in Tanzania (*Property Rights, Pastoral People and Problems with Privatization in Tanzania*. Dar es Salaam, Tanzania: Academic Books and Stationery Itinerant Trade, 2004) and has since that time been engaged in micro-financing of women's cooperatives.

Karene M. Boos is a licensed physical therapist and healthcare attorney. Karene remains active in a conflict resolution clinic she and her husband (Eric J. Boos) started at the Salvatorian Institute in Morogoro, Tanzania, and she continues to structure micro-financing for women's cooperatives there. She was awarded a

Brunnerdale Tithing Fund grant to organize workshops on micro-financing for women in Tanzania. Karene works closely with her husband to assist women in structuring co-ops and small businesses on limited capital and credit. She has a genuine interest in women's issues in developing countries because she believes women are the key to all future development.

Gabriela de Cabrera is the Director of a Pre-School and Elementary School *Happy Kids* in Quetzaltenango, Guatemala, and Vice-President of *Corporación de Inversiones E. Polanco*, S.A. (Spanish for "Ernesto Polanco's investments corporation") which rents houses and runs a radio station. She is also a Secretary of *Círculo Cultural Femenino* (Spanish for "women's cultural circle") and the Editor of the *Associated Monthly Feminine Cultural Bulletin*. The purpose of *Círculo Cultural Femenino* is to learn about culture, art, politics, science, medicine and other areas affecting women and host conferences dealing with these issues. In addition, Gabriela writes children's books. She has been interested in women's issues for a while. In particular, she truly cares about those women who have not had the opportunity to lead a good life. A native of Guatemala, she joined this project because she wanted to give voice to the Guatemalan women who suffer from low self-esteem and are vulnerable to mistreatment even in their own homes.

Azniv Eyramjyants is a Professor of Russian at Yerevan Linguistic University in Armenia. She is the author of twenty Russian language textbooks for secondary and higher education. Recently she compiled a textbook for students of tourism. In addition, she has served as interpreter and has translated works from Russian into Armenian and vice versa. Dr. Eyramjyants decided to join this project because she is interested in promoting mutual understanding of peoples from different cultures.

Ligia Gomez is a Field Service Instructor of Spanish at the University of Cincinnati, College of Romance Languages and Literatures in Ohio. She is a native of Colombia, where she obtained degrees in fine arts and psychology. Ligia came to the United States in 1984. She earned an M.A. in Spanish Literature at the University of Cincinnati. Since 2002, Gomez has worked as a healthcare coordinator for the disadvantaged Latino population in the Greater Cincinnati area. This experience has focused her attention on the challenges facing immigrant women in the USA. Ligia has developed and administered various educational programs designed to help immigrant women to adapt to life in the USA.

J. Kay Keels teaches strategic management at Coastal Carolina University in Conway, South Carolina, USA. She has been interested in women's issues since the early 1990s when she became a member of the Women and Gender Studies academic unit at Louisiana State University. Dr. Keels directed the unit's strategic planning initiative and was named outstanding member in 1994. Kay has a keen interest in how women practice entrepreneurship, especially in developing economies.

Suzanne Leclerc-Madlala is a medical anthropologist and Head of the Anthropology Program at the University of KwaZulu-Natal, South Africa. Her ethnographic work over the past decade has focused on the social and cultural dimensions of the AIDS pandemic in southern Africa where she is a well known researcher and social commentator on issues of gender and sexuality. A feminist before coming to South Africa in 1985 from the USA, her interest in women's issues grew alongside the growing AIDS crisis that coincided with the dawn of democracy in that country. Dr. Leclerc-Madlala joined this project in order to learn more about the challenges faced by other women newly emerged from authoritarian rule. Her efforts to promote women's rights has been recognized with an Amnesty International Award for the Protection of Women's Human Rights in 2005, and a 2006 listing of South African Women Achievers for her contribution to the fight against HIV/AIDS.

Mary Beth Looney chairs the department of Art and Design at Brenau University in Gainesville, Georgia, USA. She teaches studio art and art history, and conducts research on works in the Brenau University Permanent Art Collection. Since her first introduction to the history of feminist art in her undergraduate studies, Mary Beth has been interested in women's issues. As primarily the educator of traditionally and non-traditionally college-aged women for ten years, Professor Looney has witnessed the intellectual growth and development of many students. Some of these individuals—much like the subject of her contributing essay—have left behind detrimental situations and relationships, thus going forward with more empowered, independent lives. Mary Beth has developed and taught courses devoted to the history of women artists. One such course involved travel to and the study of museum spaces in Italy. Mary Beth's formerly published essay in *Transatlantic* put forth by Aalborg University Press (2005) discussed her students' experiences in their search for works by Italian women artists of history. She also recently guest-taught at Aalborg University in Aalborg, Denmark, leading Media and Culture studies students in a day-long research project involving the Nordjyllands Kunstmuseum's acquisitions of works by women artists.

Isabella Manassarian is a Lecturer at Yerevan State University in Armenia. She also serves as a section manager at SHARM Holding, LLC, where she coordinates a joint project with the UNDP on gender and politics in the southern Caucasus region. This project conducts mass media analysis and addresses gender inequality in Armenia. In addition, Manassarian investigates gender inequalities in Armenian legislation. Isabella became aware of gender issues as an undergraduate student in Cairo, Egypt. She became aware of the severity of these issues when she assisted Sudanese refugees who had suffered sexual abuse. She earned an M.A. degree in Political Science from Central European

University in Budapest, Hungary. Isabella volunteered at a Hungarian center providing legal advice to Roma women. She decided to join this project because she felt that the topic was important to her as a woman and because of the magnitude of women's problems, which she has seen with her own eyes across the two continents.

Gnimbin A. Ouattara is an Assistant Professor of History and International Studies at Brenau University in Gainesville, Georgia, USA. A native of Côte d'Ivoire, Ouattara came to the United States in 2001 on a Fulbright scholarship to study American democracy. One chapter of his doctoral dissertation (*Africans, Cherokees and the ABCFM Missionaries in the Nineteenth Century: An Unusual Story of Redemption,* Georgia State University 2007) is devoted to gender. This chapter analyzes power within the African and Cherokee gender systems, and how this power dynamic was transformed by Christian missions.

Vilana Pilinkaite-Sotirovic is a Lecturer of Gender History at European Humanities University and Project Coordinator at the Center for Equality Advancement in Vilnius, Lithuania. She belongs to the international women's activists' network that deals with issues of violence against women in post-Soviet space. She conducted research on policies to combat violence against women in Lithuania. This was part of a larger research project that covered 22 post-communist countries (www.stopvaw.org). Her interest in women's issues started during her studies at the University of Essex in UK and Central European University in Hungary where she completed a Ph.D. in Comparative History. The academic feminist environment during her studies and current employment by the NGO pursuing women's rights advocacy have made a great impact on her academic perspective and personal viewpoint regarding women's issues. Findings from her research on policies to reduce violence in Lithuania showed the lack of political will and limits of the women's movement to seriously deal with this problem. She joined this project in order to share these findings with the global women's movement and get knowledge about the diverse strategies of women's empowerment. Currently Dr. Pilinkaite-Sotirovic works on an international project on gender and equality issues in the EU that explores unemployment, intimate citizenship and gender-based violence.

Ellen Rafshoon is an Assistant Professor of History at Georgia Gwinnett College in Lawrenceville, Georgia. She teaches US history and her areas of interest are foreign policy, ethnic and race relations and intellectual history. In the past Dr. Rafshoon has worked as a freelance writer for trade magazines and newspapers. As the daughter of a pediatrician who was one of ten women in her medical school class, Ellen has always been interested in women's issues. Her undergraduate honors thesis examined newspaper coverage of the modern American women's movement. In the future, Dr. Rafshoon has plans to publish an oral history anthology covering the compelling life stories of female immigrants who have made the United States their home during the last two decades.

Jolanta Reingarde (Reingardiene) is an Associate Professor of Sociology and Head of Social Research Center at Vytautas Magnus University in Kaunas, Lithuania. Her research interests include sociology of gender, violence and women's rights, gender mainstreaming, EU and Lithuanian gender policy. Her interests in women's issues have been mainly determined by the gendered nature of the transformations in Central Eastern Europe and EU enlargement processes. Dr. Reingarde's interests have also been inspired by the famous feminists and women's rights activists she worked with in different international projects and during her Fulbright studies in the U.S. She is the author of *Gender Mainstreaming and Employment Policies in the European Union* (2004), editor of *Between Paid and Unpaid Work: Family Friendly Policies and Gender Equality in Europe* (2006) and the co-editor of *Men and Fatherhood: New Forms of Masculinity in Europe* (2005).

Dovile Rukaite is a Project Manager at WIIC (Women's Issues Information Center) in Vilnius, Lithuania. Since 2002, Dovile has been involved in various local, national and international initiatives combating violence against women and trafficking in women and girls, implementing gender mainstreaming policies, giving lectures, providing training and initiating numerous projects to promote women's rights. She is responsible for maintaining the women's information portal www.lygus.lt and updating databases on Lithuanian NGOs that focus on women's issues and Lithuanian women in politics. Dovile earned her Master's degree from the UNESCO Department of Cultural Management and Cultural Policy.

Anna Rulska is a doctoral candidate in the Graduate Program for International Studies at Old Dominion University in Norfolk, Virginia, USA. She earned her dual Master's degree in German and Political Science from Bowling Green State University in Ohio, USA. Her research includes global and collective security, European international and comparative politics and the transatlantic relationship. In 2002, Anna worked in a Caritas-operated refugee home in Salzburg, Austria, helping men and women from countries such as China, Georgia, Afghanistan, Cambodia, Sudan, Iran, Rwanda and Kosovo with doctor's appointments, job searches and immigration paperwork, while teaching them English and German at the same time. Interestingly, women were much more active, creative and initiative-driven than men. This observation fueled her interest in women's issues, initially sparked by her own experiences with responsibilities, possibilities and limitations of women in Poland, the country of her origin. She feels that this project provides a great opportunity to open the door for analysis of common problems and potential solutions for women's issues across the world.

Randall Scott has taught political science at the University of Saint Mary in Kansas since 2000. Before starting to teach, he worked as a clinical and administrative social worker for 12 years. His duties included program development, administration and serving in programs that involved outreach and mental health assessments at four Kansas City domestic violence shelters. Dr. Scott's academic interests include gender/queer gender/queer theory to analyze international issues.

Vytaute Smaizyte is a Lithuanian journalist. She was one of the founders and owners of *15min*, the first free daily in Lithuania which was later sold to *Schibsted*, a Scandinavian media group operating in 20 countries. Vytaute believes that all people should have access to free information. She gave up her former position as an international issues journalist at *Lietuvos Rytas*, a leading Lithuanian daily, to launch *15 min*. As a female journalist and entrepreneur, she tries to be open-minded to new ideas and unorthodox projects.

Ingrida Vegelyte is a Lithuanian journalist. Since 1993, she has published numerous newspaper and journal articles dealing with various subjects, including non-governmental organizations, social movements, transitional justice and women's issues. In 1997, she graduated from Vilnius University's School of Journalism. Since 2000, Ingrida has served as the Press Secretary for the Union of Politically Repressed and Deported Persons in Lithuania's parliament. Currently she is pursuing a graduate degree in Semiotics at Vilnius University.

Kate Wells is an Acting Head of the Department of Graphic Design at the Durban University of Technology in Durban, South Africa. She is the leader/originator of the *Siyazama* Project founded in 1999 which is the focus of her chapter in this volume. She is currently involved in an extension of the *Siyazama* project titled *Design, Health and Community* under the England and Africa Partnership Program. Her interest in women's issues spans nearly two decades. It was heightened when she began, mostly accompanied by her husband, touring and visiting remote and off-the-beaten-track parts of KwaZulu-Natal, South Africa. Her accomplishments have been noted by 2005 Amnesty International, International Honors Roll, contribution to Women's Human Rights. She was the 2000-2004 winner of three FNB Vita Craft awards for outstanding craft and the 2004 Winner of the prestigious Brett Kebble Award for most outstanding craft in South Africa. The *Siyazama* Project has been exhibited in various international museums and galleries including the Michigan State University Museum (2005-2006), the Museum of World Culture, Gothenborg, Sweden (2004-2005), Brandeis University and UCLA, USA (2004), and the Museum of Domestic Art and Architecture (MODA), UK (2003).

HQ 1870.9 .F44 2009

Feminist conversations

FEB 17 2009